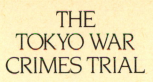

THE TOKYO WAR CRIMES TRIAL

THE
TOKYO WAR
CRIMES TRIAL

An International Symposium

•

Edited by

C. Hosoya

N. Andō

Y. Ōnuma

R. Minear

Kodansha Ltd.
Kodansha International Ltd.

To the Memory of B. V. A. Röling

Distributed in the United States by Kodansha International/
USA Ltd., through Harper & Row, Publishers, Inc., 10
East 53rd Street, New York, New York 10022. Published by
Kodansha Ltd. and Kodansha International Ltd., 12-21
Otowa 2-chome, Bunkyo-ku, Tokyo 112.

  LCC 85-80523
  ISBN 0-87011-750-5
  ISBN 4-06-202390-3 (in Japan)
First edition, 1986

CONTENTS

PREFACE

The Tokyo war crimes trial, formally known as the International Military Tribunal for the Far East, was the Pacific counterpart of the Nuremberg trial. Nuremberg captured the world's attention in 1946 and has continued to hold it in the years since: memoirs, monographs, movies, and plays have continued to deal with the trial, keeping popular and scholarly interest alive. Part of that attention is due to the notoriety of the defendants at Nuremberg: Hermann Göring, Joachim von Ribbentrop, Julius Streicher, Hjalmar Schacht, Albert Speer, Rudolf Hess. Part is due to the ignominious nature of the Nazi state and to the horrors of the European holocaust. Part is due to the prominence of the Allied personnel involved: Robert Jackson, for instance, the US prosecutor, was on leave from his seat on the Supreme Court. Part is also due to the general American and European preoccupation with things that take place in Europe, and to the perception that at Nuremberg justice was done.

The Tokyo trial, on the other hand, did not capture much attention at the time, and still remains very much in the shadow of Nuremberg. Why should this be so? Many factors suggest themselves, among them the following: that, with the possible exception of former prime minister Tōjō Hideki, none of the defendants was as famous as Göring or Hess; that the acts charged against the Japanese leaders were in no way comparable in sheer heinousness to those charged against the Nazi leaders; that few of the Allied participants were people of great standing in their home countries; that the trial dragged on so long; that by the time a judgment was reached the wartime alliance had already fallen apart; and that the rest of the world was more interested in things European than things Asian. Whatever the reasons, it remains true that today, almost forty years later, the Tokyo trial is virtually unknown outside of Japan.

In the dock at Tokyo were twenty-eight leaders of the Japanese state, both civilian and military. On the bench were representatives of the Allied powers: eleven judges in all, one each from Australia, Canada, China (the Nationalist Government), France, Great Britain, India (not an independent nation until 1947), the Netherlands, New Zealand, the Philippines (like India, independent only after the war), the Soviet Union, and the United States. The trial lasted two and a half years and ended in November 1948.

The indictment at the Tokyo trial charged that the defendants were members of a "criminal, militaristic clique" that controlled events within the Japanese government and within Japan between 1 January 1928 and 2 September 1945; and that the policies the defendants pursued "were the cause of serious world troubles, aggressive wars, and great damage to the interests of peace-loving peoples, as well as to the interests of the Japanese people themselves." The majority judgment (there were also five separate opinions) found that this charge had been proved; that indeed, beginning before 1 January 1928, a conspiracy had existed; that Japan had committed aggression as charged. In a real sense, then, the Tokyo trial sat in judgment on the history of the Pacific region up to the end of World War II.

*   *   *

Readers unfamiliar with the history of this region in the period before the Pacific War may appreciate a brief sketch of some of the factors and events that mark it. Many of the factors are those that common sense would suggest: national security in an insecure world; economic interdependence and the search for economic independence; ideological issues; anticolonial movements for national independence. These factors played a part in the actions of every major power in the Pacific—Great Britain, the United States, Japan, the Soviet Union—and of every lesser power, too—China, France, the Netherlands. Aside from these factors, which are still important in the world today, there were also issues specific to the 1920s and 1930s. They include the legacies of World War I, such as territorial issues and strategic planning for the next war; the effects of the Great Depression, among them an increased awareness of the role of economics in war and a tendency toward protectionism; the spread of Soviet military and political influence into East Asia; and the political chaos in China and the growing cohesion of Chinese nationalism that followed later.

At the Tokyo trial, it was perhaps only natural that the tribunal focused on a limited range of Japanese acts and motivations; but historians need to look at the broader picture. In this wider perspective, Japan's attempts to secure what it saw as its national interests in the Pacific are found to go back to the late nineteenth century. In the 1870s Japan began to apply pressure on Korea, then a Chinese dependency. The Sino-Japanese War of 1894-95 established Japan as the principal power on the Korean peninsula. The Russo-Japanese War of 1904-5 reinforced Japan's hold on Korea and also gave it substantial influence in Southern Manchuria (and control over Port Arthur). In 1910 Japan annexed Korea, and during and after World War I Japan fell heir to Germany's holdings in Asia, notably the Shandong (Shan-tung) peninsula and the Marshall and Mariana Islands. At times, Japanese policy-makers chose diplomatic means to achieve their goals; at times, military means. But neither means nor ends were unique to Japan: Britain, the United States, the Soviet Union, and France all had troops in Asia, and all had colonies or other forms of territorial holdings.

The Tokyo trial took 1928 as its starting point because it was in that year that Japanese involvement on the Chinese mainland led to the assassination by Japanese of Zhang Zuolin (Chang Tso-lin), then the most powerful warlord in northern China. This act was condemned by the home government in Tokyo, but it symbolized the difficulties Japan was experiencing in its search for national security in Asia: Zhang had threatened to side with the Nationalists rather than the Japanese. The year 1931 saw the Manchurian Incident, again at Japanese instigation, as well as the Japanese occupation of all of Manchuria. In 1933, Japan left the League of Nations in protest against the Lytton Commission Report, which laid more of the blame for the Manchurian Incident on Japan than its leaders felt was fair. In 1937 came the Incident at Marco Polo Bridge and the outbreak of open fighting between the Japanese armies and those of both Jiang Jieshi (Chiang Kai-shek) and Mao Tse-tung. Japan had become bogged down in what it feared most—a land war in Asia. What is more, its adversary enjoyed the moral and material support of the United States and Britain. Isolated in the international community, Japan turned to the Axis powers, signing the Tripartite Alliance in 1940. When Hitler invaded the Soviet Union in June 1941, Japan responded by concluding a neutrality pact with the Soviet Union and moving into Southern Indochina (then a French colony). The United States answered with an embargo on oil, joined by Great Britain, China, and the Netherlands: at a stroke of President Franklin Roosevelt's pen, 80 percent of Japan's peacetime oil was forfeit. The Japanese-American negotiations of 1941 failed to settle the issues outstanding between the two countries, and Japan attacked Pearl Harbor on 7 December. A little less than four years later, in August 1945, the Pacific War came to an end when negotiations led to Japan's acceptance of the Potsdam Declaration, which had been issued by the Allies after the surrender of Nazi Germany.

*　　*　　*

Having surveyed the historical landmarks of the time, let us now take a closer look at the Tokyo war crimes trial itself. The origin of the trial was to be found in article 10 of the Potsdam Declaration, which provided that "stern justice shall be meted out to all war criminals, including those who have visited cruelties upon our prisoners." And for its charter, the Tokyo trial took over virtually verbatim the charter drawn up at the London Conference (July-August 1945) for the Nuremberg trial.

The Tokyo trial opened on 3 May 1946. In the two years that followed, the tribunal heard testimony from more than 400 persons and received more than 4,000 items of documentary evidence. After several months' recess, the tribunal delivered its majority judgment in November 1948. The majority (in some cases the judges divided six to five) found the defendants guilty of one or more of the following crimes: the overall conspiracy to carry out wars of aggression in East Asia and the Indian and Pacific Ocean areas; ordering, authorizing, or permitting conventional war crimes; and not taking adequate measures to prevent the occurrence of conventional war crimes. The majority sentenced seven defendants to death by hanging, sixteen to life in prison, one to twenty years' imprisonment, and one to seven years' imprisonment. None was acquitted; two defendants died during the trial, and a third was found mentally incompetent.

Five judges submitted separate opinions. The Australian judge (and president of the tribunal), Sir William Webb, contended that in sentencing the defendants the tribunal should have taken into consideration the fact that the emperor—Webb called him "the leader in the crime"—had not been indicted. The French judge, Henri Bernard, complained of procedural shortcomings: "A verdict reached by a tribunal after a defective procedure cannot be a valid one." The Indian judge, Radhabinod Pal, pointed to the necessity of considering the past actions of the Western powers before judging Japan's acts; he argued that all defendants were innocent of all charges. Judge B. V. A. Röling of the Netherlands argued that no conspiracy existed and that five of the defendants were innocent. Judge Delfin Jaranilla of the Philippines argued that several of the sentences were "too lenient, not exemplary and deterrent, and not commensurate with the gravity of the offense or offenses committed."

*   *   *

Both at the time and since, the Tokyo trial has raised a number of fundamental questions. From the perspective of international law: Did article 10 of the Potsdam Declaration entitle the Allies to try Japanese leaders for the crime of aggression? Was aggression a crime under international law during the period at issue? Can wars of aggression be differentiated from wars of self-defense? Can individuals be prosecuted for acts of state?

From the perspective of history: Did an overall conspiracy really exist among the defendants? Was the Axis alliance a true alliance? Did American acts in the months prior to Pearl Harbor "contribute" to the Japanese attack? Did not the Soviet Union attack Japan in August 1945 and thus commit a breach of international law?

From the perspective of the quest for peace: Is the Tokyo trial a good precedent or a bad one? How should the crime against peace be applied in the international community today and in the future? Is the concept of individual (or leaders') responsibility for war a positive factor in the search for peace? In short, what is the contemporary significance of the trial?

The year 1983 seemed a fitting time to address these questions and indeed to attempt an objective and comprehensive reexamination of the Tokyo trial. For one thing, in the thirty-five years since the trial came to an end, much new material had come to light, and much research had been undertaken. For another, few of those directly involved in the trial were still alive, and each year saw the deaths of more. If those directly involved were to play any role at all in this reexamination, then the sooner the symposium was held, the better. A third factor, directly related to the second, is that the emotions the war aroused had dissipated to a considerable extent, making dispassionate judgment somewhat easier. (Readers of this volume will remark that, although emotions may have dissipated, they have not disappeared.)

The Tokyo trial itself was marked by Eurocentrism in its legal ideas, its personnel, and its historical thinking. One major contribution of the symposium was to draw attention to that Eurocentrism. A second was to develop ways to transcend it: through the make-up of the symposium (voices from the People's Republic of China, the Republic of Korea, the Union of Burma; many voices from Japan), and through the focus of its discussions.

Thus it was that the International Symposium on the Tokyo War Crimes Trial was held in Tokyo on 28–29 May 1983. It brought together former participants in the Tokyo trial and scholars, social critics, and a playwright, who came from many countries, including the Union of Burma, Great Britain, the Federal Republic of Germany, Japan, the People's Republic of China, the Republic of Korea, the Soviet Union, and the United States. The official languages of the symposium were Japanese and English. The Japanese record was published in 1984; this volume is the English record.

Among the special guests at the symposium were three of the defense counsel from the Tokyo trial: Alfred W. Brooks, George A. Furness, and Takigawa Masajirō. Though seating was limited, the symposium was open to the public, and questions from the floor became part of the symposium record. It was perhaps fitting that Sunshine City Hall in Ikebukuro, where the symposium was held, was built in 1978 on the site of Sugamo Prison, where the defendants at the Tokyo trial were held.

We have just mentioned the participation of persons directly involved in the trial and the lamentable fact that death continues to claim them. Here the editors wish to single out one person without whom the symposium would hardly have been possible and whose towering presence played a very significant role in the discussions. B. V. A. Röling was the Dutch judge at Tokyo. Thirty-nine years old in 1946, he was the youngest of the judges. After the trial he taught for many years on the faculty of the University of Groningen, concerning himself particularly with peace research. In 1977, he edited and published the judgments of the Tokyo trial. At the symposium, Dr. Röling presented a paper and contributed actively to the discussion; after the symposium he wrote the introduction to this volume. His death in 1985 makes this introduction one of his last efforts in the cause of peace and justice. In recognition of his role in the symposium and in warm remembrance of the qualities that made him such a special person, the editors dedicate this volume to his memory.

The editors wish to express their gratitude to Kodansha International and Kodansha Ltd. for the publication of this record, and to Mr. Sugiyama Shōzō of Kodansha Ltd. for his devotion to the success of the symposium. Kodansha Ltd. was the sponsor as well of the four-and-a-half-hour documentary film *Tokyo Trial*, which was released at the time of the symposium. The English-language version had its New York premiere in September 1985.

Hosoya Chihiro
Andō Nisuke
Ōnuma Yasuaki
Richard H. Minear

PANELISTS

(in alphabetical order; with titles at time of symposium)

Andō Nisuke   Professor, international law, Kobe University
Awaya Kentarō   Professor, history, Rikkyo University
Hagiwara Nobutoshi   Historian, critic
Hata Ikuhiko   Professor, history, Takushoku University
Hosoya Chihiro   Professor Emeritus, international political
                       affairs, Hitotsubashi University; vice-
                       president, Kokusai University
Ienaga Saburō   Professor, history, Chuo University
Ipsen, Knut   President, international law, Ruhr University
Kinoshita Junji   Playwright, critic
Kojima Noboru   Historian, critic
Lounev, Alexandr E.   Professor, theory of the state and public
                       administration, Institute of State and Law,
                       Academy of Science of the USSR
Minear, Richard H.   Professor, history, University of Massachusetts
Okuhara Toshio   Professor, international law, Kokushikan University
Ōnuma Yasuaki   Associate professor, international law, University
                       of Tokyo
Paik Choong-Hyun   Professor, international law, Seoul National
                       University
Pritchard, R. John   Research Associate, compiler of English
                       transcripts of Tokyo trial, London School of
                       Political Science and Economics
Röling, B. V. A.   Professor Emeritus, international law,
                       University of Groningen; former judge at
                       Tokyo trial
Than Tun   Professor, history, Mandalay University;
                       visiting professor, Kyoto University
Tsurumi Shunsuke   Philosopher, critic
Yu Xinchun   Associate Professor, history, Nankai University

EDITORIAL NOTE

This is the official English-language record of the International Symposium on the Tokyo War Crimes Trial, which was held on 28 and 29 May 1983 at Sunshine City Hall in Tokyo. The basic policy adhered to in editing this record was to faithfully reproduce the papers presented and the discussions following them. However, based on the following guidelines, emendations were made that seemed essential from the viewpoint of historical accuracy, precise legal interpretation, and readability. The sole purpose of all editorial changes has been greater clarity, and the editors have been careful not to alter the intent or the flavor of the original.

1. Written versions of the papers presented by the participants were received in advance, but in some cases the language of the actual presentation differed from that of the written papers. In these cases, the editors relied in principle on the taped presentation. Occasionally, however, the language of the written version was retained. Notes and additional materials appended to the written papers were eliminated or substantially reduced at the editors' discretion.

2. Statements concerning the management of the symposium and the progress of the various sessions were substantially abbreviated. The editors also assume responsibility for making minimal changes necessitated by problems in recording (e.g., inaudible statements), by redundancy, and by linguistic factors (some of the more elaborate expressions of politeness in Japanese were eliminated or shortened).

3. The tape recording of the proceedings takes precedence over the Japanese record published in 1984. Those preparing the Japanese record found a few exchanges indecipherable; some of those passages were subsequently deciphered. Hence the English record and the Japanese record are not always in exact accord.

4. English was one of the two languages of the symposium—Japanese the other—and most of the non-Japanese participants presented their papers and comments in English. Still, few of those non-Japanese participants were native speakers of English, and even native speakers were not always as clear as they might have been. The editors have therefore undertaken to polish papers and comments given in both languages.

5. Subheadings were provided by the editors. Notes in square brackets were supplied by the editors in the interest of historical accuracy and precision of legal interpretation. Statements in round brackets were made by the speakers themselves.

6. Chinese names of persons and places are transliterated into Pinyin, with Wade-Giles in brackets. The order of all personal names are recorded as in the language in question (e.g., Japanese and Chinese surnames precede given names).

7. Besides those who presented papers and the commentators, a number of researchers, lawyers, and others closely connected with the Tokyo trial were invited to participate in the symposium as special guests. In compiling this record, the speakers, the commentators, and the special guests are identified by name whenever they speak. Any question or statement by other invited guests and members of the audience is indicated as a "question"—that is, the speaker is not identified.

8. At the symposium, interpreters rendered papers and comments presented in Japanese into English. In the interest of even greater accuracy, all Japanese-language material has been retranslated for this volume by Mark Harbison. Editorial assistance for the English edition was given by Michael Brase of Kodansha International.

9. The editors, and they alone, bear responsibility for the changes made. Due to constraints of time, the editors were not able to clear editorial changes with participants.

INTRODUCTION

by B. V. A. Röling

Why, now, an international symposium on the International Military Tribunal for the Far East, a trial that took place more than thirty-five years ago? Why again confront the horrifying events that occurred during World War II? Why revive the humiliation of Japan and the reign of the conqueror, and, above all, why reexamine the sentencing of Japanese leaders?

The answer, perhaps, is that by examining the errors of the past we hope to prepare a more peaceful path for the future. This also can explain the renewed interest in World War II and the atrocities connected with it, as well as the study of the trials that followed in Europe, especially in Germany. Millions have seen films about the persecution and extermination of the Jews by the Nazis and about the subsequent Nuremberg trial, where Goering and his accomplices were called to account and sentenced. Several books have been published based on recently released official documents, on memoirs now available, and on the diaries of those who were involved in the trial.[1]

In Japan, too, there is renewed interest in the war and the trial in which Japanese leaders stood accused. Millions of people in Japan have seen the recent film that Kobayashi Masaki produced about the trial.

In 1983, experts from around the world gathered in Tokyo for a symposium on the Tokyo trial. This volume is the record of that event, and many of the articles contributed to it express this strong Japanese interest. The Tokyo trial has not, however, attracted a great deal of attention in the rest of the world. The most important book about the trial, Richard H. Minear's *Victors' Justice: The Tokyo War Crimes Trial* (Princeton University Press), appeared fourteen years ago, in 1971. It is exceedingly critical of the procedure of the trial as well as of the outcome. I regret that I have not been able to study the Japanese literature on the trial because it is not yet available in translation.

It took a long time for the Tokyo judgment to be published. I knew that the judgment had not appeared in print, so I decided to produce an edition myself: B. V. A. Röling and C. F. Rüter (eds.), *The Tokyo Judgment* in two volumes (University Press Amsterdam, 1977). Meanwhile, publication of the complete transcript of the proceedings was moving forward in England. Thanks to the perseverance of R. John Pritchard, this gigantic work is now completed.[2]

The Japanese edition of the contributions to the International Symposium on the Tokyo War Crimes Trial, held on 28–29 May 1983, was published in 1984. It is gratifying that now an English edition is coming out, too. It is important that the non-Japanese world also be able to study the various aspects of the Tokyo trial and the existing opinions about it.

Tokyo and Nuremberg Compared

"Nuremberg" became more widely known throughout the world than "Tokyo." This is quite understandable. The Nuremberg trial began quite soon after the end of the war, and it did not last very long. It was the first trial in which leaders of a state—among whom were such well-known figures as Goering—stood trial, not only for crimes committed during the war, but also for launching the war itself.

Nuremberg also had more allure than the Tokyo trial. The reasons are clear when one compares the chief prosecutors and the presidents, the persons who, for the general public, established the image and determined the prestige of the two trials. Robert Jackson, the American chief prosecutor at Nuremberg, was a brilliant man who assumed his function convinced that this was one of those rare moments in history that might yield a fundamental change in thought and action, and who could express that deep conviction in words reminiscent of Churchill.

The prevailing opinion in America and in England was that the Nazi leaders should be summarily shot. According to *The Nuremberg Trial* by A. and J. Tusa (p. 63), Eden had about fifty Nazis in mind. Jackson resisted this: "To free them without a trial would mock the dead and make cynics of the living"; and "undiscriminating executions or punishments without definite findings of guilt, fairly arrived at, would violate pledges repeatedly given, and would not set easily on the American conscience or be remembered by our children with pride."[3] In the same report, Jackson also remarked upon the uniqueness of the moment: "In untroubled times, progress toward an effective rule of law in the international community is slow indeed. Inertia rests more heavily upon the society of nations than upon any other society. Now we stand at one of those rare moments when the thought and institutions and habits of the world have been shaken by the impact of world war on the lives of countless millions. Such occasions rarely come and quickly pass. We are put under a heavy responsibility to see that our behavior during the unsettled period will direct the world's thought toward a firmer enforcement of the laws of international conduct, so as to make war less attractive to those who have governments and the destinies of peoples in their power" (p. 53).

Compared with Jackson, Joseph B. Keenan was a mediocre man. The evidence suggests that he saw his job in Tokyo as a way to gain a seat in the US Senate. He was clearly unqualified to lead the prosecution, and he was in part rescued in this task by the English prosecutor, Arthur S. Comyns-Carr.

The presidents of the tribunals in Nuremberg and Tokyo also differed strikingly. Sir Geoffrey Lawrence, the English president at Nuremberg, was a typical representative of the English judicial tradition, dignified, poised, courteous, certain of the manner in which the trial should be conducted. Justice must be done, but also must be seen to be done. Ann and John Tusa write: "For many people at Nuremberg—including all the defendants—he would come to personify Justice" (p. 112). In contrast, Sir William Webb, the Australian who presided at Tokyo, gave the impression of being completely unsure of his own position; hence his tendency to seek positions of power by any available means and his dictatorial behavior toward his colleagues as well as toward the prosecutors and defense counsel. Quarrelsome at times, he embarrassed many of the judges with his court behavior.

When one compares Nuremberg and Tokyo, the impression is inescapable that the Nuremberg judges assumed an attitude of greater independence from the prosecutors as well as from the states they represented. At the behest of the Soviet Union, the accusation concerning the massacre of 11,000 Polish officers in Katyn was inserted into the Nuremberg indictment. Also in compliance with Russian wishes, Fritzsche, who was a prisoner of the Russians, was included among the accused. The tribunal, however, wanted more evidence concerning Katyn than the Soviet prosecutor had originally supplied, and six witnesses were questioned who reinforced the conviction of many that the massacre was perpetrated by the government of Josef Stalin. In its verdict the IMT did not comment on Katyn. An explicit acquittal was apparently thought to be too offensive. But there was no hesitation about acquitting Fritzsche, who had met neither Hitler nor most of the accused. He had never belonged to their circle.

At the Tokyo trial, too, the Soviets had special wishes regarding the indictment and the accused. They demanded that incidents not related to World War II, namely, those of Lake Khassan ([Changgufeng, Ch'ang-ku-feng]; 1938) and Nomonhan (1939), be included in the indictment. In the Tokyo judgment these acts of violence were treated as aggressive wars perpetrated by Japan. The Russians also insisted that Shigemitsu Mamoru be included in the list. His inclusion could be partially justified in view of the uncertainty of the evidence available to the Russian prosecutor. It is incomprehensible, however, that the majority judgment should have found Shigemitsu guilty on charges including the crime against peace. According to the Nuremberg and Tokyo judgment, this was "the supreme crime." Although the majority also condemned Shigemitsu for war crimes, ruling that he had done too little as foreign minister to stop grave violations of the laws of war, he received only a seven-year prison sentence, a punishment not at all adequate to his crimes if they had actually been committed.

The tribunal's acceptance of the principle that the accused were to be held responsible for failure to prevent war crimes led to another unjust decision, namely, a death sentence in the case of Hirota Kōki. His sentence of death by hanging rested above all on the charge that he shared responsibility for the Rape of Nanjing (Nanking). In his case, the tribunal made him accountable for his failure to act effectively in preventing war crimes, although it was not at all clear that he, though prime minister, had enough authority and power to change the attitude of the military. Hirota was also prime minister when the important resolution of 11 August 1936 was issued: "The Fundamental Principles of our National Policy." The majority verdict may be right when it states: "This policy of far-reaching effect was eventually to lead to the war between Japan and the

Western Powers in 1941.'' But this does not mean that such a war was intended then or that the eruption of such a war had been foreseen at that time. It is my deep conviction that the death sentence handed down in Hirota's case was an error of justice. I also disagree strongly with the sentences given Shigemitsu, Tōgō, and Kido. The majority apparently lacked the readiness or perhaps—due to the postwar climate—the will to disagree with the accusations set forth by the prosecution.

It seems to me that the authority of the Tokyo judgment has suffered in Japan precisely because many people were not convinced that some of the statesmen found guilty were actually among those responsible for leading Japan into the Pacific War.

But there were also other factors that undermined the authority of the trial and the judgment.

The authority of the trials, in both Nuremberg and Tokyo, was eroded by a change in American attitudes as the cold war intensified. The desire grew to secure both West German and Japanese friendship and support in the test of strength with the Soviet Union: hence the release of several suspects whom many considered more guilty than some of those sentenced by the Tokyo tribunal; hence the acquittal by American tribunals of military men who were the equals in position and responsibility of the defendants at the Tokyo trial and who could be accused of crimes as bad as those of colleagues sentenced to death by the Tokyo tribunal. All this may have strengthened in many minds the impression that politics, not justice, was at stake here, that even after Japan's surrender, the war was continued for a while in order to satisfy completely the Allied desire for revenge against some Japanese leaders. In turn, all this may have obscured an appreciation of the fact that the Tokyo trial gave real life to ideas that the world needed: the accountability of those responsible for the outbreak of war, and the answerability of military and political leaders for their failure to prevent war crimes in cases where it would have been possible to oppose them and thereby end them.

The prestige of the trial has also been severely damaged by the revelation of the existence in Manchuria of a Japanese laboratory for research into bacteriological weapons. These weapons were tested on prisoners of war and cost thousands of lives. This incident would have provided a case, rare at the Tokyo trial, of centrally organized war criminality. But everything connected with it was kept from the tribunal. The American military authorities wanted to avail themselves of the results of these experiments, criminally obtained by Japan, and at the same time to prevent them from falling into the hands of the Soviet Union. The judges in Tokyo remained ignorant. The Japanese involved in these crimes were promised immunity from prosecution in exchange for divulging the information obtained from the experiments.

Thus it is not known to what extent the entire Japanese government was involved in this affair. It is not inconceivable that it was strictly a military matter, kept by the minister of defense from his colleagues in the government. But it remains a disturbing fact that this, the worst of Japanese crimes, was kept from the tribunal. It is incomprehensible that the Russian prosecutor did not reveal the affair.[4]

Centrally issued orders to commit criminal actions were easily obtained by the Nuremberg tribunal, for they were common in the criminal Nazi regime. In Tokyo such orders were rarer. Therefore, the judgment of Nuremberg could easily adhere to the opinion that only those who had personally committed war crimes and those who had ordered them should be punished.

The Nuremberg judgment hardly mentions accountability for failure to act and bring an end to known criminal practices in a battle theater for which one was responsible and where it was possible to exert influence. At the Tokyo trial, greater consideration had to be given to such accountability.[5]

It is important that this accountability for "failure to act" be expressly acknowledged. For it was formerly far too easy for a commanding officer to feel safe as long as he did not issue direct orders for the commission of war crimes. On the other hand, accountability of this type is not without danger. The danger resides in the fact that a judicial opportunity is created to arraign on this charge any military commander or statesman one wishes. I am firmly convinced that accountability for "failure to act" went much too far in the majority judgment as it related to Hirota, Shigemitsu, and Tōgō.

The Fairness of Tokyo

There is ample room for discussion on the question of whether the Tokyo trial was a fair trial. However, this is not the place to examine this question in depth. Many of the papers appearing in this book deal with the problem. It will be clear to everyone that many aspects of the trial can be attacked by well-founded criticism; moreover, many of the decisions of the tribunal concerning procedural matters were not unanimous (for example, those concerning admissibility of evidence). According to the Tokyo charter, a fair trial was to be conducted. However, the charter's rules were of a general nature. Since most of the judges were versed in Anglo-Saxon procedure, the trial increasingly took on Anglo-Saxon features. The divergence from the Continental approach was one reason that the French judge, Henri Bernard, dissented from the judgment. Personally, I can only note that, although I often disagreed with decisions about procedure, the unfairness never reached a point where I felt compelled to resign my position as judge.

It is understandable, moreover, that the judgment itself should be criticized. I expressed my view at the time in a separate opinion, dissenting in regard not only to the legal rules applied but also to the interpretation of actual events. One or the other led me to arrive at five acquittals: Hirota, Shigemitsu, Tōgō, Kido, and Hata. The subsequent publication of official documents and the papers of statesmen have confirmed my opinion about the first four. However, since the appearance of evidence concerning biological weapons, I no longer feel the same degree of certainty in regard to General Hata. For it is quite conceivable that he was involved in this criminal enterprise, or at least knew of it.

It was clear that the Japanese defense counsel had trouble with Anglo-Saxon procedure; hence the opportunity for each of the accused to be defended by American as well as Japanese lawyers. The American lawyers were better acquainted with what was permitted and what was not, and they gradually assumed an ever greater role in the trial. This situation had to lead to conflict. The American lawyers cared solely for the interests of their clients, while their Japanese colleagues, together with most of the accused, had other concerns as well—the position of the emperor, the honor of Japan, and similar matters.

One may concentrate on these and other faults in trial procedure in order to bolster the view that the accused were unjustly punished. Some of the papers in this book even suggest that Japan and the Japanese people were standing trial. It appears to me that this is a misconception. One function of a postwar trial of government leaders is to differentiate between the criminal leaders of a nation and its deceived people. This promotes the opportunity to revive normal relations with that nation and its new leaders in the postwar period.

Whatever reservations one may have concerning the trial, there is no doubt that several of the accused were definitely not innocent. This fact came out quite clearly at the time. It has also been the conclusion of many of the contributors to this conference, whose papers sometimes emphasize the crimes committed. In addition, Europeans and Americans have been surprised that some of the papers explicitly differentiate between Japanese crimes against whites and Japanese crimes against Asians, and that they condemn acts against fellow Asians more strongly. This attitude is not difficult to appreciate in Japanese and other Asians who saw the war instigated by Japan as above all a struggle for the liberation of Asia, a struggle to end colonial rule. The arrogant and criminal posture that Japanese military leaders assumed in occupied Asian countries during the war was definitely incompatible with such a goal.

In this regard, it is important to distinguish between different kinds of war criminality. It has gradually become clear to everyone that during wartime the laws and customs of war are violated by every army. These violations may be committed by individuals who use positions of power originating from the war to murder, rob, and rape solely for their own gain. This kind of "individual criminality" is sometimes punished by the perpetrator's own government, for such acts can undermine military discipline as well as intensify the hostility of the inhabitants of the occupied territory. In short, interests can be served by prosecuting and punishing this kind of criminality in courts-martial of the nation concerned.

Then there is war criminality of a more significant nature, that which is ordered, recommended, or tolerated by the authorities because they believe it furthers the aims of the war. This can be called "systemic criminality" or "structural criminality" and includes the use of banned weapons, outlawed methods of fighting, attacks on illegitimate objectives, terrorization of the population in the theater of operations or in occupied territories, mistreatment of prisoners of war, and violation of occupation law. Such criminality usually is not punished by the government of the offending troops because the government itself is involved. It is this kind of war criminality that leads to trials after the war, by national courts of the victors or by international tribunals established by them.

Some contributors to this conference express amazement that prosecutions by German courts continued for years after the Allied powers, for political reasons, had brought their prosecutions to an end. But this view overlooks the fact that the later German prosecutions and judgments concerning German conduct dealt only with "crimes against humanity," not with traditional war crimes, the grave violations of the laws and customs of war. The postwar German government and the German people dissociated themselves from Nazi policies that led to the gas chambers and similar monstrous mass atrocities. But in Germany, too, as in any country, it was and is exceedingly difficult to prosecute soldiers for conventional war crimes committed in the fight for the "fatherland."[6]

In the case of Japan, "crimes against humanity" played a less important role. It was impossible to substantiate accusations that the Japanese intended to exterminate a certain ethnic group: for example, the Europeans. Mass killings of internees sometimes occurred, but these severe crimes were carried out for military reasons, when, for instance, the enemy was approaching.

It is understandable that the procedure as well as the legal rules applied in Nuremberg and Tokyo are open to criticism. At Tokyo, this criticism focused on the new "crime against peace." Many questions arose. Was it inconsistent with the international law then in force to start a war if a nation felt that its security was ideologically or economically threatened? Were the wars started by Japan purely wars of conquest, or did genuine security considerations play a role? Finally, did the current international law imply individual criminal accountability for crimes against peace?

Some contributors to this conference answer these questions in the negative. And, indeed, it is scientifically unjustifiable to give a positive answer to all these questions. At the time there was no absolute prohibition of war, nor a total ban on the first use of violence. Such a prohibition could be found neither in the Covenant of the League of Nations nor in the Kellogg-Briand Pact (the Pact of Paris of 1928). For violence in self-defense, including military action against nonmilitary threats, was still condoned. And the state itself retained the prerogative to decide whether threats to national interests or actual infringement on national interests called for military response.

Wars of conquest were illegal. That was certain. And this was mostly the point of contention at Nuremberg. The judicial position of the principal cases there was clearer and less subtle than in Japan. For in Japan the question could be posed whether fear of Communism from the north and anxiety about dependence on raw materials from the south had played a decisive role. This does not mean that in cases where this fear led to a military reaction it was politically prudent or legally admissible. But we see now, perhaps more clearly than at the time of the trial, how an important role can be played by fear of Communism and anxiety over dependence on raw materials.

Aggressive War: Extenuating Circumstances

This fact is evident most clearly in the present attitude of the United States, where the traditional openness leaves no doubt about the motives of American military policy. This policy is determined not only by fear of the military might of the Soviet Union but also by fear of spreading Communism in the Third World and anxiety concerning dependence on raw materials from abroad.

President Reagan has openly admitted that he sees Communism as "the focus of all evil," a force that must be fought by all Christians. Again and again, articles are published about the military power of the Soviet Union, a power which is supposed to necessitate enormous expansion of the military capabilities of the United States and NATO. This expansion of armaments has been in the planning for some time and has already been partly realized. It all culminated in the plans announced in the "Star Wars" speech: the construction of an impregnable laser-curtain that would negate all the Soviet Union's offensive strategic nuclear weapons and endow America with absolute superiority. It constitutes a fundamental divergence from the ground rules adopted in 1972 in the SALT I treaty, that a certain balance of power is the basis for reasonably friendly relations in the nuclear era.[7]

American defense spending is determined primarily by data about the might of the Soviet Union. But it is clear that the function assigned American military power involves more than assuring "military security," that is, more than assuring that the weapons will not be used. Harold Brown, President Carter's secretary of defense, wrote in his report for the fiscal year 1982: "During the decade of the 1980's, our central interests include but go beyond military security."[8] Interests of the state can also be threatened by nonmilitary means, for example, by ideological developments or economic factors.

Military Intervention by the Superpowers

The superpowers are accustomed to intervening militarily when undesirable ideological developments take place. This goes for the Soviet Union (Hungary, Czechoslovakia, Poland, Afghanistan) as well as for the United States (Guatemala, Cuba, the Dominican Republic, Vietnam, Grenada, Nicaragua). Military force then assumes the function of insuring "ideological security." Caspar Weinberger, Reagan's secretary of defense, stated in his report for the fiscal year 1983 that "defense strategy" "must bring to a halt the further expansion and consolidation of the Soviet military empire, whether that expansion would proceed through direct intervention (as in Afghanistan) or through less direct intervention (as in Angola, Nicaragua and elsewhere)."[9] This last objective is disquieting. It leads to military interventions that no longer accord with the only reasonable function of national armaments today, namely, insuring that the weapons will not be used.

A second expansion of this, the only reasonable and legitimate function of national armaments, relates to the preservation of economic welfare. Here the danger lies primarily in dependence on the raw materials of other countries. Harold Brown stated it in dramatic terms: "A large scale disruption in the supply of foreign oil could have as damaging consequences for the United States as the loss of an important military campaign, or indeed a war."[10]

Caspar Weinberger probably went even further when he counted among "the nation's fundamental vital interests and the foreign policy needed to protect them" the need "to protect access to foreign markets and overseas resources in order to maintain the strength of the United States' industrial, agricultural and technological base and the nation's economic well-being."[11]

Here is a candid statement that insuring "economic security" in the sense of "economic well-being" is still considered to be a function of the military power of a state.

War, International Law, and Nation-States

It is evident that the great powers do not recognize the absolute prohibition on war, that is, the prohibition on the first use of force.[12] This absolute ban on the threat of force and on the first use of force is a fundamental rule of the United Nations, as stated in article 2, paragraph 4, of the UN charter. If the other party initiates the use of military force, one may naturally reciprocate with force, but only "until the Security Council has taken the measures necessary to maintain international peace and security" (art. 51). This ground rule is affirmed once more by the definition of aggression laid down in a resolution of the UN General Assembly (3314 XXIX of 14 Dec. 1974), article 5 of which states explicitly: "No consideration of whatever nature, whether political, economic, military or otherwise, may serve as a justification for aggression." The "provisional measures" of the International Court of Justice of 10 May 1984, concerning the American mining of the Nicaraguan coast, rest on the same ground rule.[13]

The repugnance of war expressed in this total prohibition was intensified by the events of World War II, by the atrocities (such as the gas chambers) committed then, and by the massive destruction made possible by modern weapons, which culminated in the atomic bombing of Japanese cities. The technological development of weaponry and the criminal use of these weapons emphasized the madness of modern war, strengthening the view that it is not only wrong but also criminal to launch a war.

In earlier times one could reasonably speak of a *bellum justum*. The doctrine of the just war is a doctrine concerning the right to initiate war; there was no need for a special doctrine recognizing the inherent right of self-defense against armed attack. The doctrine of the just war was understandable in an anarchic world of primitive states, in which there was no central authority or power capable of maintaining justice. In those circumstances it was natural that states acted independently to defend their interests with military force. The dubious aspect of this system was that the states themselves determined whether the circumstances permitted and required the use of force.

It was Hugo Grotius above all who developed the doctrine of *bellum justum* in detail, if not *ad absurdum*. Clothed in elegant language and inspired, it seemed, only by a yearning for justice, his theory in fact provided the state with the rationale for starting any war it desired with a clear conscience. It is understandable that his doctrine led finally to the recognition of the state's right to initiate a war—precisely because the state itself acted as sole judge. The freedom of the state to instigate a war was the starting point for the minor, almost futile restrictions imposed by the Second Hague Peace Conference held at the beginning of this century.

The maintenance of justice is an important matter. But each method recommended to achieve that end must be judged on its own merits. Formerly, in the era of limited wars conducted with more or less primitive weapons, war could be seen as the *ultima ratio*, as a test of strength to determine whose will and opinion would prevail. The character of war itself, however, changed with the introduction of weapons of mass destruction, especially atomic weapons, and new methods of delivery against which no defense is possible. War began as a method of determining who was the strongest; with nuclear weapons war became a means of annihilation. But that is not all. It is clear that nuclear weapons can hardly distinguish between the military and common citizens, nor between belligerents and neutrals, nor even in many respects between the living generation and posterity. And specialists are more and more convinced that our earth will become uninhabitable if the available nuclear weapons are used.

Precisely because of existing alliances and factual interdependence, every war entails the risk that it may escalate into a world war involving the superpowers. That risk is unacceptably great: hence the absolute soundness of the prohibition on the first use of force laid down in the UN charter. Thus, the doctrine of the just war has become in our time a fatal doctrine, although it is still heartily recommended by some theologians and moralists who apparently lack the imagination to realize what a modern war would mean.[14] The doctrine is eagerly accepted and enthusiastically praised by all those who want to continue international relations in the old way. This pre-atomic attitude means that it is power that counts, especially military power, and that power should be used to realize political aims. At present, these typical pre-atomic contentions are gaining ever more influence and support, although it should be obvious that, in this time of unusable but indispensable nuclear weapons, the only function of national military might is to prevent war.

However, a total prohibition on violence has not prevented armed conflict, as is clear from the many wars that have been fought since 1945. That war has not broken out between the United States and the Soviet Union is probably due more to the fact that they dare not risk a direct military confrontation because of existing weapons and missiles than to their respect for the ban on war. It is undeniable that the deterrence of nuclear weapons has a peace-keeping aspect. It is also true, however, that deterrence leads to the build-up of an enormous destructive power that in turn influences governments. President Eisenhower's fears and warnings were well-founded. This influence of the military world, the arms industry, research centers, and related bureaucracies led to the present over-armament and to the continued struggle for superior weaponry between the superpowers. The weapons have become a danger in themselves. This is another aspect of the system of deterrence.

In this sphere too, progressive development of international law is called for. The present international military order rests on the freedom of national states to arm themselves. Existing treaties on arms control and disarmament limit this freedom for the states that are party to them. A "nonnuclear state" which is party to the nonproliferation treaty may not acquire nuclear arms, just as the parties to the treaty concerning biological weapons relinquish the right to possess bacteriological weapons. But every state is free to decide whether or not to be party to these treaties. An even more significant point is that every important treaty on arms control and disarmament contains a special *clausula rebus sic stantibus* allowing states to cancel the treaty on short notice if, in their opinion, "extraordinary events related to the subject matter of the treaty have jeopardized their supreme interests."[15]

In short, the present-day military order is still based essentially on the freedom of states to resort to military force. However, such freedom is only compatible with comparatively primitive weapons. It cannot be rationally defended when arms exist whose use may make human life on earth impossible.

Where does the state get the right to endanger all of humanity in order to guard its own security? The age-old tradition of the state's right to resort to force may have had its function in an earlier era; but now, having become intolerably perilous, it requires our greatest vigilance. There is no doubt, however, that this tradition will be tenaciously and powerfully defended.

The prohibition of war is only one factor in the struggle for the maintenance of peace. There are others, such as legal restrictions on the state's right to resort to arms. In other words, we must work toward a new international military order that no longer rests on the traditional freedom of states to arm. If peace is to be preserved, restrictions in other areas of national sovereignty will also be inevitable: for example, in the economic sphere. Ever increasing economic interdependence demands a new international economic order. When problems relating to the scarcity of certain raw materials manifest themselves in all seriousness, international regulations will have to limit the principle of "permanent sovereignty over natural resources," now so highly regarded by national governments. The idea of the "common heritage of mankind" will gradually have to include the earth's scarce raw materials.

None of this implies the abolition of the sovereign nation-state. The slogan "One world or none" may contain elements of truth, but it represents an ideal that is not attainable politically in the foreseeable future. Nonetheless, every effort must be made to limit national sovereignty when it leads to tension and the use of violence. The extant primitive state-anarchy must become a more "mature anarchy," "where the benefits of fragmentation could be enjoyed without the costs of continuous struggle and instability."[16]

This more mature anarchy will be characterized by an international policy that is not ruled directly by national self-interest. Every living creature needs an environment in which it can thrive. The regional environment is of foremost importance for the national state, but a healthy and peaceful global environment is of overriding importance in many vital areas. Hence a national foreign policy pursuing a "better world" is completely in accordance with the traditional theory that the government of a state must serve the national interest. In the traditional theory, however, direct self-interest most often weighs too heavily. Ultimately, the welfare of the state in the near future and the welfare of the world around us are both vital parts of the national interest.

It is an open question whether national governments will be inclined to follow such a reasonable policy. Only a few countries in the world are democracies. And the governments of many countries do not have the national interest at heart, but rather the material interests of a small "elite." Even the governments of the greater democratic states are more or less the servants of powerful factions. Some of these powerful groups are virtually unassailable because they have the financial means to influence, if not determine, political outlooks. This is all the truer because in every big country nationalism exists, or is latent, in smaller or larger groups that demand that their countries have the military power to protect and promote direct national interests. In the pre-atomic era militarism and nationalism played a perilous role; today, in the era of nuclear weapons, they gamble with the very existence of mankind.

The Peace Movement

The only force capable of countering the power of the "military-industrial complex" and nationalism is mass action by a concerned or alarmed citizenry. It is precisely the peace movement that can provide governments anew with the freedom to act rationally. The question remains whether the peace movement will ever be massive enough to help influence governments to act in a rational manner. Such peace movements base themselves on anxiety concerning arms proliferation and the threat associated with it. Is the general public ready to come to grips with the existing situation? Or is it afraid to look reality squarely in the face and recognize the horrendous danger? It is a common human trait to ignore, if possible, any danger lurking in the future. And in questions of war and peace, many people are inclined to accept governmental assurances that greater military power produces greater security.

Seen in historical perspective, the significance of the postwar trials lies in their contribution to the aversion for war and to the insight that in the nuclear age war no longer has a place. These trials advanced the legal position that the launching of war is a criminal act. Individual accountability for acts of state helped to crystallize the conviction that war is by nature criminal.

During the trials in Nuremberg and Tokyo, the prosecution pointed to the deterrent force of individual criminal accountability. Supposedly it would prevent statesmen and influential military personnel from adopting a bellicose posture. It seems to me that this kind of deterrence is practically insignificant. War in the sense of von Clausewitz—war as a continuation of policy by other means—is begun in the expectation of victory. And victors are not held accountable, even though their crimes may be known. Lady Macbeth's cry, "What need we fear who knows it, when none can call our power to account?" expresses an often bitter reality.

The idea of individual criminal accountability does not mean that now, according to valid international law, individuals can be held responsible. Indeed, no trials dealing with this problem have taken place since 1945, despite the frequent occurrence of wars of aggression. It is persuading the general public that counts.

General opposition to war is understandable. But the real question is this: to what degree will war be rejected as a way of resolving conflicts? It is clear that the elimination of war—due to the ban on war or to the fear of modern weapons—will give the weaker nations greater freedom to act for good, as well as greater freedom to misbehave. In other words, the elimination of war demands tolerance and a readiness to make sacrifices on behalf of peace. The price of peace may be high and entail unpleasant consequences, such as restrictions on sovereignty in many areas.

Only the deep conviction of the absolute impermissibility of war can further the willingness to make such sacrifices. Reviving the memories of World War II, including the atrocities and the judgments, has the merit of contributing to that deep awareness of the repugnance of war that mankind needs in order to survive.

B. V. A. Röling
(Judge at the International Military Tribunal for the Far East)
Groningen 1985

THE TOKYO TRIAL FROM THE PERSPECTIVE OF INTERNATIONAL LAW

MAY 28
1983
(morning session)

OPENING ADDRESS
Hosoya Chihiro

Issues Raised by the Tokyo Trial

Nearly thirty-five years have passed since the conclusion of the International Military Tribunal for the Far East on 12 November 1948. People have gradually forgotten the great trial in Tokyo, and its impact has begun to fade. But the problems posed by the Tokyo trial are far too important for us to allow it to fade into obscurity. On the assumption that, today once again, there is much point in taking up the issues raised by the Tokyo trial, a documentary film has been made dealing with the trial and the historical period upon which it sat in judgment; and today, this international symposium on the trial has been convened.

The issues involved in a discussion of the Tokyo trial are many and varied. First, there are legal issues, issues that were hotly debated at the time and still remain unresolved today. These include the question of the significance, or one might say the relevance, of a trial in which the victors judged the vanquished. There is the issue of what legal criteria should be used to separate aggressive wars and wars of self-defense. And there is the question of whether individuals should be held accountable for acts of state. These and many other legal problems still remain unresolved. This morning, we will be looking at the trial from the perspective of international law and discussing issues such as these.

Next, we must consider the various historical problems of the period leading up to the Pacific War, the period that became the object of the International Military Tribunal for the Far East. The tribunal handed down one particular interpretation of that period. Simply stated, it is the view that Japan's wartime leaders conspired to launch a war of aggression. In the thirty-odd years since the trial, very different interpretations have emerged. In some cases, they have been based on different premises or points of view. In others, they are conclusions based on research into new materials that have gradually emerged during the postwar period. This research has been actively carried out at both the individual and group levels. I believe we have reached a stage at which we need to reexamine these interpretations and the evidence on which they are grounded. This topic we will discuss in today's afternoon session.

A third question, also asked at the time, is simply this: What on earth was the Tokyo trial? Today, nearly thirty-five years later, I think we need to ask that question once again. What indeed was the meaning of the trial? Was it—or was it not—a landmark in the effort to construct world peace? This question we will take up in the morning session tomorrow. And, in the afternoon, the contemporary significance of the trial will be the focus of the general discussion concluding our symposium.

In the entire period since the conclusion of the Tokyo trial, I do not believe there has been a symposium of this nature. I am firmly convinced that a gathering such as this, in which all of the leading commentators on the trial gather in one place to discuss its meaning, is of enormous significance. I have great expectations for fruitful discussions that can make some contribution to worldwide efforts to achieve peace.

Speakers and Panelists

I would like now to introduce the speakers and the panelists. First, Professor Alexandr E. Lounev, of the Institute of State and Law, Academy of Science of the USSR. Professor Lounev's specialties are the theory of the state and public administration. He will be speaking in this morning's session on the legal aspects of the trial. He will be followed by Professor Knut Ipsen, president of Ruhr University at Bochum, who specializes in international law.

Dr. R. John Pritchard, from the United States, presently lives in England, where he is a research fellow at the University of London. As you know, he is the compiler of the complete English transcript of the trial and the author of a number of articles on the subject.

Professor Paik Choong-Hyun, of Seoul National University, is a specialist in international law. Professor Yu Xinchun, of the People's Republic of China, specializes in Japanese history at Nankai University. Professor Than Tun, of Burma, is now a visiting professor at Kyoto University. His specialty is history. Professor B. V. A. Röling, professor emeritus of Groningen University in the Netherlands, is an eminent scholar of international law and a leading figure in peace research. He represented the Netherlands as a judge in the Tokyo tribunal. Professor Richard Minear, of the University of Massachusetts in the United States, is a historian and the author of *Victors' Justice*.

I would now like to introduce one of the most active organizers of this symposium, Professor Andō Nisuke of Kobe University. Professor Andō specializes in international law. Next, another organizer, Ōnuma Yasuaki, associate professor of international law in the faculty of law, University of Tokyo. Professor Ōnuma has written extensively on the Tokyo trial. Professor Okuhara Toshio, of Kokushikan University, teaches international law. In addition, I would like to introduce Professor Awaya Kentarō, of Rikkyo University, and Professor Hata Ikuhiko, of Takushoku University. Both specialize in modern Japanese history. I would also like to introduce Mr. Hagiwara Nobutoshi, a critic and scholar of modern Japanese history.

I now have the great privilege of introducing two special guests. First, Mr. Kinoshita Junji. Novelist, playwright, essayist, and critic, Mr. Kinoshita has written extensively on the Tokyo trial and the period in which it occurred. His play *Between God and Man* has been translated into English and other foreign languages. Mr. Tsurumi Shunsuke is a philosopher and critic who has written on Japanese war guilt and who has been active in the Japanese peace movement. Professor Ienaga Saburō of Chuo University . . . Perhaps he doesn't require an introduction.

I would now like to turn the chair over to Professor Andō Nisuke, who will preside over the morning session.

CHAIR (Andō Nisuke): I am pleased to open the first session of the Internationall Symposium on the Tokyo War Crimes Trial. The topic of this session is the trial as seen from the perspective of international law. Our three speakers this morning are Professor Lounev, of the Soviet Union, Professor Ipsen, of West Germany, and Professor Ōnuma, of the University of Tokyo. Their presentations will be followed by comments from Professor Paik and Professor Okuhara. Then, after a fifteen-minute recess, we will enter the question-and-answer period. I would like at that time to give precedence to questions and comments from the panelists seated on the stage. Next in order of priority are the approximately twenty special guests who have a direct connection with the Tokyo trial. They are seated in the front rows of the hall. If there is time remaining afterward, I will open the discussion to members of the general audience. Professor Lounev, you have the floor. [Applause.]

LEGAL ASPECTS OF THE ACTIVITIES OF THE INTERNATIONAL MILITARY TRIBUNAL FOR THE FAR EAST
Alexandr E. Lounev

The Nuremberg and Tokyo Trials

During this symposium we will discuss problems that are not only very important but also extremely complicated. In the legal literature of many countries dealing with the Nuremberg and Tokyo trials, many conflicting points of view are expressed. In this report, I will present the Soviet position concerning the Tokyo trial. To some extent, I will connect problems pertaining to the Tokyo trial with the problems surrounding the Nuremberg trial. In order to save time, my report will be read in English.

In Tokyo, the International Military Tribunal for the Far East, consisting of

Note: This paper, written by Dr. Lounev in Russian, was translated and delivered by his interpreter in English.

eleven judges (one each from the USSR, USA, China, Great Britain, France, Australia, the Netherlands, India, Canada, New Zealand, and the Philippines), tried twenty-eight major Japanese war criminals. This number included four former prime ministers, eleven former ministers, two former ambassadors, and eight high-ranking generals of the Japanese armed forces. In the course of the proceedings, two of the accused died, and their criminal cases were dismissed. The case of Ōkawa, the ideologist of Japanese imperialism and militarism, was also dropped due to his mental illness.

The Tokyo trial started about five months after the first session of the International Military Tribunal in Nuremberg, which tried twenty-two major war criminals belonging to the top leadership of Nazi Germany. Twelve of the accused were sentenced to death; three were acquitted.

Both trials carried out the will of the peoples of countries that were victims of aggression, as well as the will of other progressive and peace-loving nations. The tribunals tried former leaders of the states and their armed forces who initiated wars of aggression and committed shocking crimes against peace, war crimes, and crimes against humanity.

The Moscow Declaration and the London Agreement

The activities of both international tribunals had, and still have, an international significance. They help unmask present-day aggressors and remind the peoples of the whole world that the war criminals were tried in the name of many tens of millions of innocent victims, in the name of peace all over the world, and in the name of the security of peoples.

The Nuremberg trial, according to which German officers, soldiers, and members of the Nazi Party were found guilty, had as its legal basis the rules of international law, which included the Moscow Declaration of 30 October 1943 [or 1 November, depending on the time zone]. That declaration provided that offenders would be tried and punished in the courts and by the laws of the countries on whose territories the crimes had been committed. The declaration further provided that in the case of major criminals whose offenses had no particular geographical location, punishment would be inflicted by the joint decision of the Allied governments. In this connection we must mention also the agreement on the subject between the USSR, the USA, Great Britain, and France, signed in London on 8 August 1945 [the London Agreement, which included a charter for an international military tribunal for the trial of European Axis war criminals]. The above-mentioned international acts expressed the will of the Allies to prosecute and punish the major war criminals of the European Axis powers.

For the trial of major war criminals, the International Military Tribunal was established and its charter was approved. The charter defined the constitution, jurisdiction, and functions of the tribunal. Article 6 of the charter determined responsibility for criminal acts committed by persons individually or as members of organizations in the interests of the European Axis powers. These crimes included: (1) crimes against peace, (2) war crimes, (3) crimes against humanity.

The question of the responsibility of Japanese war criminals was discussed by the heads of governments of the USA, Great Britain, and China, who expressed the need for a trial of those criminals in the Potsdam Declaration of 26 July 1945. The USSR associated itself with that declaration some time later. Point 10 of the Potsdam Declaration stated: "We do not intend that the Japanese shall be enslaved as a race or destroyed as a nation, but stern justice shall be meted out to all war criminals, including those who have visited cruelties upon our prisoners." In point 6 the declaration stressed the fact that "there must be eliminated for all time the authority and influence of those who have deceived and misled the people of Japan into embarking on world conquest."

Japan Violates USSR-Japan Neutrality Pact

The leaders of Nazi Germany also developed an ideology of aggressive war to gain world supremacy. World War II was started in order to secure world supremacy for the powers of the Berlin-Rome-Tokyo Axis.

Sixty-one states with 80 percent of the world's population were involved in the war, with 110 million men drafted into the armed forces. Losses in human lives reached 50 to 55 million, including 27 million people killed in combat on the various fronts. The Soviet Union played a decisive role in defeating Nazi Germany. In the fighting on the Soviet front, Germany lost about 10 million soldiers and officers, that is, 37 percent of the total [military] losses in World War II. The USSR's losses in human lives totaled 20 million, including civilians. On the territory of the Soviet Union, Nazi invaders killed 6 million civilians and 4 million soldiers. More than 4 million Soviet citizens were sent to Germany for forced labor. The Soviet Union also suffered enormous material losses. The Nazi invaders destroyed 32,000 factories, 65,000 kilometers of railroads, about 100,000 collective farms . . . state farms . . . and many thousands of cities, towns, and villages. Material losses suffered by the Soviet Union totaled 2.6 trillion rubles. [In regard to the above figures, there is some question about the reliability of contemporary statistics, and other scholars advance different figures.]

The ruling clique of Japan made active preparations for an attack against the USSR. It concentrated close to the borders of the USSR a great number of infantry divisions, artillery, air force, and other kinds of armed forces. In order to protect itself from potential aggression, the Soviet Union had to keep some dozens of divisions of its troops on its eastern borders. In this way Japanese militarists and commanders of the armed forces helped Nazi Germany wage war against the USSR. They also supplied Germany with classified information about the USSR. In so doing, the government of Japan violated the neutrality agreement signed with the government of the USSR.

The Charter of the Tribunal

Since the government of Japan and the commanders of its armed forces rejected the demand of the Allies to surrender, the Soviet Union fulfilled its obligation to its allies (reached at the Yalta Conference) and entered into war with Japan.

After the surrender of Japan, the supreme commander of the Allied powers issued on 19 January 1946 the order titled "On the Establishment of the International Military Tribunal for the Far East," in which he said that the tribunal had been established on the basis, and for the implementation, of the rules of international law laid down in the Potsdam Declaration of the USA, Great Britain, and China on 26 July 1945, with which the Soviet Union also [later] associated itself.

The legal status of the International Military Tribunal for the Far East, its structure, and its procedure were defined in the charter approved by the above-mentioned order of 19 January 1946. The charter consists of five sections and seventeen articles.

The four articles of the first section define the "Constitution of the Tribunal": establishment, members, officers and secretariat, quorum, and voting. The second section defines the jurisdiction of the tribunal: jurisdiction over persons and offenses, responsibility of the accused, and prosecutors. Procedural guarantees for the defendants as well as procedures for presenting applications and petitions are laid down in the two articles of the third section, "Fair Trial for Accused." The five articles of the fourth section define rights and obligations of the tribunal, evidence, place of the trial, and procedural order of the trial. The two articles of the fifth section lay down the procedure for the conclusion of the trial: the judgment, punishment, execution of the judgment. According to the charter, members of the tribunal and its president were to be appointed by the supreme commander of the Allied powers on the basis of recommendations by states that signed the instrument of surrender of Japan, as well as by India and the Philippines.

The important legal and procedural rules were laid down in an annex to the charter: "Rules of Procedure of the Tribunal. Content of the Incriminating Points of the Indictment."

Among the legal problems which the Tokyo tribunal faced, the most important was the problem of the nature of the crimes committed by war criminals. The general task put before the tribunal by its charter was formulated as follows: "The Tribunal shall have the power to try and punish Far Eastern war criminals who as individuals or as members of organizations are charged with offenses which include Crimes against Peace."

A Judgment of Historic Significance

Crimes against peace include such acts as the planning, preparation, initiation, or waging of a war of aggression (declared or undeclared), or a war in violation of international treaties, agreements, or assurances. Crimes against peace also include participation in a common plan or conspiracy for the accomplishment of any of the foregoing criminal acts.

War crimes include violations of international laws or customs of war. The third group of crimes consists of crimes against humanity. These crimes include killings, extermination, enslavement and deportation of the civilian population, and other inhumane acts committed before or during the war, including persecution for political or racial reasons.

The crimes committed by German and Japanese war criminals during World War II are being repeated now by the Israeli aggressors in the Middle East and the aggressors of the Republic of South Africa, who provoke military conflicts, wage aggressive wars, violate international laws and customs of war, kill people, and deport civilian populations from the territories in which they were born and lived.

In Tokyo, as well as in Nuremberg, the tribunal rejected the argument of the defense that the charter of the tribunal was not an act of international law. The charters of the Nuremberg and Tokyo tribunals and the judgments given on that basis, punishing war criminals for offenses committed by them (and proved at the trial), have historic significance. They serve as an important moral and legal weapon in the struggle for peace and against the preparation and waging of aggressive wars, especially wars in which nuclear and other weapons of mass destruction are used.

It is well known that the principles of international law recognized by the charter of the Nuremberg tribunal, and also expressed in the judgment of the tribunal, were approved by the UN General Assembly in its resolution of 11 December 1946. Fifty-four states signed that resolution, which expressed the opinion of the United Nations in respect to the character and legality of international law for the trial of war criminals.

In constituting and conducting the Tokyo tribunal, the experience and the charter of the Nuremberg tribunal were widely used.

The Struggle for World Peace

Under present conditions, when progressive forces all over the world struggle for peace and the prevention of nuclear war, when in some countries aggressive tendencies are growing and military conflicts are being provoked, it is very important to strengthen friendship among peoples. At the same time, we should not forget that those persons who committed crimes on occupied territories during World War II, who committed crimes at prisoners-of-war camps, who committed atrocities against civilian populations—all of those persons must bear criminal responsibility.

Many war criminals are still hiding in the USA, some countries of South America, Canada, West Germany, and other countries. In many countries there are forces demanding that statutory limitations be applied to crimes against peace, war crimes, and crimes against humanity.

Along with many other member states of the United Nations, the USSR actively supports the international Convention on Non-Applicability of Statutory Limitations to War Crimes and Crimes Against Humanity, approved by the General Assembly on 26 November 1968. The Presidium of the Supreme Soviet of the USSR has ratified that convention.

In addition, it is necessary to ensure that all states observe the UN General Assembly resolution on the extradition and punishment of war criminals. On the basis of the Hague Convention of 1907, the Moscow Declaration of the heads of governments of the USA, the USSR, and Great Britain adopted on 1 November 1943, declarations made by other Allied states, and the charter of the International Military Tribunal approved on 8 August 1945, the UN General Assembly recommended that all member states of the UN immediately take every measure necessary to ensure that war criminals guilty of crimes against peace, war crimes, and crimes against humanity be arrested and sent back to the countries in which their crimes were committed, in order that they might be judged and punished according to the laws of those countries.

Unfortunately, the governments of some countries do not observe the resolution of the General Assembly and refuse to extradite war criminals on the demand of the Soviet government and the governments of other countries.

The Legal Grounds for Soviet Participation in the Tokyo Trial

For a correct understanding of the legal grounds for Soviet participation in the Tokyo trial of the major Japanese war criminals, it is necessary to become acquainted with that part of the judgment of the International Military Tribunal for the Far East which lays out proof that Japan planned and committed acts of aggression against the USSR.

It was proven at the trial that as early as 1924 the aim of Japanese expansion had been formulated: the occupation of Soviet territories in the Far East and Siberia.

In 1936 a military putsch took place in Japan. The main point in the program of the leaders of the putsch was the demand to adopt an aggressive policy against the USSR and China in order to make Japan the dominant power in the whole of Asia. From 1936 to 1940, Japan, together with Nazi Germany, had been preparing for aggression against the USSR on the basis of ideas laid down in the Anti-Comintern Pact. That aggressive alliance against the USSR was broadened when in 1940 Nazi Germany, fascist Italy, and militarist Japan signed a military pact [the Tripartite Pact]. Without denouncing the treaty of neutrality with the USSR, the Japanese government guaranteed assistance to Germany in case of war between Germany and the USSR. The Japanese general staff was preparing a plan of military attack against the USSR in 1941, and a plan for administration of the occupied Soviet territories from the littoral to Lake Baikal was approved.

The test of forces in 1938 near Lake Khassan [Changgufeng; Ch'ang-ku-feng] and in 1939 in Nomonhan (Halhin Gol) in Mongolia represented aggressive military actions by Japan against the USSR.

The USSR, which always has been and now remains an active fighter for peace, stood and now stands against aggressive wars. The USSR Constitution declares in article 28: "The USSR steadfastly pursues a Leninist policy of peace and stands for strengthening of the security of nations and broad international cooperation. . . . In the USSR war propaganda is banned."

Problems of Procedure and Organization

Ladies and gentlemen, from our point of view, there were some shortcomings in the organization and functioning of the International Military Tribunal for the Far East. First, the charter of the tribunal was not prepared on a collective basis by the states participating in the trial. Unlike the Nuremberg charter, the charter for the Tokyo tribunal was drafted personally by the supreme commander of the Allied forces, General MacArthur. Apart from that, it somehow contradicts legal tradition that the president of the tribunal was not elected by the members of the tribunal but was appointed by General MacArthur himself. The chief prosecutor was also appointed by General MacArthur, unlike Nuremberg where all prosecutors from participating countries had equal rights and participated on an equal footing. And, from our point of view, it does not seem a very democratic procedure when defense counsel from the United States were allowed to participate in the trial even though they were from a country that was at the same time prosecuting the war criminals. These are some remarks on the legal aspects of the conduct of the International Military Tribunal in Tokyo, which by its judgment of November 1948 punished major Japanese war criminals by sentencing seven of them to death, sixteen to life imprisonment, one to twenty years imprisonment, and one to seven years of imprisonment. Thank you very much. [Applause.]

CHAIR: Thank you very much, Professor Lounev. Professor Lounev's paper provides an overview of the entire trial, as well as the process leading up to it, and I'm sure it will prove useful to those who have little knowledge of the trial.

    I would now like to introduce Professor Ipsen, who will speak on the technical legal aspects of the trial.

A REVIEW OF THE MAIN LEGAL ASPECTS OF THE TOKYO TRIAL AND THEIR INFLUENCE ON THE DEVELOPMENT OF INTERNATIONAL LAW

Knut Ipsen

Thank you, Mr. Chairman. First of all, I should like to extend my congratulations to my learned colleagues Professors Andō and Ōnuma and to Kōdansha Limited for the excellent idea of holding this symposium, which may lead to a better understanding of what happened and of what to avoid in the future. Although there are countless problems involved in the Tokyo trial, in my legal analysis of the trial and its consequences for the progressive development of international law, I shall concentrate on two issues, which are, indeed, the most basic, most important, and most frequently disputed issues: (1) Was the Tokyo trial in conformity with international law in force at the time? (2) Have the legal principles applied at the Tokyo trial (as well as at the Nuremberg trial) been reaffirmed, or have they even been progressively developed by present international law?

Only an honest judgment of these issues, based on scholarly methods of interpretation, will produce an answer to the question of whether international criminal law can contribute effectively to the maintenance of peace.

A. THE INTERNATIONAL LAW
IN FORCE AT THE TIME OF THE TOKYO TRIAL

Analysis of the first issue has to begin with an indisputable statement: that in international law a treaty, as such, creates obligations and rights only for the contracting parties. This is a well-established general principle of international law, in force today as well as in the mid-1940s and earlier. A state that is party to a treaty is, by definition, a subject of international law, to which all respective provisions, rules, and principles of international law are to be applied. The international legal position of Japan as a subject of international law was never contested by the Allied powers in 1945 and 1946. This legal position of Japan was, moreover, the fundamental precondition for all its obligations derived from the Instrument of Surrender of 2 September 1945. By this instrument the Japanese authorities undertook "to carry out the provisions of the Potsdam Declaration in good faith, and to issue whatever orders and take whatever action may be required by the Supreme Commander for the Allied Powers or by any other designated representatives of the Allied Powers for the purpose of giving effect to the Declaration." With regard to the prosecution of crimes committed by Japanese nationals, the Potsdam Declaration stated: "Stern justice shall be meted out to all war criminals." It was from this provision of the Potsdam Declaration, included in the Instrument of Surrender, that the supreme commander explicitly derived his powers to establish the International Military Tribunal for the Far East by the special proclamation just quoted by the previous speaker, my colleague Herr Lounev. By exercising these powers the supreme commander, as an organ of the Allied powers, was of course strictly bound by the Instrument of Surrender, as well as by all other instruments and rules of international law applicable between Japan and the Allied powers. These powers and Japan were, with one exception, parties to the Hague Regulations, article 43 of which prescribes: "The authority of the legitimate power having in fact passed into the hands of the occupant, the latter shall take all the measures in his powers to restore, and ensure, as far as possible, public order and safety, while respecting, unless absolutely prevented, the laws in force in the country." Neither the wording nor the object and purpose of the Instrument of Surrender, or of article 43 of the Hague Regulations, could be taken as a legal basis for the argument that the powers of the supreme commander included the right to establish a jurisdiction that was unknown until that time in international law or in municipal Japanese law. The charter of the International Military Tribunal for the Far East was apparently not interpreted by the IMT itself as establishing a new jurisdiction. With reference to the Nuremberg IMT it was stated: "The Charter is not an arbitrary exercise of power on the part of the victorious nations but is the expression of international law existing at the time of its creation." Taking this authoritative opinion as the starting point for further analysis, we must examine whether the charter of the IMT only restated already existing treaty law or whether it codified customary law then in force. Therefore, we must take a closer look at the problem of how jurisdiction is legally established, especially in criminal matters.

I. The Jurisdiction of the International Military Tribunal

The jurisdiction of a state to adjudicate upon charges against individuals was based at the time of the Tokyo trial, as it is today, primarily on territorial authority. This well-known *principle of territorial jurisdiction* means that a state may prosecute crimes committed on its territory, whether by its own or by foreign nationals. The first exception to this principle is *personal jurisdiction*, which empowers the state to prosecute crimes committed by foreign nationals or its own nationals outside its territory when the crimes are directed against anything protected by its own legal order. [This is generally called protective jurisdiction. Personal jurisdiction is the principle whereby a state prosecutes crimes committed by its *own* nationals according to its own laws, regardless of where the crimes were committed.] The second exception is the so-called *principle of universal jurisdiction*. This principle is defined negatively by the fact that, in the case concerned, neither the principle of territorial jurisdiction nor the principle of personal jurisdiction is to be applied. Defined positively, universal jurisdiction is based on international law, either treaty law or customary law. Therefore, the crime in question must be condemned internationally by a treaty provision or a customary law rule. This provision or rule must, moreover, authorize the state to prosecute that crime regardless of where it was committed or who committed it. An example of a crime for which universal jurisdiction has long been established is piracy.

The common denominator of these three principles is that they establish *national jurisdiction* for the prosecution of crimes on the basis of the respective *national* legal order. Even the principle of universal jurisdiction presupposes that a rule or provision of international law condemning a certain crime is transformed into national criminal law. This indispensable precondition clearly prohibits making one of the three principles explained above the legal basis of the Tokyo IMT, for by its very definition the IMT was not a national tribunal (e.g., a court-martial), nor did it apply national criminal law.

Thus, we must examine whether the *international jurisdiction* claimed by the tribunal was in fact established by the charter of the IMT. If it was, it would presume that the charter contained international law applicable between the subjects of international law involved, that is, Japan, nationals of which had been accused, and the Allied powers, exercising jurisdiction. According to article 5 of the charter, the Tokyo tribunal was to have "the power to try and punish Far Eastern war criminals who as individuals or as members of organizations are charged with offenses which include Crimes against Peace." The jurisdiction of the tribunal was defined expressly in the same article: "The following acts, or any of them, are crimes coming within the jurisdiction of the Tribunal

for which there shall be individual responsibility:
a) Crimes against Peace. . . .
b) Conventional War Crimes. . . .
c) Crimes against Humanity. . . .''
If the jurisdiction thus defined was in conformity with international law, it *must have been derived* from sources of international law then in force for the Allied powers as well as for Japan. Therefore, we must analyze each of the three categories of international crimes contained in the charter to see whether it fulfills this presupposition.

1. Individual Responsibility for Crimes against Peace?

The charter defined crimes against peace as, ''namely, the planning, preparation, initiation or waging of a declared or undeclared war of aggression, or a war in violation of international law, treaties, agreements or assurances, or participation in a common plan or conspiracy for the accomplishment of any of the foregoing.''

There is no doubt that before the Nuremberg and the Tokyo trials, international customary law did not include a rule formulated as precisely as this concrete provision of the charter. In particular, there was no definition of aggression derived from general practice and accepted as law by all nations. All attempts to introduce such a definition into international law during the time of the League of Nations failed. The Geneva Protocol of 2 October 1924, which in its preamble defined a war of aggression as an international crime, did not go into force. Thus, there was no clear-cut definition of aggression in international law when the Tokyo charter was proclaimed. In order to defend its jurisdiction in spite of this legal uncertainty, the Tokyo tribunal took recourse to the same argumentation as the Nuremberg tribunal, declaring itself to be in complete accord with the latter's opinions and the reasoning by which they had been reached. The main argument was a reference to the Pact of Paris of 27 August 1928. The tribunal stated: ''The Nations who signed the Pact or adhered to it unconditionally condemned recourse to war for the future as an instrument of policy and expressly renounced it. After the signing of the pact any nation resorting to war as an instrument of national policy breaks the pact. In the opinion of the Tribunal, the solemn renunciation of war as an instrument of national policy necessarily involves the proposition that such a war is illegal in international law; and that *those who plan and wage such a war*, with its inevitable and terrible consequences, *are committing a crime in so doing*'' (emphasis added).

The tribunal was right in stating that the resort to war was a breach of the Pact of Paris and that therefore such a resort to war was illegal in international law. With regard to the Pact of Paris, resort to war was indeed a grave breach of that treaty, in fact one of the gravest breaches that could occur in international law at that time. Such a breach was—and could only be—committed by the state resorting to war, and this state, as a subject of international law, was responsible under this law for the wrongful act. At the time of the Tokyo trial, this international responsibility was clearly a state responsibility, not an individual responsibility. The aim of the authors of the Tokyo charter to establish individual responsibility deserves high respect because of its moral background. It would have been impossible, however, to reach that aim through legally conceivable and convincing argument. The Pact of Paris, like any other legal instrument, was subject to interpretation on the basis of generally accepted methods. But none of these methods could be invoked to derive from a treaty, which had created obligations only for the states party to it, an additional individual responsibility for the nationals of those states. This impossibility may be one of the reasons why neither before nor after the Nuremberg and Tokyo trials have nationals of states that broke the Pact of Paris been prosecuted by an international tribunal.

The derivation of individual responsibility from the Pact of Paris was not, however, the only argument that went beyond the generally recognized limits of interpretation. Individual responsibility does not necessarily mean criminal responsibility. It has always been a general principle of law recognized by civilized nations that acts for which individuals are responsible may lead to trial and punishment only if such acts are regulated by criminal law. As the tribunal itself acknowledged, "The maxim *nullum crimen sine lege* is not a limitation of sovereignty but is in general a principle of justice." Nevertheless, to take breaches of the Pact of Paris as breaches of international criminal law, as the IMT did, could hardly be justified using generally recognized means of interpretation.

Thus, the charter of the IMT exceeded the framework of then existing international law by two consecutive (but not legally based) steps of argumentation: first, it changed state responsibility for the breach of treaty obligations into individual responsibility; second, it took this individual responsibility as the basis for a newly created international criminal law. Therefore, the jurisdiction of the tribunal with regard to crimes against peace remains doubtful.

2. Jurisdiction for War Crimes?
Article 5 of the charter defined war crimes as "violations of the laws or customs of war." Such war crimes committed by soldiers or by other individuals may be tried and punished by the power which captures and detains the offenders. Already before World War II, this was a general practice of states. This practice was in conformity with article 45 of the Geneva Convention Relating to the Treatment of Prisoners of War of 1929, to which Japan and the Allied powers were bound, which prescribed: "Prisoners of war shall be subject to the laws, regulations, and orders in force in the armies of the detaining Power" (see also articles 60 and 63). The jurisdiction thus described is based on the well-established principle of personal [territorial?] jurisdiction, which I have defined above. In regard to the Geneva Convention of 1929, the jurisdiction of the tribunal was contested by some defendants who had surrendered as prisoners of war. They argued that as prisoners of war they were triable under the articles of the Geneva Convention only by court-martial. But the IMT agreed with the reasoning and conclusion of the US Supreme Court in the Yamashita case, which confined the jurisdiction of a court-martial to offenses that a defendant had committed while a prisoner of war. However, neither chapter 3 of the Geneva Convention of 1929 nor the subsequent practice of the contracting parties supports the view of the US Supreme Court—and certainly not the practice of the United States. I refer to the well-known Malmedy case, which was being tried at the same time the Tokyo trial was being conducted.

As far as war crimes are concerned, international law in force at the time of the Tokyo trial leads to the following findings:

First, defendants who were prisoners of war had to be treated in accordance with the Geneva Convention of 1929. It was within the jurisdiction of the detaining power or powers to try them, and to punish them, for violations of the laws or customs of war in conformity with articles 45, 60, and 63 of the Geneva Convention, as well as for offenses committed before they had been captured. Second, according to customary law already developed before World War II, defendants other than prisoners of war could be tried and punished by courts-martial of the occupying power within the limits set up in article 43 of the Hague Regulations.

These findings raise doubts about the jurisdiction of the Tokyo IMT, which clearly was not a court-martial and did not apply the law of the detaining powers.

3. Jurisdiction for Crimes against Humanity?

The charter defined crimes against humanity as "murder, extermination, enslavement, deportation, and other inhumane acts committed before or during the war, or persecutions on political or racial grounds in execution of or in connection with any crime within the jurisdiction of the Tribunal, whether or not in violation of the domestic law of the country where perpetrated." Already at that time, the general principles of law recognized by civilized nations were accepted as a source of international law applicable to the acts described above, as, for instance, in the statutes of the Permanent Court of International Justice. For decades the legal order of every civilized nation had provided for trial and punishment in cases of offenses such as murder, extermination, and similar inhumane acts. Therefore, within these limits, crimes against humanity may be derived from a recognized source of international law. Until Nuremberg and Tokyo, there was no precedent in international law for jurisdiction over such crimes to be conferred on an international tribunal; still, by virtue of the Hague Regulations it was a lawful act to establish such jurisdiction. For its article 43 empowers the occupying power to "take all the measures . . . to restore . . . public order . . . , while respecting, unless absolutely prevented, the laws in force in the country." The urgent necessity of establishing the jurisdiction of an international tribunal for such grave offenses as crimes against humanity was an exceptional case under this provision.

Therefore, with regard to crimes against humanity, the IMT had an assured basis in the international law then in force. To the extent that the jurisdiction of the IMT extended to persecutions committed in the execution of or in connection with any other crime within the jurisdiction of the tribunal, that jurisdiction exceeded the limits of international law then in force. Therefore, the definition of crimes against humanity did involve a decisive expansion of existing international law. The charter stated: "Leaders, organizers, instigators and accomplices participating in the formulation or execution of a common plan or conspiracy to commit any of the foregoing crimes *are responsible for all acts performed by any person in execution of such plan*" (emphasis added). This extension is an apparent contradiction to the *individual* responsibility established by article 5 of the charter (as described above) and is not to be derived from a general principle of law recognized by civilized nations. For the doctrine of conspiracy was to be found only in the Anglo-American legal system, and even there it had been contested by learned lawyers.

II. A Critical Summary of the Tokyo Trial

The foregoing analysis leads to the following findings:

1. The jurisdiction of the IMT for crimes against peace was not based on international law in force at that time. Individual responsibility had not been established for the prohibition against resort to war already in existence. Nor were there sanctions in criminal law against a breach of that prohibition. To that extent, the charter contained *ex post facto* legislation and was incompatible with the maxim *nullum crimen sine lege*, which the Tokyo tribunal itself recognized expressly as a "general principle of justice."

2. There remain legal doubts with regard to the jurisdiction of the IMT for war crimes, because for such crimes, which unquestionably could be tried and punished, the jurisdiction of courts-martial of the respective detaining and occupying powers was established by the Geneva Convention of 1929 and by customary law. It must be admitted, however, that a fair trial before a court-martial would have led to similar punishments.

3. The jurisdiction of the IMT for crimes against humanity, under the limitations described earlier, was based on international law in force at that time. Article 43 of the Hague Regulations empowered the occupying power to establish an international tribunal, and this tribunal could apply law derived from a recognized source of international law, that is to say, the condemnation of murder and other inhumane acts as a general principle of law recognized by civilized nations.

B. THE INFLUENCE OF THE TOKYO TRIAL ON THE DEVELOPMENT OF INTERNATIONAL LAW

Taking up now the second basic issue, it cannot be denied that international criminal law reached its culmination during the Nuremberg and Tokyo trials. Since then most attempts to reaffirm or develop this law have failed in the preliminary stages. I shall demonstrate this by reference to the main events relevant to this point.

I. The Problem of Jurisdiction

From 1948 to 1950 the International Law Commission discussed the problem of international criminal jurisdiction. The majority of the ILC regarded the establishment of a permanent international criminal court as desirable and possible. In the UN Legal Committee, however, a majority opposed such a court. Some states were of the opinion that jurisdiction for crimes was an indispensable element of sovereignty. To internationalize this element would cause an unacceptable interference in the internal affairs of states. Many other states argued that an international court could not be established unless the law such a court had to apply were determined legally. Discussion of international organs has made no progress since then.

II. The Problem of Applicable International Criminal Law

In regard to the problem of what international law is to be applied, the UN General Assembly reaffirmed the principles of the Nuremberg charter (UN GA Res. 95 I) in 1946 and then asked the ILC to formulate these principles more precisely (UN GA Res. 177 II). The ILC fulfilled this task (YBILC 1950 II, 374), but serious controversies within the General Assembly, especially over the problem of individual responsibility, prevented the General Assembly from endorsing the draft. The General Assembly then recommended that the member states give their opinions on the draft principles (UN GA Res. 488 V). Some of these principles were included by the ILC in its Draft Code of Offences against the Peace and Security of Mankind (YBILC 1951 II, 133), which of course is not in force; and in 1968 further discussion of the Draft Code was postponed within the UN.

With regard to state practice since Nuremberg and Tokyo, states are apparently hesitant to apply the law included in the two charters. I shall give only one example. In the instructions from the military judge to the members of the court-martial in US vs. Calley (the well-known My Lai incident), there was not a single reference to similar international precedents. If the judge had taken the decision of the US Supreme Court in the Yamashita case as a precedent, not only two low-ranking officers but all their superiors would have been prosecuted and punished, as Telford Taylor, for instance, has admitted.

III. Conclusions

In the light of developments and state practice since Nuremberg and Tokyo, we must conclude unhappily that the law of both charters has been neither reaffirmed by treaty law nor developed into customary law. The main problems still to be resolved are the following:

1. The problem of national or international jurisdiction has remained controversial among the states of the world.
2. The majority of states is still not prepared to accept individual responsibility for crimes in international law.
3. In order to meet the requirements of the general principle *nullum crimen sine lege*, the provisions of international criminal law and international procedural law have to be formulated as precisely and definitely as the provisions of national criminal law. In particular, international criminal law must provide exact definitions of justifications and exculpations, such as superior orders or other defenses, which were controversial at the Nuremberg and Tokyo trials.
4. The provisions of international criminal law must include exact descriptions of penalties, that is, of the type of penalty and, in the case of imprisonment, the duration of the penalty.
5. Conflicts between national criminal law and international criminal law must be resolved.

Only when these problems are solved will international criminal law contribute significantly to world peace. I hope we shall see such a development in the future. Thank you, Mr. Chairman. [Applause.]

CHAIR: Thank you. Professor Ipsen has expressed doubts concerning the legal foundations of the Tokyo trial. These doubts concern "crimes against peace," individual responsibility for acts of state, and "crimes against humanity," though this last is not directly related to the Tokyo trial. Moreover, he suggests that the practice of states subsequent to the Tokyo trial has not necessarily moved in the direction of affirming the principles of Tokyo and Nuremberg. He concludes his paper by listing a number of conditions that would have to be fulfilled before these principles could serve as effective law in contemporary international society. In this sense, Professor Ipsen has put forth a number of objections to Professor Lounev's paper.

Our final paper this morning is by Professor Ōnuma of the University of Tokyo. [Applause.]

THE TOKYO TRIAL: Between Law and Politics
Ōnuma Yasuaki

The two previous speakers dealt with the Tokyo trial from a rather traditional point of view; this holds especially for Professor Ipsen, whose paper dealt in great detail with the technical legal problems presented by the trial. Therefore, I would like to limit my discussion of the legal technicalities of the trial and focus on the historical significance of the fact that the Allied powers adopted the method of an international military tribunal in passing judgment on Japan. Specifically, I want to address the issue of the relationship between law and history from a broad perspective, and to do this in terms of our present grasp of the meaning of the trial. Let me begin by enumerating what I view as major problems of the trial.

Victors' Justice

First, the Tokyo trial was unfair. As at the Nuremberg trial, the Tokyo tribunal judged only the Axis power involved. Japan was not even allowed to raise as issues the actions of the Allied powers, which include the atomic bombing of Hiroshima and Nagasaki by the United States and the violation of the neutrality Pact of 13 April 1941 by the Soviet Union.[1] However, the fundamental condition that makes a law a law is its universal applicability. The attitude represented in the statement, "If you steal you are a thief, but I may steal with impunity,"[2] cannot hold for law. This aspect of unfairness—the fact that the tribunal had the character of a political trial—is one of the major factors leading to cynicism about the Tokyo trial. For many people, the Tokyo trial proved the maxim that "might makes right."

The political character of the trial is manifest in the treatment of the emperor, who under the Meiji Constitution bore ultimate responsibility for the war. The tribunal not only failed to call the emperor to account for Japan's war of aggression, but did not even summon him as a witness. Most people who attack the trial for its political nature remain strangely silent on this point. But this is one issue that should be clearly raised.

It is also important to point out that the postwar conduct of the countries that judged the Axis powers in the trials at Nuremberg and Tokyo has seriously detracted from the significance of the Tokyo trial. Consider, for example, America's war in Vietnam, the Soviet Union's suppression of the Hungarian revolt, the Soviet invasion of Afghanistan, and the British-French expedition in the Suez Canal incident. From the standpoint of the legal principles of Tokyo and Nuremberg, it is quite obvious that the leaders of these countries should have been called to account for the illegal use of armed force. As you all know, however, this never happened.[3]

The Allied Powers' Arrogation of "Civilization"

The structure of the postwar world is supported by the two superpowers, and I believe that the essential character of both the United States and the Soviet Union is self-righteousness. While preaching to others that wars of aggression are crimes, both nations have developed arsenals of nuclear weapons capable of destroying all of mankind several times over. Moreover, they persist in sending enormous numbers of troops to distant foreign countries. And on every occasion, they justify these actions in the name of the "Communist threat" or the "criminality of American imperialism." This is nothing but self-righteousness, and there is no doubt that this dogmatism on both sides has served to increase cynicism toward the Tokyo and Nuremberg trials.

There is also the issue of the extent to which the Tokyo trial was an expression of a norm consciousness shared universally by international society. As I will explain later, I believe that ultimately both the Tokyo trial and the Nuremberg trial did include something that embodied the norm consciousness of ordinary people. However, in terms of the process by which law is established, the charter of the International Tribunal for the Far East was promulgated under the sole authority of the supreme commander for the Allied powers, and no neutral countries were included in drafting it.

Moreover, the Tokyo trial took place during the final phase of traditional international law as it existed under a worldwide system of colonialism. As you know, Professor Röling, who is present at this meeting, was one of the judges at the Tokyo trial. Dr. Röling is among the international legal scholars I hold in greatest esteem, and I certainly do not want to be misunderstood on this point; but it is one of the significant facts of the Tokyo trial that a representative of the Netherlands, not an Indonesian, was appointed as a judge. Similarly, judges from England and France assumed seats on the bench instead of Malaysians or Vietnamese. And, "of course," there was no judge from Korea. Despite the fact that Asian peoples suffered the greatest damage in Japan's Greater East Asia War, only three of the eleven judges at the trial represented Asian countries.

Given the international law of the time, this situation was a matter of course. For Malaysia, Vietnam, and Korea were colonies. Still, it cannot be denied that this "matter of course" poses a serious problem for those who would assert the universal nature of the Tokyo trial. Both at Nuremberg and at Tokyo, the Allied powers insisted that judgment was being rendered by "civilization." Certainly, many of the acts on which these tribunals passed judgment deserved censure, whether by the standards of Western or Eastern civilization. But the question still remains: Were the Allied powers in a position to arrogate to themselves the title of "civilization at large"?

The Concepts of the Illegality of War and Leaders' Responsibility

Finally, as Professor Ipsen has pointed out, the "crimes against peace" and "crimes against humanity" applied at Tokyo and Nuremberg were unknown in international law at the time of the outbreak of World War II. Therefore, to treat them as crimes was a violation of the principle of *nullum crimen sine lege, nulla poena sine lege* [unless there is a law, there can be no crime; unless there is a law, there can be no punishment].

The majority opinion of the tribunal, as well as those who defend the trials, attempt to refute this criticism by insisting that crimes against peace, and related crimes, were already recognized in international law at the time of the outbreak of the war. However, this assertion is difficult to support. As I have demonstrated in my book *Sensō Sekinin-ron Josetsu* [Prolegomenon to a Theory of War Guilt], the logical structure of the concept of crimes against peace is a synthesis of the concepts of the "illegality of war" and "leaders' responsibility."[4] The illegality of war is based on the idea that war can be deemed illegal in principle under international law. Leaders' responsibility is the concept that the leaders of a state can be held accountable for acts of state that are negatively judged under international law. It is true that one of these, the illegality of war, had been established in international law by the time of the outbreak of the war.[5] However, this is not true in the case of leaders' responsibility.[6] Therefore, crimes against peace, which is a synthesis of these two, must be considered a new category of crime that came into existence only at the end of World War II. The same can be said of the concept of a "common plan or conspiracy to wage war."

The concept of crimes against humanity is somewhat different.[7] However, it was not known in international law at the time of the outbreak of the war, and in that regard it has the same problematic character as crimes against peace.

Of course, in origin, *nullum crimen* was a principle of human rights, intended to protect ordinary citizens from the enormous power of the state. For that reason, it is doubtful whether the leaders of a state, who are themselves in the seats of power in the state, can assert this principle in an international tribunal. However, if it is granted that *nullum crimen* is applicable to international law, it is then undeniable that the invocation of crimes against humanity at Nuremberg and Tokyo violated that principle.[8]

As I have suggested above, to the extent that we take as our criteria of judgment (1) the actions of the countries that sat in judgment on Japan, and (2) international law as it existed at the time of the trial, it is difficult to acknowledge any constructive value in the Tokyo trial.

However, is it axiomatic that the standards of countries whose own hands are bloody and the state of international law at the time of the outbreak of World War II are the proper criteria for evaluating the Tokyo trial? It is precisely this question—the issue of our posture in evaluating the trial—that I want to address today.

The Problematic Nature of Blind Faith in Existing Law

First, in regard to international law as a criterion of evaluation, it should be pointed out that international law is not immutable, not the same in all ages. In some cases, acts that are considered illegal in one age become legal in the next, and vice versa.[9] Moreover, international law does not govern all spheres of activity. In each age, there are acts totally unanticipated in the international law of that period. More important, the fact that an act is *legal* under the international law of a given period does not necessarily mean that it is *right*. Colonial rule, for example, was considered legal under traditional international law. Hence, until quite recently it was illegal under international law to provide support to people's liberation groups struggling for independence from colonial rulers. Such support was deemed unlawful interference in the internal affairs of the colonial ruler.

As this suggests, whether something is legal under the international law of a given period provides us with no absolute criterion upon which to make value judgments. Despite this fact, the great majority of those studying the legal aspects of Nuremberg and Tokyo have focused on the narrow issue of whether the trials were legal under international law as it existed at the time. I view this as a kind of closed mode of thinking—I should like to call it "faith in existing law"—in which the question of whether the trials were consistent with existing international law is seen not simply as one criterion among many, but as the sole criterion determining our evaluation of the trial as a whole.[10]

Thus, the fact that the great majority of legal evaluations take this approach—that is, whether the trials were in accord with existing international law—has exerted no small adverse influence on our grasp of the historical significance of the Nuremberg and Tokyo trials. Those who defend the trials have long been fighting an uphill battle, their arguments having little power to persuade ordinary people. On the other hand, critics of the trials are unable to reverse their judgments. The result is that the cynical view, "Might makes right," becomes dominant.

Law and the Common Sense of Justice

As I stated at the beginning of my paper, I believe that we should acknowledge frankly that the legal basis for the Tokyo and Nuremberg trials cannot be found in international law as it existed at the time. However, seen from a broader perspective, that admission is not necessarily damaging to the assessment that the trials were legal and legitimate. The problem of crimes against peace is a good example. I pointed out earlier that one of its two constituent elements, the concept of the illegality of war, had received general recognition in international society and had already been established in international law by the time of the outbreak of World War II. It is true that its second element, the concept of leaders' responsibility, had not yet been recognized in international law. As a result, even though the decision to launch an illegal war was made by the leaders of a country, the responsibility for the war, under existing international law, was considered to reside in the country as a whole. In concrete terms, this responsibility took the form of war reparations, which were paid from the taxes collected from individual citizens.[11] The country's leaders bore no responsibility, even though it was their decisions that had led to the illegal acts.

In regard to crimes against humanity, traditional international law simply did not foresee that the leaders of a state might use the state apparatus in the systematic slaughter of an enormous number of the country's own citizens—but this is precisely what the Nazis did. These acts were in fact committed. Traditional international law was deficient in this respect and that deficiency had to be corrected.

I do not know how many of you here have studied the atrocities committed at Oświecim (Auschwitz), in Nanjing [Nanking], and elsewhere during World War II. But what ordinary people first feel on learning of such atrocities is that they must not be tolerated. This reflects an extremely simple sense of justice. But it is precisely this simple sense of justice of ordinary people that is the ultimate *raison d'etre* of law. In that sense, regardless of the undeniable formal flaws in the way this law was established, crimes against peace and crimes against humanity were a legal response to actions of the Axis powers that were in fact intrinsically intolerable, a reaction based on the universal sense of justice held by ordinary people.

Leaders' Responsibility and the Duty of Disobedience to Illegal State Orders

In this way, the Tokyo and Nuremberg trials were meaningful in that they rectified deficiencies and defects in existing international law. For that very reason, they contain concepts that can play an important role in ordering international relations today. Among these ideas, the legal concepts most worthy of our attention are the concept of leaders' responsibility, discussed above, and the concept of "the duty of disobedience to illegal orders."

Traditional international law, established during the late nineteenth century and the early twentieth, took as its central principle the concept of the unity of the state as a single entity. Today, however, in the latter half of the twentieth century, this concept has been severely shaken by the rapid expansion of various human activities, economic relations, and information services that transcend national borders.[12] In the context of these trends, the concept of leaders' responsibility has an eminently modern significance. It dissolves the state logically into its constituent elements—national leaders and ordinary citizens—and holds the national leaders accountable for illegal acts of the state.

For example, South Africa's policy of apartheid is considered illegal under international law. According to traditional international law, the enforcement of apartheid would be considered an illegal act of the *state*, and legal sanctions would be applied against the *state*. However, were economic sanctions to be applied against the *state* of South Africa, the effect would be to impose hardship on the general population of the country, the majority of whom are black.

In short, the traditional conception of international law would have the ironic effect of creating hardship for the very people who are the objects of apartheid in the first place. If, on the other hand, the concept of leaders' responsibility is used as a basis for censure of and sanctions against the *government* of South Africa, international condemnation of apartheid can take place without the negative consequences suggested above.

On the other hand, the citizens of a country engaging in illegal acts should not cooperate in those acts. In today's world, all countries, even the most dictatorial, subscribe in principle to democratic forms of government. Thus, on a formal level the leaders of a country derive their authority from the will of the people. Therefore, it is necessary that the people not cooperate in illegal acts in order to establish grounds for arraigning government leaders—and not the people—for such acts. One cannot escape responsibility for cooperating in wars of aggression or in genocide by arguing that one was acting under orders. This means a repudiation of the idea that, as one member of the state, the individual is completely subsumed in the state. Accordingly, leaders' responsibility and the duty to disobey illegal orders, essentially two aspects of the same entity, deserve our attention as a concept capable of deconstructing the unity and absolute nature of the state.

The Need to Confront Reality

The Tokyo and Nuremberg tribunals, by virtue of the fact that they took the form of trials, laid bare various shameful and horrible acts committed by the Axis powers. Of course, historical scholarship today has gone far beyond the two tribunals in uncovering such facts. However, what is important is that the trials in Nuremberg and Tokyo laid bare the facts of terrible atrocities and murder (at Auschwitz, for example) immediately after the end of the war. The significance of the trials in demonstrating the tragedy and the horror of war to our generation and future generations *with concrete factual evidence*—what in a broad sense we may call their educational function—cannot be emphasized too strongly.

It is highly doubtful that the collection and publication of factual data that took place during the Nuremberg and Tokyo trials could have occurred if the Allied powers had adopted a policy of summary execution (i.e., lining up suspected war criminals and shooting them), as was advocated in some quarters at the end of the war, or if Japan had conducted trials on its own. As a Japanese, I would like nothing better than to avert my eyes from the acts the Japanese army committed on the Chinese mainland; but facts are facts. In the end, there is no alternative for us but to proceed on the basis of these facts.

This is related to a point I raised above: the problematic nature of taking the actions of the former Allied powers, who themselves have blood on their hands, as our criteria of judgment. Even those who criticize Nuremberg and Tokyo would probably not go so far as to say that Germany and Japan did nothing wrong, nor could they. The number of people killed in the Nanjing [Nanking] Incident may be smaller than the number stated by the Tokyo tribunal. But even if the number was smaller, the fact that Japanese troops slaughtered innocent Chinese citizens in Nanjing will not go away. The Soviet Union massacred Polish citizens in the Katyn Forest, and the United States dropped atomic bombs on Hiroshima and Nagasaki. But the fact that Nazi Germany systematically murdered six million Jews still remains.

Japan's Peace Constitution: Something to be Proud of

When it comes to pointing out the unfairness of the Tokyo trial, I share the perception of those who criticize the trial. The problem, however, lies in the value judgments to which this perception leads. To say "you too have done wrong, so I should be forgiven my sins" reveals, I submit, only a bleak poverty of spirit. If the actions of various countries, and especially those of the two super-powers, betray Nuremberg and Tokyo, we should use the trials as weapons in challenging these actions. Such challenges have in fact taken place, in the Stockholm trial of US conduct in Vietnam, and in the International Peoples' Tribunal on Israel's invasion of Lebanon. And these trials were conducted by ordinary citizens without power or government authority. I believe that it is precisely these responses that realize the historical significance of the Tokyo trial—and precisely these responses that are of greatest importance for Japan.

Japan launched wars of aggression, and judgment was passed on it at the Tokyo tribunal. However, when viewed in the spirit of the Tokyo trial, postwar Japan has, by means of its peace constitution, conducted itself in a manner far superior to the former Allied powers. This is a fact in which we Japanese can take pride among peoples of the world.[13]

Flawed as it may be, the law established by the Tokyo trial is law, and therefore the countries that sat in judgment on Japan should be judged by the same law. In fact, Japan—with its past history of war and its present accomplishments as a peaceful nation—has the right to accuse the superpowers of actions that endanger world peace. I believe that this is the way to assume responsibility for past wars of aggression. In short, it is our historical duty.

Despite repeated demands from the United States to rearm itself, Japan has kept its military expenditures at a low level in international terms. Moreover, despite its highly sophisticated industrial base, Japan has achieved its present economic prosperity and social stability almost entirely without exporting weapons. These facts should lend great persuasive force to our efforts to criticize the international conduct of the United States and the Soviet Union.

Issues the Tribunal Did Not Address

In conclusion, I would like to touch briefly on matters that were not directly addressed at the Tokyo trial, and again these concern Japan's historical responsibility. As I stated earlier, the Tokyo tribunal was a trial in which the Allied powers, themselves not without guilt, judged the leaders of Japan, who, all things considered, should certainly have been held accountable. Thus, the trial did not address the issue of the responsibility of the Japanese people. Moreover, Japan's right to exist as a colonial power was negated by World War II, but this issue was also not taken up at the trial. This is closely related to the fact that there was no Korean representative on the tribunal, as I mentioned earlier.

However, in at least one respect the Fifteen-Year War that began with the

Manchurian Incident was historically inevitable. That is, in a sense, it was an inevitable outcome of the path that Japan had taken since the formation of the Meiji regime. World War II was a final reckoning for Japan's "original sin" of the modern era—"leaving Asia, joining Europe" [datsu'a nyūō]. In this sense, the Fifteen-Year War was by no means carried out only by the defendants at the Tokyo trial; it was something for which the Japanese people as a whole were accountable, in which all Japanese were involved.

As a result of World War II, Japan's leaders were brought to judgment at the Tokyo trial. And at the same time, our status as the colonial ruler of Korea and Taiwan, which was a result of Japan's post-1868 policy toward Asia, was negated. We had to pay reparations to Korea and the countries of Southeast Asia. These historical facts were not addressed directly at the Tokyo trial, but I think they should occupy an important place in our consideration of the International Military Tribunal for the Far East. Thank you very much. [Applause.]

CHAIR: Thank you very much. Professor Ōnuma follows Professor Ipsen in pointing out that there are various problematic aspects of the Tokyo trial. Having recognized these problems, he goes on to discuss the stance we should adopt in evaluating the trial. He suggests that international law has changed in the past and will continue to change throughout history. If we consider the trial in this light, it is possible that the fact-finding carried out by the tribunal and the principles applied in judging these facts can have a positive function in limiting future wars. Legal scholars speak of *lex ferenda* and I think Professor Ōnuma has addressed the trial from this perspective—that is, the possibility of creating new law.

I would now like to ask our two discussants, Professor Paik and Professor Okuhara, for comments on the papers. Professor Paik, you have the floor.

COMMENTS BY PAIK CHOONG-HYUN

A Product of Political Compromise

Mr. Chairman, learned scholars, and distinguished guests. It is a real pleasure and a privilege for me to comment on the opinions presented by these distinguished specialists. The day before yesterday I was informed that this conference site is the place where the war criminals were imprisoned. Professor Ōnuma says that it's a coincidence. Today is the twenty-eighth, and twenty-eight people were indicted at the Tokyo trial. This is apparently another coincidence.

My comments are based on two assumptions: first, that the legal aspects of the process of the trial were viewed differently at the time of the trial than they are today, after a lapse of more than thirty-five years; and second, that the political aspects of the Tokyo trial are quite apparent. Indeed, the Tokyo tribunal may be characterized as a product of political compromise, a quasi-judicial body. Compared to the alternative of summary execution, this characteristic of the trial removed to some extent the dangers of political arbitrariness and increased the chances that objective legal standards would be applied. I will make some general comments on each speaker's approach. Of course, these comments will reflect my personal views based on the assumptions outlined above.

I would like to begin with Professor Lounev's paper. Professor Lounev's approach is so policy-oriented that it reminds me of the general attitude displayed by the Allied powers at the time of the Tokyo trial itself. His high evaluation of the judgment as an important moral and legal weapon in the struggle for peace is impressive. But Professor Lounev also offered a lengthy justification of Russia's involvement in the war against Japan, and of Russia's acts leading up to that involvement. It seems to me that logic similar to his could be employed to justify the Japanese attack on Pearl Harbor. Such a double standard of justice clearly undermines the very basis of the authority of international law.

The Neglected Issue of Crimes against Humanity

I will now turn to Professor Ipsen's paper. Professor Ipsen raised two fundamental issues, but he employs such strict legal logic to arrive at his answers that legal technicality seems to obscure the substance of the law. Nevertheless, his proposals for the development of international criminal law point to the very problems we face at the present time.

Finally, I would like to comment on Professor Ōnuma's presentation. His review of the Tokyo trial is quite comprehensive, and I think his position is appropriate at this point in time. The issues he raised, his critique of the trial, and his suggestions for the future all reflect changes in international law and society.

I cannot agree with the opinions of the speakers on some specific issues, but since it would be impossible to discuss all of these in the time allotted, I will pose two broader questions.

First, in connection with the principle of *nullum crimen sine lege*, Professor Ipsen and Professor Ōnuma, with some differences in interpretation, seem to share the opinion that the principle of the responsibility of individuals for crimes against peace had not been accepted into international law at the time these crimes were committed by the accused or at the time of the Tokyo trial. However, they did not address the question of whether or not *nullum crimen sine lege* itself was ever adopted into international law. I understand that even in domestic legal systems there are some exceptional cases in which this principle is not applied to certain categories of crimes.

My second question suggests itself because Professor Ōnuma, although not going into detail, mentioned it briefly at the end of his paper. It is the problem of how the Tokyo trial dealt with crimes against humanity. It should be noted that while the Nuremberg trial placed great emphasis on crimes against humanity, the Tokyo trial apparently failed to recognize the importance of these crimes. All of the speakers this morning seemed to ignore this issue.

As Professor Ōnuma pointed out, historical evidence demonstrates that there was a large number of cases of crimes against humanity: murder, extermination, enslavement, deportation, and other inhumane acts committed by the then existing Japanese government, or with the acquiescence of that government, against minority populations in Japan, Korea, Manchuria, China, the Philippines, and the other Asian regions under Japanese control. But the victorious Allied powers paid very little attention to crimes committed against these colonial peoples, perhaps because the victims of these crimes were not nationals of the victorious nations. All the same, this neglect of crimes against humanity is, I think, one of the most serious defects of the Tokyo trial. Many of the victims of these crimes were left helpless by the injuries they suffered, and they have been left without redress to this day. Thank you. [Applause.]

CHAIR: Thank you very much. Professor Paik has raised two important issues. First, he questioned whether the principle of *nullum crimen sine lege* can be fully applied in international society. Second, he pointed out that the Tokyo trial failed to deal directly with crimes against humanity, despite the fact that many of the acts of the Japanese government amounted to crimes against humanity.

I would now like to ask for some comments from Professor Okuhara.

COMMENTS BY OKUHARA TOSHIO

Crimes Against Humanity and International Law

I would like to begin by thanking the three speakers for their highly informative papers. I was particularly struck by the contrasts in their approaches.

First, a few comments about Professor Lounev's report. The impression I received from Professor Lounev's paper was that basically it was a reaffirmation of the Soviet position at the time of the Tokyo trial, when the Soviet Union was one of the Allied powers. Other specialists on the Nuremberg and Tokyo trials probably noticed this too. However, Professor Lounev made one point that I found very interesting. This was his position on the neutrality pact between Japan and the Soviet Union, an issue that is often discussed in Japan. In Japan, the argument is usually that the Soviet Union violated the pact by attacking Japanese troops without declaring war. But as Professor Lounev has presented it, the Soviet position is that Japan had already violated its obligations as a neutral country. Therefore, the neutrality pact was, in fact, null and void at the time of the Soviet attack. He argues further that even if the Soviet Union did commit a technical violation of the neutrality pact, it was immune from responsibility because of Japan's previous violations. I find this argument very interesting.

Professor Ipsen's paper states the conclusions that must be drawn when one considers the various problems of the Tokyo trial from the standpoint of international law in force at the time. There is almost nothing in his analysis to which I might take exception. However, his assertion that crimes against humanity had already become part of customary international law by the time of the Nuremberg trial is problematic. That assertion may reflect Germany's difficult position in regard to such acts. However, as is true in the case of crimes against peace, it is impossible to conclude from a strict interpretation of international law then in force that crimes against humanity were crimes under international law.

Professor Ipsen's analysis relates largely to the rules of land warfare. To the extent that crimes against humanity overlap with conventional war crimes, we may be able to say that they existed in international law. In fact, however, the action at issue here is the mass slaughter before the war of one's own nationals, as if they were pieces of coal to be thrown into an incinerator. These acts were committed simply because the victims belonged to a particular "race." Ultimately, even at Nuremberg, acts committed before the war could not be dealt with at the trial. Both the tribunal itself and one of the Allied powers that took part in drafting the Nuremberg charter recognized that unless a relevancy could be established to crimes against peace, crimes against humanity were not crimes under international law. Therefore, it became a matter of the relevancy to crimes against peace. In this sense, my understanding in regard to the legality of crimes against humanity differs from Professor Ipsen's analysis. I should point out, however, that I share Professor Ipsen's opinion that, today, crimes against humanity are an established part of international law.

Is "Responsibility" Responsibility Under International Law?

I was familiar with the main points of Professor Ōnuma's paper from his book and his articles. Today he has stated his position very clearly. As in the past, however, there is one aspect of the analysis he presented today that is not clear to me. Briefly stated, it is not clear to me how Professor Ōnuma is using the word *responsibility*. Is he referring to "responsibility" under international law? Or is he using it as a basis for political criticism or moral condemnation—simply to say that the leaders did bad things? If he is referring to rights, responsibilities, or duties under international law—this session of the symposium, after all, concerns international law—I would appreciate it if he would explain his position a little more clearly from the point of view of international law.

Finally, I would like to state briefly my own view, namely, that it is still too soon to reach any conclusive evaluation of the Nuremberg and Tokyo trials. For the evolution of customary international law is characterized in part by its transcendence of existing international law. So if, in the future, the concept of crimes against peace actually becomes a part of customary international law, the Nuremberg and Tokyo trials will take on enormous significance.

It is easy to criticize the trials on the basis of existing international law. But I think we must look at what role they can play in the ongoing formation of new customary international law.

The Motives for Holding the Nuremberg and Tokyo Trials

There is one more point I would like to make. I think it is slightly off the mark to criticize the Tokyo and Nuremberg trials on the grounds that the principles they developed are never applied today, in a generalized form. I think it is essential to consider the motives that led to the trials. The Nuremberg and Tokyo trials were convened in the aftermath of an extraordinary war that engulfed the entire world, unparalleled in scale in the degree to which it involved planned aggression, and in the horrors that accompanied it. In this sense, it was an exceptional war. It was not, after all, your ordinary local or regional armed conflict.

Until we reach a period in which an international criminal court has been established and its compulsory jurisdiction recognized, as Professor Ipsen suggests, it would be impractical to apply the legal principles of Nuremberg and Tokyo to cases of ordinary local military clashes or regional conflicts.

But in the case of world wars, the establishment of such a court had already been attempted at the end of World War I. It ended in failure. The idea was finally realized in the aftermath of World War II, in an exceptional set of circumstances. If a worldwide war were to occur today, more than one billion people would perish. In the aftermath of such a war, would it even be possible to carry on a discussion like this? I think not.

And for that reason, it seems problematic from a realistic viewpoint to apply something so exceptional to this stagnant stage in the development of international society. [Applause.]

CHAIR: Thank you, Professor Okuhara. After commenting on the papers of our three speakers, Professor Okuhara expressed his own opinion that it is too soon to take up the problem of the Tokyo trial, particularly given the nature of customary international law. He suggested further that in view of the scale of the war and the subsequent actions of each country involved, we must broaden our perspective to include such issues as the establishment of an international criminal court, as suggested by Professor Ipsen.

I would like to remind the participants that the purpose of our gathering here is not to take nationalistic positions against one another. Please bear this in mind in making statements.

[Recess]

QUESTION-AND-ANSWER PERIOD

CHAIR: Do any of the panelists wish to speak? Yes, Dr. Pritchard.
DR. PRITCHARD: Regarding the address by Professor Ipsen, I was extremely impressed by his presentation. I feel that there were several points which may have been overlooked.

One is the obvious fact that customary law does not require universal acquiescence in order to have universal application. Secondly, in regard to the principle of territorial jurisdiction, one has not only jurisdiction over one's own territory, but also any occupied territories. This is confirmed in the military codes of the several belligerents, including Japan. Finally, there is the question of national jurisdiction, the legal basis as a national court. Nothing, of course, bars military allies from reaching agreements to hold military courts in collaboration with or in co-participation with each other.

With regard to Dr. Lounev's remarks, particularly his postscript to the written remarks, he is in fact wrong on three matters of fact. The charter was not unilaterally drafted by MacArthur. MacArthur did not appoint Webb.

That in fact was an American appointment, which was then confirmed by the Far Eastern Commission. The amended charter was a Far Eastern Commission document—well, it was agreed to by the Far Eastern Commission. Finally, MacArthur did not appoint Keenan. He was an American appointee, but the appointment was made by the president of the United States in the first instance, and, again, was confirmed by the Far Eastern Commission.

It was very interesting to hear Dr. Lounev, in a very partisan discussion, confirm that, with regard to war criminals or suspected war criminals hiding in various countries, as he puts it, he finds as a spokesman for the Soviet Union that the Soviet Union, along with other states, feels that the universality of human rights protections must be suspended when overriding political considerations are involved. That is all I have to say.

CHAIR: Thank you. If possible we would like to limit individual questions, and the responses, to about five minutes. We will first recognize speakers who wish to respond to questions regarding their papers. Professor Ipsen?

PROFESSOR IPSEN: Yes. As far as the question of a common court of several occupying or detaining powers is concerned, this is of course possible. But the Tokyo trial was not such a common court-martial. It was, by its very definition in its charter, an international tribunal, which had no precedent in international law up to that time. As was expressly stated in its charter, the tribunal derived its jurisdiction from international law, and, therefore, it cannot be called a common court-martial, conducted, for instance, by the occupying powers.

CHAIR: Thank you. Next, I would like to call on Professor Lounev.

PROFESSOR LOUNEV: I would like to respond briefly to the remarks by Dr. Pritchard of the USA, uh, Britain. Well, Britain, the USA . . .

UNIDENTIFIED PARTICIPANT: They're not the same.

PROFESSOR LOUNEV: It is not established, exactly. [Laughter.] In preparing for this symposium, I visited the Attorney General of the Soviet Union and asked him, "What is the current state of affairs concerning the prosecution and extradition of the forty war criminals that committed crimes during the war period and that are presently hiding abroad?" It turns out that all these forty war criminals are living in the United States of America. According to the information we obtained at the Attorney General's office, only seven criminals have been extradited in the last six years. The rest are living in the United States, unpunished for their crimes. I think the extradition of war criminals should not be conditional on any other considerations whatsoever. Indeed, I was astonished to learn that not all states are following the decision of the United Nations in this matter, and that not all states have complied in extraditing war criminals to the countries in which they committed their crimes.

CHAIR: Are there other questions from the members of the panel? Yes, Mr. Furness.

Differences of Opinion Concerning the Japan-USSR Neutrality Pact

MR. GEORGE A. FURNESS (one of the defense counsel at the Tokyo trial): Russia had a neutrality pact with Japan, and the pact was still in effect at the time Russia crossed into Manchuria. It had been denounced, but it had a year to run from the denouncement. It is true that Japan had a concentration of troops in Manchukuo. It was for protection. Russia had a concentration of troops on the border of Manchukuo. They attacked without any declaration of war, and they crossed the border and conquered the Japanese in Manchukuo in less than two weeks—just at the end of the fighting. I wonder what comments he wants to make on that. Mr. Lounev?

CHAIR: This question concerns relations between the Soviet Union and Japan at the end of the war. As Professor Lounev explained in his presentation, and as was concluded in the Tokyo trial itself, Japan carried out a war of aggression against the Soviet Union. However, the problem remains of how to evaluate attacks by the Soviet Union against Japanese forces just before the end of the war. Professor Lounev, would you like to comment further on this issue?

PROFESSOR LOUNEV: Thank you, Mr. Chairman. Before declaring war on Japan, the Soviet Union, in consultation with the Allies, proposed to the Japanese government that it surrender and stop fighting. The Soviet government wished to avoid heavy casualties on both sides—both our side and the Japanese side. At the time, we had already suffered heavy casualties in fighting against Nazi Germany. Unfortunately, the government of Japan rejected that proposal, and the Soviet Union fulfilled its obligations to the Allies.

MR. FURNESS: What obligations did the Soviet Union have toward the Allies with regard to Japan?

PROFESSOR LOUNEV: Here, we would rather simply discuss the problem, without questioning only one side.

MR. FURNESS: Well, I heard his side, and I am now stating the Japanese side. [Laughter.]

CHAIR: I think we would all like to avoid one-sided statements of the facts. I don't think we want to reenact World War II, so for the moment, let's consider it a difference of opinion . . . In his paper, Professor Lounev elucidated the position that Japan had already abrogated the neutrality pact by its own actions before Soviet attacks on Japanese forces. This is a problem of historical fact, and I would like to defer it to the next session of the symposium.

CHAIR: Mr. Furness, I would like to close . . .

MR. FURNESS: It was just a statement of facts, too.

CHAIR: Thank you very much. Dr. Takigawa, would you care to comment?

Disputing the Rape of Nanjing

DR. TAKIGAWA SEIJIRŌ (one of the defense counsel at the Tokyo trial): Professor Ōnuma spoke of the Nanjing [Nanking] Incident. I would like to say something about his remarks.

I do not recognize the so-called Rape of Nanjing. At the time, the Jiang Jie-shi [Chiang Kai-shek] army had created guerrilla units called *ben'itai* (C. *bianyidui*)—un-uniformed soldiers wearing the same clothing as civilian non-combatants. These guerrilla units attacked Japanese troops constantly, and were responsible for heavy casualties. General Matsui repeatedly issued warnings that such actions on the part of Jiang's army would necessitate killing civilian noncombatants, but Jiang refused to heed these warnings. The activities of the guerrilla units were a considerable threat.

At the time, I was in Beijing [Peking], an instructor at the military academy established by the People's Provisional Government in Beijing. Immediately after the fall of Nanjing, I went there. While I was in Nanjing, I witnessed members of the Japanese army killing Chinese suspected of being members of guerrilla units. But I also observed that adequate measures had been taken to protect Chinese citizens who had been proven not to be guerrillas. Moreover, I witnessed the initiation of policies by the Japanese military commander of Nanjing for the reconstruction of the city. This is what I wish to point out.

I presented this evidence at the time of the Tokyo trial, but the so-called Rape of Nanjing was an accepted fact throughout the world; evidence such as mine, which contradicted this fact, was not deemed necessary, so it was all dismissed. I agree with the opinion of Professor Ōnuma that "massacres," whether at Nanjing or elsewhere, would have been morally inexcusable. But in the case of the "Nanjing massacre," Japanese military forces killed Chinese who were suspected of being un-uniformed guerrillas. Certainly, there were mistakes, and there is no question that innocent civilians were killed. But given the situation, I think these mistakes were unavoidable.

CHAIR: Dr. Takigawa's remarks were not a question concerning the facts of the Nanjing Incident, but a presentation of his own personal knowledge of the facts. Again, I would like to defer discussion of the points he raised to the next section of the symposium, that on historical fact. . . .

Protection of Fighters in Wars of National Liberation

PROFESSOR ŌNUMA: I would like to respond to Mr. Takigawa's remarks as they relate to international law.

CHAIR: Very well, but please limit your remarks to points of international law. And please try to be brief.

PROFESSOR ŌNUMA: As the Chair has pointed out, the issues raised by Dr. Takigawa are questions of historical fact, and research into the historical facts of the Nanjing Incident is being actively pursued both in Japan and in the People's Republic of China. Therefore, I am confident that this point, as well as other points of historical fact that will be raised in the second session this afternoon, will eventually be settled. But I would like to add one word here. Dr. Takigawa spoke of Chinese civilians who were suspected of being guerrillas. However, women and children were also killed *en masse* in this incident. I think that this is a point he cannot possibly explain with the logic he has presented.

I will limit my remarks now to points of international law. Under traditional international law, there is a strict distinction between soldiers and civilians. It is one of the principles of traditional international law that when civilians participate in acts of war they no longer enjoy the protection of international law as civilians. However, World War II occurred at a time when traditional international law was undergoing upheaval. The struggle of the

Chinese people was similar to the wars of national liberation that we are witnessing all over the world today. The people of China were resisting Japanese aggression in a *people's war*.

Today, international law is moving in the direction of giving the same protections to this kind of fighter in wars of national liberation—so-called freedom fighters—as are afforded to ordinary soldiers. Just as Dr. Takigawa pointed out, it may be difficult in practice to distinguish between these combatants and ordinary citizens; but one of the developments, or trends, in international law has been to recognize the legitimacy of wars of national liberation. This, I think, is the legal and factual response to Dr. Takigawa's remarks.

CHAIR: Thank you, Professor Ōnuma. The difference between guerrilla activity and fighting on the front lines of a war of national liberation is an important issue. I would welcome any other opinions. Professor Okuhara.

The Duty to Protect Civilians in International Law

PROFESSOR OKUHARA: I hesitate to speak of my own experience, but I was in Changchun [Ch'ang-ch'un] in 1946, shortly after the war. There I experienced the savage urban warfare raging between the Guomindang [Kuomintang, or Nationalist Party] and the Communist armies. The strategy of the Eighth Route Army, the Communist Party army, was to appear like smoke, out of nowhere, and then disappear in the same manner. It would be difficult for anyone who has not seen this kind of fighting to understand what it is like.

I well understand what Dr. Takigawa is talking about. But from the perspective of international law, when soldiers of the Japanese army encountered a person in civilian clothing whom they suspected of being a soldier of the People's Government Army, they should have disarmed that person and treated him or her as a prisoner of war. At the very least, they had the duty of dealing with that person under the international law pertaining to the detention of civilians. There is absolutely no legal principle that would have made it right to kill such a person.

CHAIR: In the case of Japan, the word *ben'itai* was used, but the problems of guerrilla war, spy activity, and people's wars of national liberation are extremely complex. Therefore, I would like to return the discussion to more general problems concerning the legal aspects of the Tokyo trial. Professor Ipsen?

The Distinction Between Combatants and the Civilian Population

PROFESSOR IPSEN: Thank you, Mr. Chairman. First, I would like to make just one small comment on the preceding discussion concerning the distinction between combatants and civilian population. Since 1977, we have had a clearcut definition in international law, contained in the First Protocol Relating to the Protection of Victims of International Armed Conflicts. The relevant passage, article 43, paragraph 2, reads as follows: "Members of the armed forces of a party to a conflict are combatants." That is to say, they have the right to participate directly in hostilities. This by itself states quite clearly that the civilian population is not permitted to take part deliberately in armed conflicts, that is, in hostilities.

In addition to this, I would like to draw your attention to a point made by my distinguished colleague Professor Lounev. He has made the factual statement that many war criminals are still hiding in some countries, including the Federal Republic of Germany. As a matter of fact, when the Federal Republic regained its sovereignty, all prosecutions were submitted to German courts. Since that time, several hundred war criminals have been prosecuted and punished by German courts—far more than were punished by the Nuremberg trial or by courts-martial conducted by the occupying powers. Of course, all the defendants had a fair trial, as is prescribed under our legal system. The latest trial began in 1982 and is still pending.

CHAIR: Thank you. Professor Ipsen has responded both to a question posed by Professor Lounev and to the preceding discussion of guerrilla warfare and people's liberation fronts. In regard to the latter, he pointed out that the first of two protocols to the Geneva Conventions adopted in 1977 clearly established a distinction between combatants and civilian populations.

I will now call on former Ambassador Matsudaira.

Soviet Violation of the Japan-USSR Neutrality Pact

MR. MATSUDAIRA KŌTŌ: I would like to address a question to Dr. Lounev. I was in the Japanese embassy in Moscow at the time and was personally responsible for political affairs relating to the neutrality pact. I would like some clarification from Dr. Lounev concerning factual matters which I have heard today for the first time.

The point of my question is this: on what points did Japan violate the pact? What specific clause of the neutrality pact did Japan fail to observe? At no time during my entire tour of duty in Moscow did the Soviet Union ever lodge a protest against alleged Japanese violations of the pact.

CHAIR: We are back to the question of Japan-Soviet relations. Mr. Matsudaira has asked for clarification of the specific points of the neutrality pact alleged to have been violated by Japan. I would like to end discussion of this issue with Professor Lounev's response.

PROFESSOR LOUNEV: The question was very short, and I shall answer it briefly. Having concluded a treaty of neutrality with the Soviet Union, the government of Japan proceeded at the same time to conclude a pact with Nazi Germany. The government of Nazi Germany declared war on the Soviet Union. Unfortunately, even before the neutrality pact was concluded, the attitude of Japan toward the Soviet Union was by no means friendly. If you will remember the events at Khassan Lake [Changgufeng, Ch'ang-ku-feng] and Halhin Gol [Nomonhan], there had already been local clashes between Japanese and Soviet armed forces. To be sure, these events occurred before the signing of the treaty, so they are not formal violations of it; but they happened nonetheless.

Today there are a great many Japanese present, and it may not be very polite of me to say these things. But it is essential that we see past events as they were. In addition to the events I have mentioned already, it is a fact that, during our war with Nazi Germany, Japan concentrated a large body of troops on our borders and was ready to attack at any moment if Nazi Germany succeeded in conquering the Soviet Union.

MR. MATSUDAIRA: I am not asking about the background leading up to Japan's pact with Germany. What I am asking you is which specific clause of the Japan-Soviet neutrality pact was violated by Japan. If you cannot answer, then . . .

CHAIR: Mr. Matsudaira, I apologize for interrupting your question, but I would like to close this discussion with Professor Lounev's response.

MR. MATSUDAIRA: It was hardly a response.

CHAIR: I am sorry, but at this point I would like to leave the issue of Japan-Soviet relations and return to the broader issues raised by the speakers' papers. I think the main points under discussion are crimes against peace and personal responsibility for international crimes. I will entertain questions relevant to those two points.

The Soviet Position on Japanese Experiments in Bacteriological Warfare

QUESTION: I am a correspondent for *Vision* magazine. I would like to direct my question to Mr. Lounev. In regard to the Tokyo trials, did the Soviet Union attempt to bring to the attention of the tribunal the bacteriological warfare unit 731, which had existed in Manchuria? And, if you did try to bring this to the attention of the Tokyo tribunal, what was the reaction of the tribunal to this?

Later, you tried the Japanese that you captured in Manchuria who belonged to this unit, which experimented on Chinese and some Caucasian prisoners of war.

CHAIR: I apologize again for interrupting, but I would like to limit the discussion to the two points I outlined earlier. I think your question concerns problems of historical fact, and I wonder if you could hold it until the afternoon session.

QUESTION: The question is: in the judgment of the Russians at their trials, did they find the individuals collectively guilty, individually guilty, or was the judgment based on the fact that they had followed the orders of the state? In the judgment of the Soviets in the trials of the Japanese connected with the unit 731, how did you judge them guilty: on the basis of individual guilt, or a collective guilt, or the fact that they had carried out orders from the state? And, if they had done this on orders from the state, what was the ultimate responsibility of the state? In other words, at what level did they receive the orders?

CHAIR: I understand the intent of your question. However, Professor Awaya touches on these points in the paper he will be delivering this afternoon. Therefore, I think they can be discussed more fruitfully at that time. As for your question, perhaps you could discuss it privately with Professor Lounev in the lobby.

As I said earlier, the important issues of crimes against peace and personal responsibility still remain. If there are comments on these points . . . Professor Takano?

The Significance of the Tokyo Tribunal in Establishing the Illegality of War in International Law

PROFESSOR TAKANO YŪICHI: Listening to the reports by Professors Lounev, Ipsen, and Ōnuma, I found myself in agreement with much that was said. However, there also are a number of points on which I disagree.

Professor Lounev emphasized the positive significance of the trials and the Soviet Union's role in them. But I wonder if there also are not problems on the side that judged Japan and Germany, including the Soviet Union.

Professor Ipsen, basing his analysis on international law in force at the time, pointed out a number of technical legal problems related to the Tokyo trial. Other problems he indicated concerned *lex ferenda*. However, international law has been in a state of great flux. In this respect, I think there must be other problems, over and above those of *lex ferenda*, that should be raised.

Professor Ōnuma, while recognizing these legal problems, expressed his view of the significance of the trial from a standpoint one step removed, as it were, from the problem of international law in effect at the time. However, I believe that in addressing this issue it is possible, indeed essential, to return to points of existing international law in a slightly broader sense. I would like to base my own comments on such a perspective.

There are a great number of issues, and I too am aware of their complexity. However, from the point of view of international law, I think the Tokyo trial has one aspect that can be considered to have legal significance. Moreover, the international law established by the trial is related to postwar, that is, current international law.

In regard to the first point, the Tokyo trial marked a widening dissemination of the idea that war is illegal. And, of course, the German trial had the same significance. In China and elsewhere, Japan launched wars of aggression, the history of which can be traced from the Twenty-One Demands, through the Manchurian Incident, the China Incident [beginning with the Marco Polo Bridge Incident], and so on. Indeed, it can be traced further back in history to Japanese actions in Korea. Japan drove out Russia and China, only to step in then to take their place as a colonial ruler, reducing Korea to the status of a Japanese protectorate. World War II was an extension of this pattern. Thus, while there are of course debates about which country was the aggressor, I think the legal judgment that Japan launched aggressive wars can be made.

The Unfolding of International Law

Addressing the issue of personal responsibility, the idea of trying the kaiser of Germany had already entered international law at the end of World War I (though no trial actually took place). Moreover, in the period before and after World War II, the concept of individual responsibility rose to the surface of international law, not necessarily in terms of responsibility alone, but also in terms of individual rights. I think the concept of individual responsibility has significance in the context of developing international law.

Current international law springs from two sources: the aftermath of World War II, and the modern international community itself. The Tokyo trial is profoundly relevant to both. What is new in the postwar development is that the rights of a people to self-determination and to equal treatment under the law have become principles of international law. Further, respect for the freedoms and rights of human beings without discrimination according to race, sex, language, or religion has become a norm in international law. And these are principles of substantive international law that developed partly in reaction to the acts of Japan, Germany, and Italy, which launched aggressive wars under extremely militaristic conditions. On the other hand, within the context of modern international law and society, actions that are diametrically opposed to the principles of self-determination and equal rights have been committed by countries such as England and France. It is such acts as these that have given birth to present-day international law.

In this light, it seems to me that the significance of the Tokyo trial must be sought precisely in the context of the evolution of international law—in the movement from the past to the international law of the present and the future. The issues raised by the trial must be resolved in international law yet to be formed. At the same time, in exactly the sense I have just stated, the responsibility for actions by the former Allied powers now being challenged by other members of the international community, while not direct "responsibility" in terms of existing international law, is responsibility that has legal connotations. I would be happy to hear reactions from the three speakers concerning these points.

CHAIR: Thank you very much. The points raised by Professor Takano are related to Professor Ōnuma's paper as commented on by Professor Okuhara. Professor Ōnuma, would you care to respond?

PROFESSOR ŌNUMA: I would like to respond while making reference also to Professor Okuhara's comments.

I think Professor Okuhara's comments were directed against the concept of leaders' responsibility. He questions whether this is a concept in international law. I am firmly convinced that it is. As Professor Ipsen pointed out in his paper, individual responsibility under international law is not necessarily limited to *criminal* responsibility. In this sense, it is possible, for example, to censure South Africa's policy of apartheid by means of an official condemnation of its leaders by an international body.

Moreover, it is necessary for us to recognize the importance of introducing into international law the idea that "responsibility" rests ultimately with the population of a country as a whole. We are accustomed to thinking of a country, or a state, as a substantial entity. But the state is only a framework. It is its people that constitute its substance. Ultimately, unless we consider where responsibility actually lies we will not be able to give a realistic explication of international law.

Professor Takano made one statement with which I agree completely: that this is not simply a question of *lex ferenda*. In other words, as I stated in my paper, international law is not a fixed entity; the law itself changes constantly. Considered in this context, the traditional framework of *lex ferenda* versus *lex lata* itself becomes problematic. What today appears at first glance to be a violation of law may in fact reflect the normative consciousness of ordinary people and, in fact, may be perfectly legal. And what appears at first glance to be legal may be contrary to the norm consciousness and the sense of justice of ordinary people and eventually become illegal. It is important, therefore, that we be aware of elements that do not appear on the surface.

CHAIR: Thank you, Professor Ōnuma. I believe Mr. Brooks has a comment.

The Educational Function of the Tribunal

MR. ALFRED W. BROOKS (one of the defense counsel at the Tokyo trial): I think we should rise to a point of order. Our purpose here, as I understood it, is to discuss what we need to do in the world today. Do we need another Asiatic *saiban* [trial]? . . . a European *saiban*? . . . possibly an American *saiban*? . . . to restore peace among nations? We have been talking about international law. In the past, international law has been created by treaties, and by the actions of nations. We're not here to justify history. It's unjustifiable. We're still living like animals. In the past, enforcing our will sometimes with bullets instead of ballots—or with bayonets. Civilized men don't do that. We were not here to punish the Japanese war criminals—alleged war criminals I'll say (of course, I've always said they were alleged war criminals, because there had not been any written code of international criminal law)—but we were here under an unconditional surrender, with a supreme commander of Allied powers representing a majority of civilization that was calling for order in the world. We were here to *deter* their leaders of the future, and to deter the leaders of the past—temporarily if possible—to allow a pause, a pause for the creation of a great economic power. But this great achievement could only be realized by giving up all their fat former destructive armies, navies, and air forces and saying, now I'm going to live in peace with the rest of the world—like the Philippines and the Japanese are doing today—to be the leaders of the world. That's what this is about.

We're here to say: why was this policy adopted by the supreme commander? His word set aside the law in that situation. He was creating international law. He created a policy of forgiving your enemies, not punishing them necessarily, but temporarily holding them back.

A long trial that cost millions of dollars—and most of the world has ignored it. Why? Because most of the countries of the world have been too busy with their own machinations to enforce their will upon, in many cases, unwilling subjects.

We must come back—or we're going to destroy the world—to creating something from this past experience. Not punishment for criminals. You don't punish criminals if you're civilized. You deter them so that they can't act that way. You correct their habits. They are supposed to be an example made—that we don't want this kind of practice. And I think General Koiso, General Minami, who I represented, and General MacArthur would agree with this. I talked with General MacArthur about setting up this so-called law. He said,

"Is it legal?" I said, "It doesn't matter whether it's legal or not. You have an unconditional surrender. You have the power to enforce upon the world for one time Peace." Forgive the enemy, and get a nation here that can create constructively what Japan has created today, after nearly forty years of peace.

CHAIR: Thank you. Are there other questions?

Establishment of Leaders' Responsibility

DR. RÖLING: I would like to have some explanation from Professor Ipsen about his second conclusion, where he states that the majority of states is still not prepared to accept individual responsibility for crimes in international law. I thought that later developments in the United Nations, such as the acceptance of the definition of aggression and the acceptance of the treaty on the nonapplicability of statutory limitations, all presupposed the criminal responsibility of the individual for international crimes. I think these were all positive developments, and it seems to me that the significance of the Tokyo trial lies precisely in helping to develop a world in which there is individual responsibility, which aims, and I think Professor Ōnuma stressed this point, to make a distinction between the responsibility of the state and the population—to make a distinction between the responsibility of leaders and that of the more-or-less misled population. It is a concrete means of establishing peace when only the responsible leaders of nations are punished as the ones who have resorted to war and as the ones who have committed violations of the laws of war. Therefore, I would like to have some clarification of the statement that the majority of states is still not prepared to accept criminal responsibility. We know that, between the First and Second World Wars, there was a movement to accept the concept of crimes of the state, and I think the state and the population are punished by the war itself. In Germany and Japan after the war, there could have been no question of further punishing their populations, who had suffered so much already from the misdeeds of their leaders. Therefore, I think the concept of the responsibility of the individual for international crimes is a correct development, and one that has in fact taken place. I would like to have some explanation of this point.

CHAIR: Thank you Professor Röling. Professor Ipsen argues that even today the concept of individual responsibility has not been accepted by the international community, or entered international law. Professor Röling suggests, however, that it is precisely this concept that was one of the new viewpoints introduced by the Tokyo trial. Professor Ipsen, would you like to reply?

The Problematic Nature of Defining Aggression

PROFESSOR IPSEN: Thank you, Mr. Chairman. The examples just given by Professor Röling provide quite a firm proof for my position. First, the Convention on the Non-Applicability of Statutory Limitations has twenty-two members to date. There are presently one hundred and sixty-eight states in the world. Thus, less than 14 percent are members of the convention. The great majority of states has explicitly refused to become members of the convention. Moreover, the convention refers to only two of the crimes tried at the Tokyo trial, crimes against humanity and war crimes. Crimes against peace are not included.

Secondly, Professor Röling mentioned the UN General Assembly Resolution 3314 of 14 December 1974, the definition of "aggression." First, we must note the fact that this definition has only the form of a resolution. As every international lawyer knows, a resolution does not by itself create law, unless it is included in a relevant convention. Moreover, many states had great misgivings about this resolution, because it defines aggression only in terms of military means of force. These facts show that the result of the work of fifteen years in the United Nations to reach a definition of aggression had only a rather small success.

Besides the examples given by Dr. Röling, I shall add a third example confirming my position. I mentioned earlier the draft offense code elaborated by the International Law Commission. This would have been a sort of international criminal code, had it become a convention. But in 1968, the United Nations postponed the treatment of this draft code. This is firm proof that the majority of states expressly refuses to accept international individual responsibility at this time.

CHAIR: Thank you very much. I am sure that there are still many questions and comments, but I am afraid it is time to close this morning's session. A great many points were raised in our speakers' papers, the comments of our panelists, and the questions of the audience. It seems clear that one of the central points of today's discussion was the problem of the tribunal's jurisdiction. The issue of Japan-Soviet relations will be raised again in Professor Awaya's paper this afternoon, and I will defer my own comments until then.

The issues that have dominated our discussion this morning are clearly those of the "crimes against peace" and "individual responsibility" for acts of state. And, certainly, we have reached no definite conclusion. As is clear from the papers, it would be difficult to contend that these concepts existed in international law in 1945. However, where do we go from that point? Do we take Nuremberg and Tokyo as starting points, accepting these concepts into international law as cases of *lex ferenda*? Or do we insist on strict, rigorous legalism? Our answer to these questions will of course depend on our interpretation of international law; it demands our continuing study.

I am painfully aware of my inadequacy as chairman, and I want to apologize for my poor efforts. Thank you all for your patience and cooperation.

THE TOKYO TRIAL IN HISTORICAL PERSPECTIVE

May 28
1983
(afternoon session)

INTRODUCTION TO THE SESSION

CHAIR (Hosoya Chihiro): I would now like to open the afternoon session. This morning several papers were presented concerning the legal aspects of the Tokyo trial, and a lively discussion followed. In this afternoon's session, we will be hearing three papers on Japan's prewar political process, which became an object of the trial's judgment.

Mr. Kojima, who will present the first paper, has not yet been introduced. He was working on his paper until three o'clock this morning and was therefore unable to attend the morning session. However, Mr. Kojima needs little introduction. I am sure you are all aware of his books on the Tokyo trial. Nevertheless, he worked until 3:00 A.M. this morning on a new paper specifically for this symposium. This is ample indication of his interest in the subject.

Following Mr. Kojima, Professor Awaya and Dr. Pritchard will present their papers, and then I will ask for comments from our discussants. These presentations alone are scheduled to take about two hours, and we have less than four hours for the entire session. I am looking forward to a lively discussion following the papers and comments, but please bear in mind that time is limited.

Actually, Mr. Kojima pleaded for more time, insisting that he could not possibly say all he wanted to say in twenty-five minutes. But I have been forced to ask all the speakers to confine their presentations to twenty-five minutes and then expand on their remarks during the discussion.

CONTRIBUTIONS TO PEACE
Kojima Noboru

Some Basic Doubts

Thank you, Mr. Chairman. As directed, I will do my best to see that I don't speak too long.

I hesitate to speak of personal experiences at the very beginning of my paper, but the fact is that I attended the trial two or three times a week when I was nineteen years old. In part because I was very young at the time, I had a number of doubts concerning the proceedings. For instance, while the Allied countries conducting the trial numbered eleven (the United States, England, China, the Soviet Union, Australia, Canada, New Zealand, the Netherlands, France, India, and the Philippines), I had the definite feeling that some of them were not among the countries that Japan had directly fought against and been defeated by. In fact, I wondered if there weren't too many victorious countries.

Moreover, it was said at the Tokyo and Nuremberg trials that Japan and Germany had launched wars of aggression, destroying world peace, and that the tribunals would call them to account for these wars. But taken from that point of view, why wasn't there a Rome trial? Was it because the Italians had surrendered earlier, or what? These were the kinds of doubts I remember having at the time.

The reason I bring them up at the beginning of my paper is that I believe a great number of doubts still remain concerning the Tokyo trial. If we understand the Tokyo trial to have been carried out with future world peace as one of its objectives, I would like to place special emphasis on the influence the trial has exerted on historical research.

In no way is it possible to make a whole country—its entire population or its history—the object of judicial proceedings, and of course in the case of the Tokyo trial, it was only the leaders of Japan and one part of its population that were put on trial. However, insofar as the tribunal sought to determine whether Japan had waged a war of aggression from 1928 onward and whether the leaders who took part in executing that war were responsible for it, it made an issue of Japan's entire history. This is particularly true in the case of "crimes against peace." I believe that in this sense the trial is an extremely special case.

Emphasis on Condemning the Vanquished

The Tokyo trial was unprecedented, and I doubt that a similar trial will ever be held in the future. Yet, precisely because of its special character as a trial that made Japan's history one of its basic issues, the Tokyo trial potentially had great significance in promoting understanding and mutual reflection between East and West.

That is to say, Germany and Japan, the objects of the so-called war crimes trials, were respectively representative countries of Europe and Asia. The very act of tracing the steps of Japan's past history with care and dispassion should have created a deeper understanding of Japan, as well as of the actual situation in the various Asian countries into which Japan advanced under its "mainland policy" and its other policies. At the same time, it should have been an opportunity to promote mutual understanding between the countries of Asia, as well as understanding of the relationship between Asia and the West. Given the fact that war often arises from a lack of mutual understanding, I believe that promoting understanding of Japan and Asia can become an important basis for the prevention of future wars and the preservation of peace, which was the goal of the Tokyo trial. As you know, however, this was not the perspective adopted at the Tokyo trial. Instead, emphasis was placed on the hasty trial and punishment of the atrocities that had been committed by a defeated Japan.

The Prehistory of the "Manchurian Incident"

For example, in asserting that Japan invaded China, the prosecution argued to the effect that a "criminal military clique" and "criminal leaders" had conspired to incite the Manchurian Incident and to commit countless acts of atrocity throughout the war.

However, in order to understand Japan's actions on the Chinese mainland, and particularly in taking up the Manchurian Incident, one must not ignore the relationship that existed between China and Japan before the incident. Japan did not suddenly pounce on Manchuria one day like a tiger or a wolf. The Manchurian Incident had its origins in the fact that Japan had already established a position in China, particularly in Manchuria.

The principal rights Japan had obtained on the Chinese mainland were based on a protocol signed by the United States, England, and ten other countries after the Beiqing Incident [the so-called Boxer Rebellion] of 1900. This protocol recognized Japan's right to station troops in Beijing [Pei-ching; Peking], Tianjin [T'ien-chin; Tientsin], Shanhaiguan [Shan-hai-kuan], Qinhuangdao [Ch'in-huang-tao], and elsewhere. Further, under the terms of the Manchurian Rehabilitation Pact, which Japan concluded with the Chinese government in 1905 after the Russo-Japanese War, Japan obtained the South Manchurian Railway between Changchun [Ch'ang-ch'un] and Lüshun [Port Arthur], a concession in Guandong [Kwan-tung], and the right to station a garrison to defend the South Manchurian Railway. This pact gave Japan the rights and interests that had been held by Russia under the Sino-Russian Pact of 1898, which was not set to expire until 1924.

However, what I especially want to emphasize here is the fact that there were severe restrictions on Japan's movements in Manchuria after the Russo-Japanese War, in the event, say, that Japan were to exhibit territorial ambitions there. First, at the time of the Russo-Japanese War, Japan had publicly pledged that it would protect the rights and interests in Manchuria of any country that allied itself with Japan or took a neutral position. Second, as you all know, in setting national defense policy after the Russo-Japanese War, the Japanese army made Russia the hypothetical enemy, while the navy assumed that the enemy would be the United States. However, this defense policy rested on the absolute requisite of the defense of the Korean peninsula. As for Russia, the possibility that it might once again launch an invasion of Manchuria had decreased as a result of its defeat in the Russo-Japanese War.

The Maintenance of Rights, as Opposed to Territorial Ambitions

A third restriction on Japanese movements was the condition of the Japanese economy after the Russo-Japanese War. Japan's economic power had declined drastically due to the burden of military expenditures, and it is a well-known fact that Japan simply did not have the reserve strength to undertake the administration of Manchuria. Finally, even during the Qing [Ch'ing] dynasty, Manchuria was called the "land without a lord." As this label indicates, in a certain sense Manchuria had been neglected, and it was undeveloped. Even if Japan were to take over such a Manchuria, what was there to be gained . . . ?

Thus, there were international, military, economic, and environmental conditions that obstructed Japan's advance into Manchuria, and these four restrictions continued to exist thereafter.

Nevertheless, Japan had to concern itself with the preservation of the rights and interests it had secured in Manchuria. Therefore, when the Qing dynasty was overthrown in the Xinhai [Hsin-hai] Revolution of 1911, Japan presented the new Chinese government with its Twenty-One Demands, which sought the continuation of Japanese rights and concessions in the region. In fact, there were sixteen articles in this document; but putting that aside, the main thrust of the demands was for an extension of concessions and other rights and privileges in the region for ninety-nine years. Internationally, the Twenty-One Demands were sharply criticized. Within China, 9 March, the date on which they were accepted by the Beijing government, came to be observed as a "day of national humiliation," and was thereafter a rallying point for the anti-Japanese movement.

However, the Japanese thought that Japan's rights and privileges in China were of the same nature as those held by other countries and that their continuation had been formally negotiated and accepted by the Yuan Shikai [Yüan Shih-k'ai] government in Beijing, internationally recognized at that time as the government of China. Certainly, the Twenty-One Demands were extremely one-sided. But I want to repeat that even if Japan sought an economic base in Manchuria, it had no territorial ambitions there at that time.

Anxiety Over the Northern Expedition

Japan began to pay special attention to Manchuria after Sun Yixian [Sun I-hsien; Sun Yat-sen] launched the Northern Expedition [1926–28]. The Northern Expedition presented two problems for Japan. First, while the Beijing government was recognized internationally, there were also governments in Kuandong [Canton], Nanjing [Nanking], and elsewhere. Therefore, the advent of a unified national government as a result of the Northern Expedition would be a welcome event. The problem, however, was whether the Sun government would in fact be friendly toward Japan.

Sun's Three People's Principles (Sanminzhuyi)—nationalism, democracy, and the people's livelihood—were viewed as extremely dangerous ideas in Japan at that time. In fact, the word *democracy* itself was taken to be virtually synonymous with Communism. Moreover, Sun had adopted a united front policy, welcoming Soviet advisers and leaders of the Chinese Communist Party. If the Northern Expedition were successful, and Sun eliminated or co-opted the local warlords and established a central government, would Sun's government agree to the continuation of Japan rights and privileges in Manchuria? That was the first problem for Japan.

The second problem, related to the first, was the fate of the Japanese who had settled in China and Manchuria. The Northern Expedition was a civil war, yet it occurred against a background of exploding nationalism. There was a great deal of anxiety among the Japanese leadership that the spreading flames of war and rising nationalist sentiment would result in violence against Japanese residents in China.

Troops Sent to Protect Japanese Residents

If violence occurred, Japan did have troops stationed in China and Manchuria under the terms of the agreement described above, but their number was extremely small. Moreover, most of the Japanese living in China at this time were people who had been extremely poor and who had given up what little they possessed to seek a new life in China. They were petty merchants or manual laborers or prostitutes, and not a few were utopian dreamers, dropouts from Japanese society. Other countries had acquired concessions in China, and people from these countries had also settled there. But even though technically receiving the same rights and privileges as other foreigners, the Japanese were looked down on even by the Chinese. Thus, on the one hand, these people could not return easily to Japan if the situation deteriorated, and, on the other, they were the most likely objects of violence—Japanese residents, the prime target of Chinese nationalism, and people whom the Chinese considered to be of a lower social status than the Chinese themselves. And, in fact, anti-Japanese, "humiliate Japan" incidents of violence did occur during the course of the Northern Expedition, resulting in a number of deaths. Some of these incidents involved soldiers of the expedition or the opposing armies, and others, opportunistic civilians.

Of course, the Chinese have their own side of this story, but so do the Japanese; and because the Japanese had also felt superior to and contemptuous of the Chinese since the Sino-Japanese War [of 1894–95], the two peoples were bound to clash. As a result, the Japanese repeatedly dispatched troops, but at this time the purpose was merely to protect Japanese residents in China. The troops were withdrawn as soon as that objective had been achieved.

Tanaka Gi'ichi and the Eastern Conference

However, with the progress of the Northern Expedition, its implications for Manchuria became a serious problem for Japan. Of course, Manchuria was Chinese territory, and foreign countries could not prevent the expeditionary force from extending its campaign into Manchuria to eliminate warlords and unify the country. For Japan, the overriding goals at this time were the maintenance of its rights and privileges and the protection of Japanese residents; so if a policy could be discovered that would solve these two problems, that would be sufficient.

At this juncture, the government of Tanaka Gi'ichi was formed, in April 1927, and in June Tanaka convened the Eastern Conference [tōhō kaigi]. People often point to the existence of a "Tanaka memorandum," which supposedly summarizes the results of this meeting. Indeed, at the Tokyo trial, the prosecution argued that it was the basic document of Japan's policy of aggressive war, citing the following passage: "He who would conquer China must first conquer Mongolia. He who would conquer the world must first conquer China." However, it has already become clear that this "Tanaka memorandum" was a clumsy fake—indeed, more obviously a fake than the "Hitler diary" that caused such a stir recently.

The absurd "confessions" of Cai Zhikan [T'sai Chi-kan] have been published. This intrepid character claims to have infiltrated the Imperial Household Agency and copied the "Tanaka memorandum" by bribing the Lord Keeper of the Privy Seal and the Palace Minister with opium and Chinese rice wine. Even before the publication of these confessions, the fact that the "Tanaka memorandum" was circulated in a "Chinese translation" instead of in Japanese, as well as the large number of factual mistakes in it, should have made its authenticity highly suspect.

In fact, two main policies were decided at the Eastern Conference: (1) In the event that the disorder resulting from the Northern Expedition spread to Manchuria, Japan would dispatch troops to maintain law and order; (2) Japan would support influential persons in Manchuria who understood Japan's position there.

Meeting with Jiang Jieshi [Chiang Kai-shek], who came to Japan shortly after the conference, Tanaka emphasized two points: (1) Japan would not interfere in China's internal affairs, but it opposed the spread of Communism; (2) Japan earnestly hoped for the maintenance of law and order in Manchuria.

Personally, Tanaka hoped for a political situation in which China proper would be ruled by Jiang Jieshi and Manchuria by Zhang Zuolin [Chang Tso-lin], the Manchurian warlord whose life Tanaka had spared during the Sino-Japanese War [of 1894–95]. Through such a formula, he sought to preserve Japanese interests in Manchuria.

Relations with Zhang Zuolin

Of course, Tanaka's policy, which amounted to a plan to separate China proper and Manchuria, was a clear case of interference in China's domestic politics. Moreover, it was based on an unrealistic assessment of the situation. For if China proper were unified, Zhang would be placed in the position of controlling Manchuria only with Japan's backing. He would be considered a traitor to China, and would have to choose between leading a rebellion against his Japanese patrons or fighting a war of resistance against the Chinese army.

In fact, events did not wait for such a situation to develop, and Tanaka's plan for a Zhang government controlled by Japan collapsed even more quickly than might have been expected. Shortly before the Eastern Conference, Zhang appointed himself "Supreme Commander of the Army and Navy of the Republic of China." He announced that he considered Jiang's government to be "red," and that he was raising an army to attack it. He also boasted of his intention to become the emperor of China. Moreover, even while maintaining a friendly posture toward Japan, he adopted a series of anti-Japanese policies designed to rally support among the people. He imposed heavy taxes on Japanese merchants in Manchuria and on Japanese products, and also planned construction of a system of five railroads that would have surrounded the Manchurian Railway, [which was controlled by Japan].

At the same time, his preparations for war with Jiang's army included buying up rice supplies and issuing an absurd volume of currency. High taxes and raging inflation caused a great deal of hardship for ordinary citizens, so Zhang's program had the contradictory result of stirring up strong anti-Zhang sentiments. For Japan, this created a situation in which further support for the Zhang government might well add impetus to the anti-Japanese movement and increase the possibility that the Northern Expedition would effect Manchuria.

Moreover, Zhang had suffered one defeat after the other in China proper, and it seemed likely that he would soon be forced to flee over the Great Wall and retreat into Manchuria. Japanese policy-makers deliberated long and hard about how to react.

At that time, the Guandong [Kwan-tung] Army in Manchuria was limited to a force of about ten thousand. It was estimated that Zhang, retreating to Manchuria in defeat, had three hundred thousand troops. If the retreat of this huge army were accompanied by the same atrocities, looting, and violence that had characterized Zhang's tactics in China proper, it would be totally impossible for the small Japanese force to maintain law and order and protect Japanese citizens.

Moreover, if Jiang's army entered Manchuria in pursuit of Zhang, clashes with the Guandong Army might well lead to war between Japan and China. Japanese policy-makers considered various ideas, such as disarming Zhang's army at the Great Wall before it entered Manchuria or halting Jiang's advance at the Great Wall; but Zhang insisted on making a stand at Beijing. But this also could lead to war: if Beijing became a battleground and the Japanese residents and military personnel stationed there were endangered, this too might well invite the dispatch of Japanese troops, increasing the possibility of a full-scale confrontation between China and Japan.

Faced with this situation, the Tanaka government decided in May 1928 on a new policy: "Japan has no intention of supporting Zhang Zuolin. What is essential is to leave Zhang to his own devices and to support the northern forces." Essentially, this policy entailed replacing Zhang with another Manchurian warlord favorable to Japan, who would block Jiang, with the support of the Japanese army, and prevent him from advancing into Manchuria, thus insuring Japan's rights and interests.

The basic stance was still that of separating Manchuria from China proper. Moreover, Tanaka was considering no measures to deal with Zhang other than his forced retirement from public office. However, the army, fearing further complications, plotted and carried out Zhang's assassination.

Behind this event was an analysis of the situation based on little more than wishful thinking. It was assumed that Zhang was the only powerful figure in Manchuria and that if he were deposed, the military clique in Manchuria would disintegrate; or that, at the very least, without Zhang the military clique's influence would break up into smaller units that could be manipulated at will by Japan. Just how misguided this thinking was became clear when Zhang Xueliang [Chang Hsüeh-liang], Zhang's son, assumed his father's position as warlord and, changing his colors, pledged his loyalty to the Nationalist government. [Zhang did this in a ceremony in which he struck the five-colored flag of his own government, raised the flag of the Nationalist government, and saluted it.]

The Hamaguchi Cabinet and the Policy of Rapprochement

The government of Hamaguchi Osachi, which took over from the Tanaka cabinet, did a complete about-face and adopted a policy of rapprochement with China. Even after the conclusion of the Northern Expedition, the government adopted a policy of formally recognizing the Jiang government, which it had refused to do previously, and maintained a friendly posture toward Zhang Xueliang. Moreover, in Manchuria, it concentrated solely on strengthening economic investment.

Japanese investment in Manchuria was an enormous one for that time. At the beginning of May 1930, it had reached ¥1,468,450,000. This investment sparked rapid economic growth in Southern Manchuria. The number of factories, hotels, hospitals, schools, and other facilities increased rapidly. Its impact may be seen, for example, in school attendance statistics for Chinese children. The rate of school attendance in China proper at that times was 15.13 percent, but in Manchuria as a whole it had risen to 21.72 percent, and in the Southern Manchurian concession controlled by Japan, it was 31.72 percent.

The Impossibility of a Conspiracy

In China, however, this policy of conciliation was interpreted as a sign of weakness and heightened anti-Japanese sentiment. This in turn fueled a backlash of Japanese public opinion, which, together with the army's warnings about the Soviet Union—now more of a military power than Imperial Russia had been—strengthened fears that Manchuria could not be secured through diplomacy, and that if it could not be held militarily, Japan would be driven out. It is already clear that these anxieties led to the Manchurian Incident and eventually to the policy of partitioning China by creating a "Manchurian Empire" under Puyi [P'u-i], the last Qing emperor.

The Japanese policies that surfaced in this process were both extremely selfish and extremely maladroit. Particularly striking were the poverty of Japan's society, the confusion of its politics, and the complexity and vagueness of decision-making institutions under the political order established by the old Constitution of the Empire of Japan.

At the Tokyo trial, Japanese leaders were charged with a "conspiracy" to launch and wage an aggressive war. However, I think it is clear from the analysis above that the elements of confusion, of tangled complexity, in Japanese policy-making at this time made any unified conspiracy quite impossible. In this sense, the situation in Japan was very different from that in Nazi Germany, where a single dictator and the group surrounding him were in constant control of policy decisions.

The prosecution at the trial also spoke of a military dictatorship, but, in fact, the army and the navy acted as quite independent entities in advocating policy. The result was a series of *ad hoc* measures designed to treat the symptoms of a steadily deteriorating situation. Precisely because the Japanese government was ultimately incapable of the kind of "conspiracy" that would have enabled it to formulate national policies based on a wide perspective, it was forced in its progress thereafter from Manchuria into China proper to rely on policies that were narrow, short-sighted, and unilateral. When we look back on Japan's past, it is this aspect that most invites reflection.

Chinese Weakness Invites Japanese Aggression

However, there are also problems on the Chinese side. Even if it can be argued that Japan's actions were designed to protect rights and privileges obtained in the past, the fact that it attempted to do so by the use of military force, by expanding the area under its military occupation, constituted aggression from the Chinese point of view. These actions did, after all, take place on Chinese territory. But the next question is, why did China allow this aggression to continue?

Looking back at Jiang Jieshi's achievements, and tracing them through his own records, it seems to me that he had four major internal enemies throughout his career: warlords, the Communists, the left wing of the Guomindang, and corruption in the government and the military. One comes to the conclusion that he was never able to overcome these enemies. Even after the establishment of a unified central government, and even after the beginning of large-scale warfare against Japanese forces, they continued to show themselves whenever the occasion presented itself, impairing political stability, obstructing improvement of the people's living standards, and preventing the spread of education. Of course, these negative elements were exacerbated by Japanese aggression, but at the same time they were themselves factors that invited Japanese aggression. In other words, if there was a mistaken "logic," a mistaken "psychology," among Japanese leaders that gave rise to mistaken policies, there were also important factors on the Chinese side that laid the country open to aggression.

Effects of the "War-Crimes View" of Japanese History

The same thing may be said of the appearance of Nazism and Fascism in Europe. It is clear that there were also important factors in the countries of Europe other than Germany and Italy that allowed Nazism and Fascism to rise. Therefore, if it is necessary to promote international understanding in order to prevent war and maintain peace, we must not view history simply as a confrontation between the "evil strong" and the "saintly weak." If at the same time that we point out the faults of other countries we do not reflect on the immaturity of our own countries, it will be impossible to achieve mutual understanding in international relations. As I stated above, I believe the Tokyo trial should have been a starting point for "mutual understanding based on mutual reflection." Unfortunately, however, it has had the opposite effect of putting a brake on dispassionate research on the history of the period. And, at least up to the present, that is the only effect it has had.

In the case of Japan, the view of Japanese history put forward by the prosecution and expressed in the majority opinion—that is, the "war-crimes view" of Japanese history—continues to be accepted totally and uncritically. Of course, the Tokyo trial was conducted under military occupation, a continuation of the state of war, so to speak; moreover, it was convened for the express purpose of punishing Japanese war criminals in a period when the bitter passions of the war had not yet cooled. In that sense, anything like mutual reflection was out of the question. It is unreasonable to seek mutual reflection in the trial itself; and perhaps mutual reflection was completely irrelevant to the trial. However, in Japan at that time, the Tokyo trial was not perceived merely as a trial that brought certain wartime leaders to account, but rather as a condemnation of Japanese history itself. Moreover, while the terms have a bad connotation, the trial gave birth to an atmosphere in which Japan was viewed as a "criminal state" and the Japanese people as a "criminal people." As a result, there has even been a tendency, alive in some circles to this day, to emphasize that Japan is a "country with previous historical convictions." That this tendency to treat Japan as an "ex-con" has deep roots in some foreign countries, too, is evident from the accounts of Japan in their schoolbooks.

This is clearly the influence of the "war-crimes view" of Japan's past. For Japan, as well as for other countries, this concept shrouds the most important aspects of history and leads us to forfeit opportunities for reflection and research.

Freeing Ourselves from the "War-Crimes View" of History

Studying history by calmly looking back at the past is a rigorous task; sometimes it is like tearing out one's own heart. But if we do not do it, history becomes nothing more than *ad hoc* political positions, and its lessons for the future are lost. The Tokyo trial itself is already only a page in history. And at the same time, I have the feeling that the door has been left unopened that the Tokyo trial could have and should have opened—the door to "mutual understanding through mutual reflection." Looking back at the Tokyo trial, what I feel most strongly today is the need to free ourselves from the "war-crimes view" of history, the view that it is enough merely to stipulate that Japan and Germany are solely responsible for modern history.

As I stated above, attempting to evade important issues by accepting this historical view *in toto* also has the effect of closing the way to genuine research on international history. What might come next is an attempt simply to reject the Tokyo trial and the Nuremberg trial *in toto*.

In this sense, the Tokyo trial is not simply an object of retrospection or something that concerns Japan only. Nor should it be the object of endless exchanges between defenders and critics. Rather, it should become a kind of stimulant, or starting point, for historical research, showing all of us the unvarnished reality of each other's past. That is precisely what would give renewed life to the Tokyo trial, which has become a brake on international understanding, and give the trial a role in contributing to world peace.

Even though I promised to adhere to my allotted time, I see that I have exceeded it. I apologize. With this, I conclude my remarks. [Applause.]

CHAIR: Thank you, Mr. Kojima. Overwhelmed by Professor Kojima's earlier entreaty and by his vigor, I was unable as chair to cut him off, and we have fallen far behind schedule. I ask the later speakers please to stick strictly to the time allotted. I think the main point of Mr. Kojima's paper was that it is impossible to understand the historical period that was the object of the Tokyo trial, the period between 1928 and Pearl Harbor, unless it is set in the context of Japanese history from the beginning of the twentieth century. He asks if it is not necessary to view the development of Japanese policies toward mainland China within this larger historical context. Viewed in this way, Japan's actions after 1928 are seen in light of Japan's treaty rights in China and Manchuria, and the need to protect Japanese residents on the mainland. He did not use the word *self-defense*, but I think his first point was that Japanese actions had an aspect of defense.

His second point was that while there may have been inconsistencies in Japanese policies and *ad hoc* elements in diplomacy and policy making, there were also problems on the Chinese side. In short, there is a need for reflection on both sides. These, I think, are the major points Mr. Kojima wished to make. I think others here will have their own opinions on these points.

Professor Awaya, the next speaker, has recently been conducting research on the history of the Tokyo trial itself, and I think this will be the main theme of his paper. Professor Awaya, you have the floor.

IN THE SHADOWS OF THE TOKYO TRIBUNAL
Awaya Kentarō

Thank you, Professor Hosoya. Due to time limitations and the fact that the content of my original paper overlapped with that of another speaker, what I will present this afternoon differs somewhat from my draft paper, which you have before you. During the discussion period this morning, there was a good deal of talk about Japanese-Soviet relations, and Professor Andō suggested that I would be dealing with that problem this afternoon; but I will not be dealing with that subject. However, I will have something to say about Unit 731.

Now, what was the Tokyo trial? The problems involved are immense and cover a wide range of issues. The Tokyo trial is a particularly up-to-date subject, for it suggests a virtually endless list of problems concerning war and peace that are still unresolved today. In my presentation, I will not be dealing with the proceedings or the judgments of the trial, both of which took place before the footlights. Instead, as one entree into the debate about the Tokyo trial, I would like to focus on problems that remained in the shadows, problems that in fact never made their appearance on the stage of the trial, and by so doing bring into relief some of its special characteristics. That is the reason I have titled my presentation *In the Shadows of the Tokyo Tribunal*.

Conflict among the Allied Powers

First, I would like to consider the significance of the fact that the Tokyo trial took the form of an international military tribunal conducted by the Allied powers. In pursuing the responsibility of Japan's leaders for the war and punishing them, the Allied powers adopted the format of an international trial. I would like to consider the significance of this trial in light of the fact that there were other possible ways of punishing the defendants; specifically, summary execution and trials conducted independently by the postwar Japanese government itself.

An examination of the postwar attitudes of the Allied powers reveals that, immediately after Japan's defeat, there was no basic conflict among the Allies concerning the decision to reject the summary execution of Japan's wartime leaders and conduct instead an international trial modeled on Nuremberg. The problem was rather in the concrete form the trial should take. In the case of the Tokyo trial, conflict among the Allied powers arose from the fact that the United States seized the initiative in the management of the trial, including the preparations, the appointment of judges and prosecutors, and all the other details of setting up the court. The fact that the Soviet Union delayed for a long time before sending its delegation was in retaliation for this. As you know, an even greater problem was the question of who should be indicted as Class A war criminals. In any case, the Tokyo trial was convened in the form that it finally took only after a great number of complicated twists and turns.

Summary Executions Carried Out by the Japanese Army

Summary execution was rejected by the Allied powers from the very beginning. It is rather in the military operations of the Japanese army during the Fifteen-Year War that a large number of summary executions can be seen. In China and other Asian countries, the Japanese army meted out severe punishment for participation in people's resistance movements and guerrilla activities on the grounds that these constituted acts of hostility toward Japan. In many cases, persons arrested, whether they were combatants or noncombatants, were not treated as prisoners of war under the laws of war or subjected to "tedious" trials or courts-martial, but executed on the spot. A small number of these acts were taken up in the Tokyo trial and dealt with as atrocities committed by the Japanese army in the regions involved.

It should also be noted that the trial and punishment of the crews of American warplanes taken prisoner by the Japanese army during the Pacific War, while they took a form resembling war crimes trials, were in fact summary executions. After the air raids on Japan by the Doolittle Squadron in April 1942, the army issued a directive titled "On the Treatment of the Crews of Enemy Planes Engaged in Aerial Bombing." This directive established the policy of trying "persons among the crews of enemy planes who are suspected of having committed major crimes in a time of war" in "courts of military law" [gunritsu kaigi], which were quasi–courts-martial. Looking over the new military code promulgated in October 1942, what is interesting is that, in addition to the bombing of the civilian population and nonmilitary targets, "acts that are atrocious and inhumane in disregard of the basic principles of humanity" were also subject to punishment, said punishment being death. Of course, the new military code itself, promulgated after the Doolittle raids, is a perfect example of ex post facto law. Nevertheless, it is important to note that the text of this law contains a concept corresponding to that of the "crime against humanity" established at the Tokyo trial. In short, even the Japanese army considered indiscriminate bombing carried out by an enemy force—its own operations were a different matter—a heinous atrocity opposed to basic principles of humanity. And, on the basis of an ex post facto military law, the Japanese army actually meted out severe punishments.

Ōoka Shōhei, in his Nagai tabi [A Long Journey], has depicted an actual case of one of these military trials. Of course, as Ōoka himself emphasizes, the indiscriminate aerial bombing of the Japanese islands by American forces at the end of the war—and even more the atomic bombings of Hiroshima and

Nagasaki—qualify as atrocious and inhumane acts. In the last days of World War II, with the aim of bringing the war to a quick end, the Allied powers often employed military tactics designed specifically to kill or wound huge numbers of ordinary people in the Axis countries; those actions can only be considered inhumane tactics. But the reality of the military trials conducted by the Japanese army in response to these acts of indiscriminate bombing is that they were trials carried out by courts composed only of judges and prosecutors, with no defense counsel. Admittedly, these trials were conducted in wartime, but they were, nonetheless, nothing more than summary executions, their verdicts a foregone conclusion. Indeed, as the Allied powers indicated in their trials of Class B and Class C war criminals, the system of summary execution as a judicial form was highly unfair.

The Japanese Scheme to Hold Autonomous Trials

Next I would like to touch on the concept of autonomous trials put forward by the Japanese government.

While there may have been some lack of clarity, Japan was aware for the most part that articles six and ten of the Potsdam Declaration did not refer simply to the punishment of "conventional war crimes," but that the political responsibility of wartime leaders would be pursued in a war crimes trial. On this point, my view differs from that given by defense counsel Kiyose Ichirō in his motion on jurisdiction at the beginning of the trial, but I base my judgment on a careful reading of contemporary documents. Reports on conditions in Europe were still being sent from Japanese diplomatic officials stationed in Switzerland and other neutral countries, and the government, including the foreign ministry, concluded from them that, aside from the question of the emperor's responsibility, which was the most important concern of the government, the methods of punishment for war crimes stipulated by the Potsdam Declaration would be the same in general as those of the Nuremberg trial. However, there was a strongly rooted movement at the highest levels of the government to preempt an Allied international tribunal by having Japan conduct its own trials. The so-called four-conditions faction of the Army Ministry and the high command had advocated autonomous trials on the occasion of the acceptance of the Potsdam Declaration, but that proposal was not accepted. The idea was revived by the Higashikuni cabinet immediately after defeat. On 12 September, the day after GHQ issued the first Directive for the Arrest of War Criminals, which listed Tōjō Hideki and other major figures, the Higashikuni cabinet passed a resolution directing the government to proceed with all haste to investigate war crimes and conduct autonomous trials. Needless to say, however, this cabinet resolution was not accepted by GHQ.

Draft for an Emergency Imperial Decree

Actually, in a small number of cases, autonomous trials were conducted. In courts-martial conducted by the army between September 1945 and March 1946, four cases of criminal acts by Japanese soldiers were handled by administrative disposition. These cases, which involved eight persons, concerned acts that corresponded to GHQ's Class B and Class C war crimes. Sentences ranged from ten months of confinement to life imprisonment, but considering that the crimes in question were murder and torture, the sentences were comparatively light. I think the true purpose of these punishments was to preempt trials by the Allied powers, by exploiting the principle of double jeopardy. Ironically, the soldiers involved were later retried in military courts conducted by the Allied powers on Class B and Class C war crimes, and received unusually severe sentences on the grounds that they already had been proven guilty by their own country.

Even after the failure of the Higashikuni cabinet's resolution, the idea of independent trials remained strongly rooted among the Japanese leadership. As one example of this, I would like to introduce an interesting document. This document [see pages 87–88], which has never been published previously, is in the collection of documents titled *Makino Nobuaki monjo* [Makino Nobuaki Papers] in the National Diet Library. Titled "Emergency Imperial Decree for the Purpose of Independently Establishing the National Ethic Necessary for the Stabilization of Public Sentiments and the Maintenance of the National Order (Draft)," this draft decree has twelve articles and provides for trials. I believe it was drafted by someone in the government during the Shidehara cabinet. It is of enormous interest. I will omit the details, but the basic outline of the decree is that those who defied the emperor's "spirit of peace" by launching foreign wars of aggression were guilty of treason, and that these people would be punished with death or imprisonment by Japan. What is interesting here is that this document, in a manner that is both straightforward and, read in a certain way, comic, displays a logic whereby responsibility for war could be sought under the emperor system, and also a reverse logic of immunity; this was the logic of the "defense of the national polity," as it was called at the time. It was a scheme that had no chance of being realized, and when compared with the charter of the tribunal, it looks like a silly dwarf.

The idea of autonomous trials came to an end in March 1946, when GHQ issued a total prohibition on any investigation or trial of war crimes by the Japanese government. Thus the plans of the Japanese leadership to hold autonomous trials collapsed, and the International Tribunal for the Far East was convened on 3 May 1946.

Problems Concerning the Conclusion of the Tokyo Trial

I would now like to turn to a discussion of problems surrounding the conclusion of the Tokyo trial, as an additional clue to its special nature. Of course, this is the opposite of the usual approach, for it does not touch on the proceedings of the trial itself.

First, consider the actions of the Allied powers that were sitting in judgment. Already in 1947, the leaders of the United States and Great Britain had reached an understanding that there would be no further international trials of Class A war criminals. Beginning in August of that year, GHQ issued one order after the other for the release without indictment of suspected Class A war criminals already in custody. In 1948, as part of the overall reversal of its occupation policies, the US plan to end war crimes trials of Japanese was made national policy. This policy was outlined in the now famous document *Recommendations with Respect to US Policy Toward Japan* (NSC 13/2), which was drafted by G. F. Kennan, director of the Policy Planning Staff of the Department of State.

By 1948, the cold war between the United States and the Soviet Union had intensified even in the Far East. The United States and Great Britain quickly lost their zeal for pursuing Japan's responsibility for the war and for punishing wartime leaders. This led to the policy of ending Class A war crimes trials. As can be seen in the statements of Kennan and Chief Prosecutor Joseph B. Keenan, American officials had grown impatient with the long, drawn-out trial and almost sorry that the trial had been conducted in the first place. Indeed, Kennan argued that summary executions of Japanese wartime leaders might have been preferable.

The United States executed the *fait accompli* of terminating the prosecution of suspected Class A war criminals by simply releasing them one after the other. In doing so, the United States exploited what may be called its peremptory rights of leadership, which it had maintained since the beginning of preparations for the trial, in particular exercising Keenan's power as sole chief prosecutor and the functions of the Legal Affairs Bureau of GHQ.

Reading of the judgment of the tribunal began on 4 November 1948, and the sentences for individual defendants were handed down on 12 November. On 23 December, the seven defendants who had been sentenced to death were executed. On the following day, GHQ released all the remaining seventeen suspected Class A war criminals, including Kishi Nobusuke and Kodama Yoshio, without indictments, and announced that there would be no more trials of Class A war criminals. The explanation given at the time by A. C. Carpenter, chief of the Legal Affairs Bureau of GHQ, was extremely vague. It was not an amnesty, a voiding, founded on a recognition of their responsibility as war crimes suspects; but it was rather a matter of simply ignoring the crimes.

The Tokyo Trial as an Aspect of US Occupation Policy

Previously, in a meeting with American officials, Carpenter had stated that among the fifty suspected war criminals then in custody, twenty-five should be tried for Class A war crimes. In March 1948, Chief Prosecutor Keenan, too, had told a meeting of the Far Eastern Commission that "if the tribunal attempts to try every person who comes within the purview of 'crimes against peace,' the trials cannot be concluded within a single lifetime." In short, there was clearly a large element of opportunism in the later American policy of terminating the trials of suspected Class A war criminals.

After his release, Kishi Nobusuke returned to political life and, in 1957, became prime minister. Kodama Yoshio established a connection with American intelligence agencies and was active behind the scenes as one of the "shadow shōguns" of Japanese politics. Recently, the significance for postwar Japanese history of the release of these suspected war criminals has been increasingly emphasized, the Lockheed scandal being a good case in point. It is certainly true that the manner in which the Tokyo trial was concluded had the ironic effect of granting immunity from prosecution to precisely those people who should have borne responsibility for the war, and accelerating the return of the prewar and wartime ruling class to Japanese politics.

On the other hand, there was heated debate within the Far Eastern Commission during the same period over the termination of trials of suspected Class A war criminals, particularly in Committee No. 5, which dealt specifically with war crimes. The Soviet Union and the Philippines strongly resisted any measures to discontinue war crimes trials. However, just as in the case of setting up the Tokyo trial itself, the FEC had no choice but to recognize the *fait accompli* engineered by the US government and GHQ, and, on 24 February 1949, approved the policy of terminating the trials. The tribunal had been closed since 29 December 1948.

Even a cursory reading of FEC records demonstrates that while the Tokyo trial had both the form and the substance of an international trial conducted by the Allied powers, it was also an "American court," one aspect of the American administration of the occupation. Reading these documents, one is left with a poignant sense of the two-sided, political nature of the Tokyo trial.

It is true that the Soviet Union consistently opposed the policy of discontinuing war crimes trials, but aside from the truth and justice of its official position, I sense a kind of national egoism in its position. I will not go into detail here, but I think Soviet opposition to ending the trials is deeply related to the issue of the 570,000 Japanese who were sent to Soviet territory and forced into hard labor, and to the unique circumstances of the Soviet Union's trials of Class B and Class C war criminals. In short, I think the Soviet Union had an extreme aversion to interference from other countries in any of these actions.

Tokyo and Nuremberg

I would like to turn next to a comparison between the conclusion of the Tokyo trial and that of Nuremberg. In the case of Nuremberg, article 10 of the IMT charter specifically recognizes the criminal nature of certain groups. Thus, the judgment of the Nuremberg tribunal also recognizes the criminal nature *as groups* of the political control group of the Nazi Party, the *Schutzstaffel* (SS), the Gestapo, and the German high command. Therefore, even though the Nuremberg trial itself was concluded quickly, trials of Nazi war crimes based on the judgment of the tribunal have continued in the various countries concerned. Moreover, both West Germany and East Germany established domestic legislation stipulating punishment for Nazi war crimes that do not contain statutes of limitation. On the basis of this legislation, anti-Nazi war crimes trials were conducted by the German people themselves, and such trials continue up to this day.

As Murase Okio, a noted scholar of German history, has pointed out, these anti-Nazi trials are problematic in important respects, but the main point to be made here is that war crimes trials have continued. In contrast, while it is true that the structure of Japan's wartime leadership was significantly different from that of Germany's, neither the charter of the Tokyo tribunal nor the indictments recognized the criminal nature of groups. Apparently, once the Tokyo trial had ended, some thought was given to the idea of holding summary proceedings for Class A suspects that would take the Tokyo judgment as a model, but the plan was never realized. In the end, no such war crimes trials were conducted.

While the matter of whether to recognize the criminal nature of specific groups did not become an issue at the Tokyo trial, one of the aims of this concept was in fact carried out in the Occupation purges of public officials. Moreover, while it is true that no war crimes trials were conducted under Japanese domestic law, there was, as I pointed out earlier, a movement among postwar Japanese leaders to hold autonomous Japanese trials; and it was perhaps because of this movement that GHQ moved quickly to order the prohibition of such trials in 1946. The Tokyo trial thus turned out to be a one-time affair.

Failure to Prosecute Crimes against Colonial Peoples

Another important difference between the two trials may be found in the fact that the Nuremberg tribunal placed greater emphasis on "crimes against humanity." This was of course because of the seriousness of the Nazis' mass slaughter of Jews. As a natural result, acts of persecution and murder of German Jews were prosecuted as war crimes, so acts of persecution committed by national leaders against their own countrymen became objects of judgment. In the case of the Tokyo trial, however, the tribunal failed not only to prosecute criminal acts committed by Japanese leaders against Japanese nationals, but also to try acts committed against the peoples of Japan's colonies, such as the forced mobilization of Koreans. It is extremely important to take note of this failure, for it led to such tragic results as the prosecution, for Class B and C war crimes, of Koreans and Taiwanese who had worked in Japanese POW camps, even though they had been there in a form very near forced mobilization.

Unit 731 and Unit 1644

Speaking of "crimes against humanity," perhaps the most horrible acts of the Japanese army were not prosecuted by the Tokyo tribunal. I am speaking here of the case of Unit 731. Under the leadership of Lieutenant General Ishii Shirō, Unit 731 of the Guandong [Kwan-tung] Army conducted germ warfare experiments, including vivisection, on more than three thousand prisoners of war from China and other countries (these prisoners were apparently called *maruta* [literally, logs] by the Japanese involved). Moreover, this unit actually employed germ and chemical warfare on the front lines in China. These horrible crimes have become widely known recently through the publication of Morimura Sei'ichi's best-selling series *Akuma no hōshoku* [Predator Devils].

At the time of the Tokyo trial, the Soviet Union vigorously demanded the investigation and punishment of Ishii and his staff. GHQ did not respond to these demands. It is said that Ishii and others escaped prosecution by turning over to the United States the data on their experiments and their use of germ and chemical warfare in the field.

In the huge collection of materials gathered by the International Prosecution Section, I have discovered a document, never submitted to the tribunal, that provides evidence of the actual use of germ warfare on the Chinese mainland by Unit 1644, the counterpart of Unit 731 in the Central China Expeditionary Army. It is the testimony of a member of that unit who, ashamed of the inhumane acts of the unit, fled to the Chinese side. The Tokyo tribunal uncovered and prosecuted many of the atrocities committed by the Japanese army in Asia, including murder, torture, and rape. For some reason, however, the tribunal did not take up cases of the use of germ and chemical warfare. Critics of the Tokyo trial often point to the issue of the emperor's responsibility for the war as one of the important issues not taken up at the trial. I would suggest that germ and chemical warfare is an equally serious issue that the trial failed to address. Moreover, behind the immunity granted Unit 731, I detect the national self-interest of the United States, which was willing to grant immunity to criminals in order to secure a monopoly on the most up-to-date information concerning techniques of warfare. I cannot help feeling that this mentality has something in common with the decision to place the dropping of atomic bombs on Japan outside the jurisdiction of the court.

The Japanese Response to the Trial

To what extent did the people of Japan perceive the Tokyo trial as their own problem? Positive support for the trial at the time is reflected in contemporary newspaper editorials, which argued that the trial should not stop with the punishment of individual leaders for war responsibility, but should also be an opportunity for the Japanese people as a whole to reflect on Japan's responsibility as a nation for launching a war of aggression. Moreover, not only the newspapers, but also a large number of Japanese intellectuals, stated at the time of the Tokyo trial that Japan must now move steadily forward as a peace-loving nation, as proclaimed by the new war-renouncing constitution.

But what has happened since then? What has been the relationship between the Tokyo trial and subsequent Japanese peace ideology and peace movements? Mr. Tsurumi deals with this problem in his paper, and I would like to reserve my own opinion until the discussion following his presentation.

The Movement for Abdication by the Emperor

Finally, the question of whether the emperor should abdicate flared up again around the time of the conclusion of the Tokyo trial. The emperor's responsibility for the war had been placed outside the jurisdiction of the tribunal and only rarely became an issue during the proceedings. As you know, however, it was the most important theme in the give-and-take and the agreements between the Allied powers and Japan throughout the course of the trial. Much is unclear about the handling of this problem in the period around the close of the trial; but on 12 November 1948, the day sentence was passed on the defendants, the emperor issued a message to the effect that he would not abdicate. It is now known that this took place in response to a request from MacArthur.

It is clear that a political solution had been reached. The emperor did not abdicate, and the issue of his responsibility for the war, which had been the most hotly debated issue outside the court itself, was settled at about the same time as the conclusion of the trial.

The emperor's message at the ceremony marking the occasion of the peace treaty in the United States on 3 May 1952 put an end to all talk of abdication. According to a memo of Terazaki Yoshinari, an official of the Imperial Household Agency at the time, the original draft of the message contained words suggesting a deep apology to the Japanese people for the emperor's war responsibility. However, in the message that was finally issued, the wording had been changed to this: "Particularly on this occasion, we should reflect deeply on the course of past events, engraving firmly on our hearts that together we should exercise great caution that the past shall never be repeated."

This is the extent of my report. [Applause.]

(Appendix)

From *Makino Nobuaki monjo* [The Makino Nobuaki Papers] in the collection of the National Diet Library (Kensei Shiryō Shitsu)

Emergency Imperial Decree for the Purpose of Independently Establishing the National Ethic Necessary for the Stabilization of Public Sentiments and the Maintenance of the National Order (Draft)

Article I. The purpose of this decree is to try and punish those persons and to dissolve those bodies and social organizations that, unable to distinguish loyalty to the national polity from treason, have erred in their capacities as counsellors to the emperor, have failed to serve the emperor's great spirit of peace, and have guided the politics and administration of the national polity and the opinions of the people on the basis of bellicose and aggressive militarism, as well as those who have abetted their leadership. In defiance of the instructions of the Meiji Emperor, these persons brought into existence government by a military clique, based on factionalism and elitism, or as accomplices knowingly assisted and supported this government. They provoked and incited the Manchurian Incident, the China Incident, and the Greater East Asia War, destroying the lives and fortunes of the Japanese people and of people in other countries, thereby imperiling the national polity of Japan. This decree has the purpose of punishing such persons and eliminating or dissolving such organizations for the sake of independently establishing the national ethic necessary for the stabilization of public sentiments and the maintenance of the national order.

Article II. Any person falling under the purview of the following provisions shall be found guilty of treason and punished with death or life imprisonment.

1. Any person who made unavoidable the Manchurian Incident, the China Incident, and the Greater East Asia War by mobilizing troops without the order of the emperor, instigated military actions without authority, or led aggressive actions.

2. Any person who defied the imperial instructions issued to military men by the emperor in 1882, bringing about a condition of government by a military clique, who destroyed the essence of the national polity and indulged in despotic politics, or who by engaging in political activity in collaboration with the latter, defied the emperor's spirit of peace and made inevitable the Greater East Asia War.

Article III. Any person falling under the purview of the following provisions shall be found guilty of treason and punished with domiciliary confinement for life or for ten years or less.

1. Any person who participated directly in the crimes described in Item 1 of Article II.

2. Any person who supported government by military clique, as outlined in Item 2 of Article II, who conspired to strengthen such government, or who knowingly abetted it.

3. Any person who knowingly supported the bellicose propaganda of Army politicians

and others or participated in movements to cooperate with these persons, creating a public sentiment that favored war in violation of the emperor's spirit of peace and making inevitable the beginning of war.

Article IV. Punishment will not be carried out on any person who falls under the purview of Article III if he voluntarily states his penitence publicly, resigns from all his public positions, and refrains from exercising his civil rights.

Article V. Persons falling under the purview of Articles II and III shall be indicted by a Minister of State and turned over to the Chief Public Prosecutor. Citizens may call for indictments under these provisions by submitting to a Minister of State a petition signed by one hundred persons or more.

Article VI. Citizens may bring charges against any person falling under the purview of Article III by submitting a petition signed by at least one hundred persons to the Chief Public Prosecutor through the Prosecutor in Chief. When such charges are brought, the Prosecutor in Chief shall immediately open investigations. However, such criminals cannot be physically detained on the basis of such charges.

Article VII. The venue of trials under this decree shall be the Daishin-in [Supreme Court of Japan under the Meiji Constitution]. There shall be only one trial.

Article VIII. Persons sentenced to confinement shall be subject to suspension of civil rights and deprivation of ranks and privileges during the period of the sentence.

The sentence of death or life imprisonment may be accompanied by confiscation of assets.

Article IX. The government may break up or close educational, religious, economic, or other institutions and organizations that have conducted activities described as treasonous under the provisions of this decree. It may also order changes in the activities of such organizations or take other measures.

Citizens may request the government to issue such orders with a petition signed by at least one hundred persons outlining the facts and the reasons for the petition.

Article X. For the purpose of issuing orders as outlined in Article IX, the government at such times as it deems necessary may appoint judges from among persons of learning and experience to confirm the facts and reasons. The judges will tender their findings after allowing the accused and those related to confront one another and state their respective cases.

The same procedure shall apply when the government deems it necessary to issue orders based on requests from the public as specified in paragraph two of Article IX.

Article XI. Any person who does not comply with orders or obstructs measures under Article IX shall be sentenced to not more than ten years of confinement.

Article XII. The Minister of State referred to in Article V shall be the Prime Minister, the Minister of Home Affairs, the Minister of Justice, or the Minister of Education.

The government referred to in Articles IX and X shall be the Minister in charge of the relevant institution or organization and the Minister of State as defined above.

Summary of Professor Awaya's Paper

CHAIR: Thank you. I particularly appreciate your keeping exactly to the time limit.

Like Mr. Kojima, Professor Awaya is critical of the trial. However, I think it is clear that their positions are quite different. Moreover, though they discuss the same historical issues, their approaches are very different. Professor Awaya pointed out that in the period between the end of the war and the beginning of the Tokyo trial, there existed the possibility of trials different from the form the tribunal eventually took: that is, summary executions or autonomous trials by the Japanese government. Comparing the trial with them, he went on to discuss the beginning of the trial and its character. Finally, he pointed out a number of the problems surrounding the conclusion of the trial, among them the fact that the cold war between the United States and the Soviet Union cast a shadow over the final days of the trial.

I am sure that Professor Awaya's paper will occasion a good deal of debate in the discussion period. I would now like to turn the floor over to Dr. Pritchard.

AN OVERVIEW OF THE HISTORICAL IMPORTANCE OF THE TOKYO WAR TRIAL
R. John Pritchard

An International Political Trial

Thank you. Mr. Chairman, colleagues, and guests. Shortly after the International Military Tribunal for the Far East convened, its president and member for Australia, Sir William Webb, having announced the tribunal's "joint affirmation to administer justice according to law, without fear, favour or affection," went on to declare that "there has been no more important criminal trial in all history."[1]

That boast will be etched in the memories of most of you. But it will raise only an embarrassed smile or quizzical expression on the face of most historians or criminal lawyers today. Even allowing for a bit of hyperbole (for Sir William then, of course, had no idea of how protracted an undertaking he was embarking upon), the "Tokyo trial" did develop into an enormous affair which dwarfed the activities of its far more famous sister-tribunal sitting at Nuremberg. But the German trials, not the Japanese, had already captured the world's attention at the time and have held it since. Even in historical and legal circles—not to mention throughout the world at large—there is widespread ignorance about the Tokyo trial and its significance.

Like its Nuremberg counterpart—and every other international war crimes proceedings—the Tokyo war trial was a product of the highly-charged emotional atmosphere of its time. It is axiomatic that "international" criminal prosecutions are broadly political as well as juristic causes. Few of the defendants at the Tokyo trial could have expected fairness, tact, or understanding, once they had comprehended the indictment.

The Concept of Major War Criminals

Contemporary newspaper accounts, together with private correspondence monitored by SCAP censors, demonstrate that the Japanese public understood that the primary object of the trial was the identification and punishment of the so-called major war criminals, and appreciated that there was a secondary object, which was the moral reconstruction of the world in general but especially the moral reconstruction of the Japanese people.[2] On these points the Japanese and Allied publics (who had little enough mutual comprehension) were in accord: whether or not the Japanese leadership had been "criminal," there was little doubt that the accused in the dock all had something to answer for, even if only as surrogates or scapegoats for the Japanese nation as a whole. To the outside world, all the accused were presumed "guilty": as an Australian representative declared at a meeting of the UN War Crimes Commission (when submitting the first list of sixty-two persons for trial as "major war criminals," including the name of the emperor), "it would be unnecessary to compile a voluminous documentation concerning each of these persons as their activities were notorious." When the former British ambassador in Tokyo, Sir Robert Craigie, who was then in the chair, protested that "in his opinion, it would be unfortunate to put on the list persons who, though not with success, had nevertheless opposed the war of aggression," and then suggested that "listing people for what they had done before the war" seemed to be inappropriate, he won no support. In most people's minds, it was less important that the accused arraigned before the tribunal were "suspected" than it was that they were "major." Nothing dispelled public confidence that the Allied powers were determined to observe very carefully the terms of the Potsdam Declaration that "stern justice shall be meted out to all war criminals."

The Amendment of the Charter

Concern about whether the Allied powers came to the proceedings with hands sufficiently clean to render true judgment or a fair result mostly misses the point: the Allied prosecutors might well demonstrate hypocrisy or show themselves willing to "break a few eggs" for the sake of a better world tomorrow, but they had resorted to a judicial exercise which they could have chosen to forego. Even if that did not vitiate their intention to exact retributive justice at the earliest moment consistent with "due process," it nevertheless gave the defendants a better forum from which to explain their actions than is accorded most fallen public figures or military leaders of whatever country.

Consider who was involved, how they were selected, and by what criteria. Everyone involved must have expected to gain or lose something from the experience. How far were their expectations fulfilled? Well, for lack of time I hope that you will forgive me for merely suggesting that this is a suitable framework for discussion or reflection.

Originally, as recorded in a Draft Summary of Recommendations composed by the Special Far Eastern and Pacific Sub-Commission of the UN War Crimes Commission on 29 August 1945, it was envisaged that "one or more international military tribunals" for the Far East would be conducted, each composed of five judges nominated by the ten member states. By the time General MacArthur promulgated the charter of the tribunal on 19 January 1946, nine countries were named.

Those named in the original charter were joined—very late in the day—by India and the Philippines. Washington had come under heavy Allied pressure to include India, the only one of the ten nations involved in the Special Far Eastern and Pacific Sub-Commission originally deprived of a seat on the tribunal. The United States had resisted the appointment but finally gave way when it was agreed to appoint a Filipino as well. General MacArthur implemented these changes by issuing an amended charter on 26 April 1946 to include India and the Philippines on the list of prosecuting nations and, as Justice Röling noted disapprovingly in his papers, "to change the law to be applied by the Tribunal three days before the Trial started!"

Prerequisites for Membership on the Tribunal

Considering the importance which the Allied powers attached to Japan's flagrant disregard for international treaties, it is interesting that neither Portugal nor Belgium, both of whom were signatories to the very important and critical Nine Power Treaty of 1922, took part in the proceedings. Argentina, Switzerland, and Sweden, although actively involved as "protecting powers" in efforts to restore peace and to reduce suffering experienced by Allied captives of the Japanese, similarly were excluded. One is forced to conclude that military participation in the Pacific or Greater East Asia War was a prerequisite for membership on the tribunal.

One may equally well ask why Burma was not represented at the trial in any national capacity. Administratively, Burma, like India, was treated by Britain neither as a dominion nor as a colony, but unlike India, the Burmese had felt the full weight of Japanese occupation during the Pacific War. Neither India nor the Philippines was yet a sovereign state when the trial began. Both latecomers had been assisted towards independence by the rise and fall of Japan, which also, of course, led directly to the dissolution of the British, Dutch, and French colonial empires. But gratitude was a commodity in short supply.

The Judges

As for the members, I shall not speak of their various findings: in general they are a matter of public record, to be read either in their majority judgment or through their separate opinions. One of the English assistant prosecutors, Christmas Humphreys, said of the members that "only the President, Sir William Webb of Australia, spoke in court, and we had no means of assessing their worth as lawyers, or as judges of facts and men." But by close inspection one can examine, for instance, Justice Northcroft's skillful handling of his peripatetic commissions to take the testimony of Ishihara Kanji and Baron Shidehara.

Then there was Sir William Webb's notorious leave of absence to attend the sessions court in Australia, when the proceedings in Tokyo were left in the care of Major General Myron Cramer, the member of the tribunal then representing the United States. Cramer did not much impress his colleagues on the bench: "he must have had qualities," one member said later, "but I never discovered them."[3] Age, perhaps, had been unkind to Cramer: it had affected Northcroft and Lord Patrick in other ways. Nevertheless, Cramer's period as acting president was a breath of fresh air, and he conducted the business of the tribunal with brisk efficiency, wasting neither time nor words.

One can also occasionally glimpse the views of some members of the tribunal from comments which they uttered during proceedings in chambers, which form part of the official "Record of the Tribunal" but which have not been subjected to much scrutiny by Western scholars. Lord Patrick, particularly, emerges as a man very conscious of the greater freedom which defense counsel at Tokyo enjoyed compared to their German counterparts at Nuremberg. I am afraid that time, again, precludes me from sketching the other members individually, apart from the president himself.

President Sir William Webb

Sir William Webb, by all accounts, was coarse, ill-tempered, and highly opinionated. He was hard-working and endeavored to be conscientious, however.

Despite his abrasiveness, he could be courteous (as he was towards an attractive female assistant prosecutor at an early stage in the proceedings), and there were occasions when he displayed considerable sensitivity, particularly in chambers.

One such instance should suffice (and it may correct certain misimpressions encountered elsewhere): I refer to the compassion which Webb showed when responding to an application by Hirota's Japanese counsel, seeking parole for that defendant to attend Mrs. Hirota's funeral, under guard, in May 1946. Although the application was refused, it appears that Webb himself was sympathetic—until the defense first ineptly indicated that it might not be possible to keep hundreds of people from flocking to the ceremonies, then revealed that Mrs. Hirota's body had already been cremated anyway, and finally assured Webb and several of his brother judges that it would not offend Japanese propriety under the prevailing circumstances if the memorial services were postponed (as they would have been had Hirota been a soldier posted overseas) until Hirota's eventual release, if it ever came.

On the other hand, there were frequent and embarrassing occasions when the president demonstrated his poor grasp of substantive law, whereupon heavyweights in the prosecution could generally be relied upon to spring to his rescue: Judge Mansfield of Australia and Sir Arthur Comyns-Carr of Great Britain both showed a particular genius for ingratiating themselves. Mansfield seemed to be regarded by Webb almost as a crony, but Comyns-Carr's thinly veiled contempt for Webb comes across starkly in the transcripts.

Reservations by Members of Tribunal

Before we leave the justices so that we may look at the part played by the attorneys rather more closely, I should like to emphasize that whatever moral or judicial reservations members of the tribunal felt about their own tasks were really of little consequence: there was no way in which the tribunal could have dismissed itself. Under the charter, the tribunal could "determine the mental and physical capacity of any Accused to proceed to trial," and by those powers Ōkawa was released and the charges against Nagano and Matsuoka were dismissed following their deaths during the trial. But by no means was the tribunal empowered to dismiss the indictment as a whole or to abort the proceedings. They would have to do the best they could or resign—leaving to others the task of sifting the evidence and reaching a decision. While several members did consider taking such a step, not one member concluded that his conscience, abstract justice, or his political and juridical functions would be best served by taking such drastic action.

The Role of American Attorneys

At this point, let us shift our view to the overburdened attorneys. Both sides complained of having too few attorneys to cope with their workload, yet the prosecution had the benefit of at least 82 lawyers, and the defense relied upon more than 150 lawyers (counting only those whom I have been able to identify by name), not to mention their clerical assistants. Not all of these men and women were first-rate: some were a joke. Many did not serve throughout the trial, but the raw figures help to indicate the measure of what was involved.

Each of the accused had a Japanese chief counsel and at least one Japanese associate counsel of his own choosing. Other than Uzawa Sōmei, Kiyose Ichirō, and Takayanagi Kenzō, no Japanese defense counsel attracted much attention among outside observers. However, all of the Japanese attorneys worked under terrific linguistic, procedural, and social disadvantages in appearing before the Allied court.

Within the courtroom, Japanese counsel rarely came to the microphones: there were few whom the court found tolerable, and as a general practice it was up to American defense counsel to speak up in support of their clients. Indeed, the Americans who appeared on behalf of the accused dominated the proceedings. They seemed to be cast as underdogs, but most of them put forward a convincing case in the defense of their clients.

The presence of the American attorneys was a significant improvement over the practices adopted at Nuremberg, where the accused were defended only by German nationals. According to General MacArthur, the initial suggestion that British and American lawyers should be associated with Japanese defense counsel was made by Ōta, whom I presume was Ōta Kinjirō, who was to serve as counsel for Doihara Kenji during the trial. British law made it impossible to recruit qualified barristers from the United Kingdom or British Commonwealth nations,[4] but General MacArthur gave support to the proposal and on 21 February 1946 asked the Judge Advocate-General's Department in Washington, D.C., for "fifteen to twenty [American] Attorneys of suitable experience and qualifications to act as a panel from which might be drawn by selection or by Court appointment Counsel for Defendants charged." On 19 March, MacArthur advised Northcroft, then acting president of the tribunal, that he had asked the JAG Department to increase the number to twenty-five and to make certain that those selected were "of suitable experience and qualifications to assure the Japanese Defendants proper representation and adequate defence."

The Defense's Handicaps

Whatever their handicaps, these men (or almost all of them) proved their worth. However, there were only twenty-five, or eventually twenty-eight of them, a relatively small fraction of the whole defense team, and they could not attend a full-day's hearings in court and complete their "homework" on the defense at the same time. Many of them nearly burnt themselves out with exhaustion, working almost round the clock: those who had to prepare a defense on behalf of more than one accused or who had to deal with allegations involving the whole span of the period covered by the indictment were particularly overburdened at various times. Others left Tokyo from time to time, collecting vital evidence from abroad: they tried to share out their workload among themselves, and one may find many traces of their journeys and difficulties in the Record of the Proceedings in Chambers. The heavy strain told. They lacked not only time and a large enough staff but the political clout to obtain all of the evidentiary documents and witnesses they needed and desired to present a truly definitive case. Moreover, much of what they did offer in court was rejected by members for trivial or specious reasons. The rulings of the tribunal concerning the provenance of documents, hearsay, cumulative evidence (indeed the whole idea of "probative value") deprived the defense of a great deal of valuable evidence.

Far more insidious, however, was the difference between assistance that the prosecution had from Allied governments in the discovery of documents from official archives, or in permission for key officials to appear in court, and restrictions or refusals that attended similar efforts made by the defense. This proved counterproductive in the long-run, for the release of historical archives over the years since the trial has given additional credence to many of the defense contentions, particularly over matters such as the Russo-Japanese border clashes, relations with the French in Indo-China, Anglo-American intercepts concerning Japanese efforts to terminate the Pacific War, Allied contingency plans and preparations for war against Japan, the extent of Allied foreknowledge about the probable consequences of Allied economic pressure against Japan, and so on.

Difficulties Occasioned by Chief of Counsel Keenan

Meanwhile, the shape of the International Prosecution Section took almost as long to define. Joseph B. Keenan, appointed chief of counsel by an American directive only on 27 November 1945, arrived in Tokyo scarcely a fortnight later with forty-five lawyers and a number of clerical assistants. This was an astonishing feat of speed. Much to the disgust of his senior aides who tried unsuccessfully to restrain him, Keenan promptly handed control of the whole of his operation to General MacArthur. Little more than a month afterwards, the first charter was published. Shortly after that, legal contingents from the other Allies arrived, and Keenan expressed the hope that Japanese might take a share in the prosecution. His suggestion was greeted with consternation in Allied circles.

As prosecution teams began arriving in Tokyo from the various Allies, their disparity in size was obvious. Most were composed of two or three lawyers and a small clerical staff. The Russians arrived three months late with a delegation of forty-seven: as Christmas Humphreys put it, "Their doings thereafter were a source of amusement to everyone but themselves." It became evident that the Americans, too, were having great difficulties, largely because of the inability of Keenan to organize his team: Comyns-Carr, the British associate prosecutor, is credited with having remarked that Keenan was "incapable of distinguishing between black and white even when they came out of the same bottle." Several American and Allied prosecutors asked MacArthur to dismiss Keenan: Robert Donihi notes that MacArthur lacked authority to do so.

Selection of the Twenty-eight Defendants

In the end, twenty-eight defendants were selected by a majority vote of an executive committee of Allied prosecutors under the chairmanship of Comyns-Carr. Each of the Allied powers played a part in the process. Considerable insight into what some of the members of the prosecution felt about individual suspects can be gleaned from the pretrial briefs and IPS case files. As for the indictment itself, Keenan reportedly had not even bothered to read it until at least mid-April 1946.[5] But it has long been known that several of the accused, notably Hirota, Shigemitsu, and Umezu, were only added at the last minute, due to the insistence of the Soviet Union. Keenan probably had these men in mind (and possibly also Admiral Nagano and Lieutenant General Mutō, whose names appeared on none of the four short lists prepared by the American team) when he told a special session of the War Crimes Committee of the Far Eastern Commission, meeting in Washington, D.C. (while he was absent from the trial during June 1946, shortly after he had given his opening address in Tokyo), that "we can look forward to the probability of acquittals in one or two, perhaps three, cases."

Nevertheless, the defendants were intended to stand only as a representative cross-section of those whom the Allied powers collectively regarded as responsible for Japanese policy before and during the Pacific War. It was still the intention of the Allies that other major war crimes trials should follow the first Tokyo trial, and this policy was not abandoned until December. In the event, the Allies prosecuted no less than 5,570 so-called minor war criminals and executed about a thousand of the 80 percent they convicted, but the IMTFE stands in a class by itself.

Looking over the evidence tendered to the tribunal, I think we need to remind ourselves that it was not the purpose of the Tokyo trial to distill the history of the entire period between 1928 and 1945. It was a criminal trial. From the historian's point of view, the fact that the alleged crimes involved a supposed "conspiracy" had great benefits. Professor Awaya has given us an excellent demonstration of the range of that evidence, and pointed to the Japanese and foreign reluctance to examine evidence to the extent that one might wish. But there are great opportunities.

Only rarely has new evidence come forth which lends substance to suggestions that some of the accused—or witnesses—committed acts more heinous than the misdeeds for which they were prosecuted. The horrifying story of Japanese bacteriological warfare is to my mind the most significant case to come to light to date.

The court quite rightly found there was nothing in the evidence produced by the *prosecution* which substantiated rumors of Japanese work in bacteriological warfare. But the court *did* hear evidence produced by the *defense* which would have substantiated these rumors. However, the true significance of these documents, which were not read in full, was not made apparent to the court in the defense presentation: I have some doubt that defense counsel even knew what was involved. Certainly the cross-examination was conducted by one of the less able members of the prosecution's team, and nothing was disclosed to the court that might have led it to regard the defense evidence in a different light.[6] For lack of time, I will have to reserve any elaboration on that until the period for questions or private comments.

The English Records of the Trial

There has long been a vogue among historians to deride the quality of the English-language text of the Tokyo war crimes trial records. It is an easy way to call into question the value of the trial, but I suspect that much of the criticism from Western scholars is intended to establish the individual historian's claim to Japanese language expertise. While many of the particular criticisms are amply justified, others are trivial. We should not underestimate the magnitude of what the trial attempted nor the degree of care that went into efforts to ensure that the record was as accurate as possible.

About 175 translators and "checkers" were employed in the prosecution section and another 55 worked in the defense division. Admittedly, many of the language officers at the trial were relatively inexpert (although I would hesitate to guess the proportion of their latter-day critics who are better qualified). However, President Webb was assured in chambers that documents offered in evidence had not only been translated but checked, double-checked and treble-checked—four separate processes of scrutinizing that absorbed the equivalent of one man per page per day. Taking this into consideration, I think it is fair to say that reasonable care *was* taken—certainly more care than the average solitary historian can take in screening large numbers of unfamiliar documents in a foreign language which presents as many difficulties and subtleties as Japanese!

Achievements of the Trial

What did the tribunal achieve? In the narrow sense of judgment, my personal opinion is that expressed by Justice Bernard of France and echoed by Richard Minear: "A verdict reached by a Tribunal after a defective procedure cannot be a valid one." Eric Gangloff, in his introduction to the English edition of Kinoshita's play *Between God and Man*, goes even further: "The right to judge rests on the facade of legitimacy that the court has maintained . . . and if that facade is torn away, the court will have no right to exist." I envy the playwright's privilege to create facsimiles of the truth, but as a statement of fact, that proposition misses the point. The court's right to exist rested upon more than one pillar, and there was a certain historical inevitability about the circumstances in which a trial *had* to take place. Perhaps Brendan Brown, one of the prosecutors, was right: "The emerging and functioning of the Tokyo Tribunal afford not only a fascinating study of a unique 20th century jural process, but also a vivid example of a cyclic and perennial phenomenon. Its prototypes exist in the ancient domains of half-forgotten systems of law. It represents modern man's effort to do for the international social order what his primitive ancestors did for their racial civilizations."

Historical Significance of the Trial

As for the general historical importance of the trial, I believe that its evidence provides means by which the West may approach a greater understanding about the East, a step towards the inevitable fusion of differing world cultures. There is, perhaps, a philosophical divide between those who call it the "Tokyo war crimes trial" and those who call it the "Tokyo war trial." I prefer the latter. The biggest benefit to accrue from the discredited "conspiracy" theory promoted by the prosecution comes from the fact that both the prosecution and the defense had to cast their nets so wide that detailed evidence was collected from every nook and cranny of Japanese public life—and was then packaged in the very best English that the war-weary occupationaires could produce.

What would we do differently, had we the chance? As for me, given a totally impractical, ideal world: I'd hold the Class A trial, collect and process the evidence, apply historical rather than legal criteria to the admissibility of documents and testimony, prepare compilations and briefs of substantive law, then publish and disseminate the transcripts, adjourn *sine die*, seek understanding—and write no judgment at all! Alas, that was never possible in the past. It's a job for the historian!

Thank you. [Applause.]

New Facts Revealed by Dr. Pritchard's Paper

CHAIR: Thank you very much. As you all know, Dr. Pritchard has published the stenographic record of the trial proceedings in twenty-seven volumes. In his paper today, Dr. Pritchard has given us a detailed and meticulous description of the scenes and setting of the trial based on this record. His discussion of the backgrounds of the judges and the problems surrounding the evidence has revealed many facts new to us. Dr. Pritchard concluded his paper with an assessment of the trial, but I think the main theme of his presentation was to bring those facts to light.

I would now like to ask our commentators for their reactions to the presentations. First, we will hear from Professor Yu, who teaches modern history at Nankai University in China.

COMMENTS BY YU XINCHUN

The Chinese View of Japanese Aggression

I learned a great deal from all of the papers given this afternoon. I think the most important aspect of the Tokyo trial was its character as an international tribunal on the Pacific War and the war between Japan and China. In the papers this morning and this afternoon, much of the discussion was centered on the issue of Japan's aggression against China. This afternoon, Mr. Kojima dealt with the problem systematically, and I would like now to state briefly my own opinion of how the Chinese view this issue.

The Tokyo trial dealt with both the Pacific War and the China-Japan War. However, both in terms of the amount of debate on the two wars and in the priority attached to each of them, the Pacific War received a good deal more emphasis. Thus, while the trial did deal with the subject, I believe that greater priority should have been given to the issue of Japanese aggression against China, particularly in view of the fact that it had a history of half a century.

Mr. Kojima developed a systematic argument concerning the history of Japan's aggression against China, stating that Japan began to entertain territorial ambitions toward China around the time of the Northern Expedition. However, I believe that Japanese aggression based on territorial ambitions began with the invasion of Taiwan in 1874. Furthermore, I think territorial ambition was directly linked to the invasion of the Liaodong [Liao-tung] Peninsula during the Sino-Japanese War [of 1894–95], the Beiqing [Pei-ch'ing] Incident [the so-called Boxer Rebellion], the Russo-Japanese War, and World War I. In short, the protection and expansion of Japanese rights and interests in China was absolutely linked over time to the territorial issue. Depending on the balance of international power, one or the other aspect of the issue emerged—either protection and expansion of privileges or the seizure of territory. Fundamentally, Japan had territorial ambitions in China, and when they could not be fulfilled within the international diplomatic structure, they led to the protection and expansion of privileges and concessions.

Resistance Arises Because of Aggression

Professor Hosoya pointed out that Mr. Kojima's position on the China issue differs sharply from that of Professor Awaya, and I too felt this very strongly. I come to Japan quite often, and one thing I notice is the way the China-Japan War is written about in some Japanese books. The argument is that there was first a surge of Chinese nationalism and that Japan had no choice but to react in the way it did. Even in the case of the Northern Expedition, they write, there was an upsurge of bourgeois nationalism, and it was detrimental to Japanese interests; so Japan had no choice but to send troops into Shandong [Shan-tung]. However, when viewed from the Chinese standpoint, or from that of interna-

Note: Professor Yu was the only non-Japanese participant to give his comments in Japanese.

tional justice, Japanese aggression came first and was then answered by anti-aggression. Therefore, the argument that Japanese aggression escalated because there was a reaction against aggression does not hold.

I am not saying that this is the standard view in Japan. As a Chinese, however, I cannot acquiesce to this way of writing history, which holds that Japan had no choice but to act as it did because China was anti-Japanese. Committing aggression and suffering aggression are two sides of a contradiction, and the opposition of the two sides is mutual. However, in this mutual contradiction, there are both the main contradiction and the subsidiary contradiction. No matter what the era, we cannot blot out the distinction between these two contradictions, that is, between committing aggression and suffering aggression, the fundamental principle of reaction against aggression.

In addition, Japan's anti-Soviet position exerted a substantial influence on its policy of aggression against China. I believe it is true that anti-Soviet sentiments and the perception of a Soviet threat were held by the Japanese leadership during this period. But I also believe we should not overlook the fact that one aspect of this stance was its usefulness as an excuse for Japan's aggression on the Chinese mainland.

The Question of Conspiracy

Next, I would like to turn to the issue of a conspiracy among the Japanese leadership. Mr. Kojima argued that there could not have been a conspiracy in Japan's policies toward the mainland and its policies during the war and that, therefore, he had strong doubts concerning the judgment of the tribunal on this point. Surveying the entire period, from Japan's early policies toward the mainland, to its aggression against China, and finally to the Pacific War in Southeast Asia, I believe that in the case of certain wars the argument for a common plot may be untenable in some respects; for example, the Manchurian Incident and the China-Japan War—that is, the early stages of the so-called China Incident.

The Manchurian Incident was a war provoked at the beginning by soldiers of the Guandong [Kwan-tung] Army, led by staff officers such as Ishihara and Itagaki. At first, the ruling circles and the government of Prime Minister Wakatsuki were opposed to expanding the war. Seen in this light, it may appear that there was no conspiracy. However, while this was true at this early stage, in the subsequent invasion and occupation of Qigihaer [Tsitsihar], I think the Guandong Army, the general staff, and the Wakatsuki cabinet acted in concert. Therefore, while we may not be able to see a common plot in the early stages of the Manchurian Incident, or even the China-Japan War, I firmly believe that in the subsequent progress of these wars there was in fact a conspiracy.

Moreover, the existence of a conspiracy in the Pacific War is proven by historical events and is clearly obvious in Japanese diplomatic documents.

The Two Faces of Mutual Reflection

As to the issue of mutual reflection, I think it is proper if divorced from the Tokyo trial and seen as each country reflecting on itself. On a recent trip to Japan, I was quite surprised at first to find that Japanese historians were publishing a great number of reflections, both books and articles, on the consciousness of the Japanese masses concerning war itself. The idea of the people reflecting on their own responsibility for war is unthinkable in China. But I think this kind of research is outstanding. A nation's people have no direct criminal or political responsibility for war, but from the point of view of preventing another war, the idea of rethinking why the people did not oppose the war in that period—why they allowed themselves to be dragged into the war—can be very beneficial for future peace in Asia and in the world, both in terms of its educational effect and its ideological implications. This is the people themselves reflecting wholly apart from the Tokyo trial, and I think it can be extremely beneficial.

However, I cannot agree with the criticism of the Tokyo trial on the grounds that it did not involve mutual reflection. The Tokyo trial was a trial of the defeated by the victors and dealt with a specific, limited time period. In fact, the victors at that time were of three types: an international antifascist alliance opposed to Germany, Japan, and Italy; anticolonial national liberation movements; and the winners in a struggle among the great powers. These three elements joined together to oppose the fascism of the three defeated countries. And I feel that, from the perspective of that period, the victors were after all in the right, that they were "just victors."

However, looking at mutual reflection from the perspective of the power struggle among the great powers, it seems possible that we may be losing sight of the distinctions between committing aggression and suffering aggression, and between engaging in provocation and suffering provocation, as well as reacting to provocation. It seems to me that such mutual reflection and mutual reflection in the context of the Tokyo trial belong to different categories.

US Influence on the Trial

Professor Awaya's discussion of the "shadows" of the Tokyo trial was extremely interesting. The Tokyo trial, in fact, involved a variety of elements. As I said earlier, among the victors there were the forces of the so-called anticolonial national liberation struggles as well as the great powers struggling among themselves for territory and influence. There was also the confrontation between the socialist state of the Soviet Union and the bourgeois states. It is a fact that, among these various elements, the United States seized the leadership in the Tokyo trial. This was based on the power relations that existed at the time. I also think it is true that the effects on the trial of the reversal of US occupation policy and its Far East policy remain as one of the shadows cast on the trial.

Consider, for example, the problem of selecting judges and prosecutors from China for the trial. It is true that in the period of the war of resistance against Japan there were two main forces in China: the People's Liberation Army (the so-called Eighth Route Army) led by the Communist Party, and the troops and political cadre of the Guomindang [Nationalist Party]. Obviously, it would have been fair to select representatives from each side as judges and prosecutors for the trial. Based on American policy in the Far East at that time, however, Keenan and Truman excluded the anti-Japanese resistance forces led by the Communist

Party from participating in the administration of the Japanese occupation and from the Tokyo trial. Certainly, this is one measure of the influence of the United States on the trial.

In general, as was pointed out this morning, the number of representatives from colonies and anticolonial countries was small. And I think this fact, that there were only three representatives from the [Asian] countries that suffered most in the war, is another aspect of American influence.

Finally, Professor Awaya pointed out that the tribunal prosecuted individual criminal responsibility but did not address the issue of the responsibility of the state, and I think that this fact is also linked to America's occupation policy and its Far Eastern policy. Thank you very much. [Applause.]

CHAIR: Thank you, Professor Yu. Professor Yu has offered opinions that stand in sharp contrast to those of Mr. Kojima, especially concerning Japan-China relations and Japan's policies on the mainland. I expect a great deal of discussion on their views. Professor Yu seems to agree basically with Professor Awaya's position. I think the discussion we have heard so far can be divided into two broad topics. On the one hand, the speakers have addressed issues concerning the period of history that was the object of the trial. On the other hand, they have discussed the history of the trial itself. I would like to ask for comments from our other three commentators. But since two hours have elapsed, let us first take a short break and then reconvene in ten minutes.

[Recess]

CHAIR: I would now like to introduce Professor Than. Professor Than comes from Burma and specializes in history at Mandalay University. Professor Than, you have the floor.

COMMENTS BY THAN TUN

The Burmese Desire for National Independence

Mr. Chairman, ladies and gentlemen. After the Pacific War ended with the surrender of Japan, the peoples of countries like Burma, who had suffered enormously during the war, wanted nothing more than restoration, reconstruction, and recovery as quickly as possible. Our biggest problem was that of achieving national independence without too much delay. The British were coming back with the Allied forces, which meant that we had to begin our anti-British activities all over again. What followed were long and arduous negotiations to obtain our freedom, which the Burmese had lost when our last king was dethroned in 1885. Of course, we had been granted independence by the Japanese on 1 August 1943, but that no longer held good after Japan lost the war. The Nuremberg and Tokyo trials, however, attracted the attention of our people—

because we hoped that punishing those responsible for the war might possibly prevent another major war in our region in the future.

Distrust of the Tokyo Trial

We were also interested in the reaction of the Japanese people to these trials. Some of the accused pleaded that they had only obeyed orders. In the West, Hitler was the only person who could not make such a plea; and here in Japan, the one person who could not claim to be following orders was the emperor. But the judges found it very convenient to conclude that the emperor had not been properly advised by his ministers and generals, so it was these ministers and generals who were to be held responsible. I would like to ask: If Hitler had been alive at the time of the Nuremberg trial, would he have escaped conviction on a similar excuse?

There are four other reasons that the people of Burma lost faith in the proceedings of the Tokyo trial. First, a considerable number of suspected war criminals were pardoned before the trial, and even more during the trial. When a person is accused of a crime, he first must be proved guilty or not guilty. If he is found guilty, he should be punished to the extent of his crime. This simple concept constitutes our understanding of crime and punishment. There is no justice in letting an accused person go free without a trial. We were amazed to find later that these people went free for reasons of international politics, rather than international justice.

Secondly, there was the problem of the language barrier. How could the Japanese lawyers of the defense counsel speak to good effect before a tribunal composed of judges from a great number of foreign countries?

No Judge Appointed from Burma

Third, we doubt that the tribunal could have had time to collect all the necessary evidence from all the theaters of war. For crimes committed in Burma, a trial should have been held in Burma. And Burmese should have been appointed judges rather than people from a number of other countries. Fourth, we wonder why Burma could not send representatives to the trials while India and the Philippines did. As you know, Burma became a sovereign state on 4 January 1948, before the trials were over. Neither India nor the Philippines were free states when the trial began.

Finally, I would like to point out that the trials failed to make a strong or lasting impression on those who would take up arms and cause trouble in the future. In the past thirty-eight years, more people have been killed in insurrections and civil wars than during World War II.

This is the extent of my comments. Thank you. [Applause.]

CHAIR: Thank you, Professor Than. Professor Than's comments seem to be related more to the trial itself than to historical interpretation. Nevertheless, the four doubts he has raised will certainly invite comment in the discussions to follow.

Next, we will hear from Professor Hata of Takushoku University.

COMMENTS BY HATA IKUHIKO

Responsibility for Starting the War and Responsibility for Defeat

In principle, I think historians should refrain from making value judgments. Still, aside from the Pacific War, I believe it would be difficult for Japan to justify the Manchurian Incident or the Japan-China War. But it is very strange that Ishihara Kanji, who masterminded the plot that led to the Manchurian Incident, was not indicted at the Tokyo trial as a Class A war criminal, or even as a Class B war criminal.

I think there are two kinds of responsibility for the war. One is the responsibility for starting the war. The other is the responsibility for Japan's defeat. The main purpose of the Tokyo trial was to call Japanese leaders to account for starting the war. What then of responsibility for defeat? Consider General Stessel, who led the unsuccessful defense of Lüshun [Port Arthur] during the Russo-Japanese War, or Admiral Rozhdestvenskii, who was defeated in the battle of the Japan Sea. Though both fought well, they were put on trial in the name of the Tsar for their responsibility in Russia's defeat and punished. Assuming that the Tokyo trial had not been conducted by the Allies, would the Japanese have independently pursued the responsibility of Japanese leaders for defeat in the war? I think not; I do not think they could have.

Moreover, if we could not even pursue responsibility for the defeat, we could not possibly have pursued the responsibility of government leaders for starting the war. Therefore, the way the lessons of the war were perceived was substantially altered, and the direction and character of Japan's subsequent postwar development changed greatly.

The Influence of the Tribunal's View of History

The Tokyo trial took as its object Japanese acts of aggression from 1928 to 1945. As you know, even in 1945, the great majority of the Japanese people had been told virtually nothing about what had happened in this period. In this sense, the trial was a wonderful source of information for the Japanese. Indeed, it amounted to lifting a sort of ban on history.

Moreover, the trial was not only a rich source of information, but also carried out the task of interpreting and providing an overview of the period. I need not tell you what a great shock the picture painted by the tribunal was for the Japanese people. In fact, it was this picture that gave birth to the expression "the Tokyo trial's view of history."

More than thirty years have passed since the trial, and research into the historical facts of the period have advanced a great deal. Indeed, there are now few areas in which it is necessary to rely on the transcripts of the trial itself for data. For historians, in fact, it is now extremely dangerous to rely uncritically on these transcripts, which were prepared and submitted from the standpoint of courtroom technique. However, the interpretation of history embodied in the trial is an entirely different story. I sometimes think that, consciously or unconsciously, we are all bound by this view and have not escaped its influence. [Applause.]

CHAIR: Thank you, Professor Hata. Professor Hata suggests that we should make a distinction between responsibility for starting the war and responsibility for the defeat. He argues further that the tribunal removed a ban on history and offered one framework in which the history of the period could be interpreted. In that sense, the trial had great significance.

I would like next to ask Mr. Hagiwara for his comments.

COMMENTS BY HAGIWARA NOBUTOSHI

Doubts Concerning the Tribunal's Interpretation of the Pacific War

My comments will be very short. I would like to make just two points.

My first point is related to Mr. Kojima's paper. Mr. Kojima stated that the trial should have been an opportunity for mutual reflection—both by the country that was judged and by the countries that handed down judgment. That would have been the most desirable outcome of the trial. But what I want to emphasize here is that, unfortunately, it was not that kind of trial. Moreover, what moves me even today is the self-sacrificing dedication of the American defense counsel— Mr. Furness, who is here today, Mr. Blakeney, and the others—and the existence of the minority opinions, one of which was written by Dr. Röling, who is also present today. These two facts cannot be stressed too much.

Mr. Kojima did not, I suspect, have time to say this. The overall tone of the trial was one of condemning the wrongdoings of the vanquished, but I cannot forget the dedicated activity of the American defense counsel and the existence of the minority opinions. Each time I read the transcripts of the trial, I feel that in a human sense the existence of these people was the saving grace of the Tokyo trial.

My second point is extremely vague. I study history, but my knowledge is limited pretty much to the Pacific War. I can't say I have studied the history of the prewar era. Nevertheless, it seems to me that there is a general tendency to view the war begun by Hitler in Europe and the Pacific War launched by Japan as being the same—to see the two separate wars too much in the same light. This was true at the Tokyo trial, and the same tendency exists today. Japan's Pacific war was quite different from Hitler's war in Europe, which was planned with a clear purpose. This too is a hazy notion, but it seems to me that Japan's war was in many respects comparable to World War I. In this sense, I have considerable doubts about the tribunal's interpretation of the war years, and particularly about its interpretation of the Pacific War. Thank you. [Applause.]

CHAIR: Thank you. Mr. Hagiwara's comment was brief, but very familiar to those who know his work. In short, he suggests that Hitler's war in Europe was different in nature from Japan's Pacific War, and that the war in Asia is perhaps comparable in many respects to World War I. Mr. Hagiwara is well known for this theory, and it is a highly interesting one.

QUESTION-AND-ANSWER PERIOD

CHAIR: We have heard the three papers and the remarks of our commentators. I would now like to open the floor to free discussion. A number of issues have been raised, and I am at somewhat of a loss as to how to organize the discussion.

Incidentally, as for the time, we have a little more than an hour left. I would like to finish by 6:30 P.M.

As I said before, I think the issues can be divided into two general themes. First, a number of problems were raised concerning the history of the period from 1928 to 1945, which was the object of the trial. Mr. Kojima, however, questions this dating, preferring 1900 for the initial figure. Second, there is the problem of the period surrounding the trial itself.

I am sure that Mr. Kojima is eager to respond to Professor Yu's comments. Therefore, I would like to begin with the first topic, that of the period taken up by the trial. If there is time, I would also like to entertain comments on the problems that were passed on to us from the morning session, particularly the problem of Japan-Soviet relations and the neutrality pact between the two countries. I would like to begin the discussion with those who delivered papers and wish to respond to the commentators. First, Mr. Kojima.

The Necessity of Mutual Reflection

MR. KOJIMA: I have no intention of refuting the points made by Professor Yu. However, I would like to clarify a few points on which there seems to have been some misunderstanding.

As Professor Yu pointed out, it is obvious that, in the relationship between committing aggression and suffering aggression, committing aggression comes first. I had no intention in my analysis of attempting to turn that relationship around. What I wanted to say is that if the significance and the purposes of the Tokyo trial include the theme of international mutual understanding for the sake of maintaining peace in the future, countries that were the victims of aggression must not only recognize the wrongdoing of the aggressor but also admonish themselves on account of the internal elements that laid them open to invasion—that such reflection is necessary. I was not suggesting that the Tokyo trial itself be rejected, and I emphasized that reflection on the part of the aggressor was an obvious necessity. In short, my emphasis on mutual reflection was by no means intended to be one-sided.

CHAIR: Thank you. Professor Ōnuma, I believe you have a comment.

The Rationale of Nineteenth-Century Imperialism

PROFESSOR ŌNUMA: Yes, I have a question that relates to some extent to the statement Mr. Kojima has just made. Mr. Kojima explained the fact that Japan repeatedly sent troops to China by referring to the need to protect Japanese residents there. But this is precisely the stale rationalization used repeatedly by the imperialist powers of the nineteenth century when interfering in the internal affairs of underdeveloped countries.

Mr. Kojima suggested further that, unlike the citizens of the other great powers then residing in China, the Japanese were from the lowest social classes. I have not studied this issue in detail, and he may be right on this point. But regardless of how underprivileged these people may have been, it was a mistake to send them abroad in the first place, then to send soldiers, and finally to deploy troops under the pretext of protecting these people or preserving rights and privileges.

On the other hand, I completely agree with Mr. Kojima that Japan was not the only criminal state. The great powers that judged Japan all had committed similar acts. On this point, I am also in complete agreement with Judge Pal of India, who in his minority opinion pointed out that before Japan committed aggression in Asia, the various countries of Europe had already committed repeated acts of aggression in the region.

However, this fact cannot be used to justify aggression on Japan's part. At the very least, to explain away this aggression by saying that it was "self-defense" is to use legal terminology that was not even recognized in the traditional international law of the period. I would like to hear a little more of Mr. Kojima's opinion on these points.

MR. KOJIMA: I agree completely with Professor Ōnuma that the mentality and the perceptions I outlined in my paper were those of the nineteenth century. This means that, if he would look back at Japan in that period, he would be forced to recognize that people with the knowledge of international affairs that we have today were quite rare. Nineteenth-century modes of thought were in fact the rule.

A second point: what I said about protecting Japanese residents in China was intended not as a justification of Japan's actions, but to point out that we should attempt to understand the actual conditions at the time.

I do not think that the protection of Japanese civilians was always merely a pretext for a policy of aggression, or that, in the very beginning, Japan sent troops to the mainland based on this pretext. Rather, as I suggested earlier, what we really see in Japan's China policy are the escalation of conflict in stages, panicky *ad hoc* decisions, lapses into anxiety and fear, and thinking based on exaggeration. These tendencies are clearly distinguishable in the policy making of that time. In a very real sense, it may be said that "policies" were made only after events had already outrun them. This was one of Japan's weaknesses at the time. Moreover, in terms of Japan's institutions, there were many aspects that invited independent action of an arbitrary and fragmented nature.

CHAIR: Thank you very much. I wonder if there are any other questions or opinions on these issues. I would like to entertain a question from the floor.

The Japanese Translation of *Aggression*

QUESTION: Thank you, Mr. Chairman. Frankly, I have doubts about the use of the Japanese word *shinryaku* as a translation of "aggression." This is the word that is used by today's international legal scholars, such as Professors Ōnuma and Okuhara, historians like Mr. Kojima, and political scientists. It was also used at the Tokyo trial, where "aggressive war" or "war of aggression" was translated *shinryaku sensō*. However, listening to Professor Ipsen's paper this morning, I felt quite strongly that there are grave problems with such a translation.

In any English dictionary, *aggression* is defined as "unprovoked attack." As Professor Ipsen pointed out, however, it was only with the decision concerning the definition of aggression by the UN General Assembly on 14 December 1974 that the word came to have something approaching a universal definition. And, as he also pointed out, this definition is not legally binding; at best it has only a kind of exhortative significance. Even now, it is extremely doubtful whether the definition of aggression has been fixed. Moreover, the resolution of the General Assembly declares that wars of aggression will henceforth be crimes against peace; it does not touch on the issue of personal responsibility.

However, since this statement that aggression is a crime in international law is not a treaty stipulation, it is still doubtful today that it has been established that wars of aggression are international criminal acts.

Furthermore, after studying a great number of English and American dictionaries, I have personally reached the conclusion that the word *aggression* should really be understood as "offense" or "attack," and that *aggression* should be translated into the Japanese words that correspond to these two terms. Besides English dictionaries, I have also studied the original meaning of the Chinese characters for the term *shinryaku*. In classical Chinese, the characters meant pushing forcefully into another country, stealing its territory and assets, and plundering it. As a translation for "aggression," therefore, this term is, in essence, somewhat inappropriate.

In his separate opinion, Judge Pal questioned whether "aggressive war" was actually a criminal act in the international law of the time. As Professor Ipsen explained in some detail, it was not.

International Criminality of a Nondefensive War

In the case of the Pact of Paris [Kellogg-Briand Pact], even today people like Professor von Glahn of the University of Minnesota argue persuasively that the pact did not make aggressive war a violation of law. Professor von Glahn's analysis suggests that the Pact of Paris made any nondefensive war a war of aggression but did not make such wars illegal. Indeed, as Secretary of State Kellogg, the American proponent of the pact, stated, each country would determine whether a war was self-defense or aggression, that is, defensive or offensive. In short, each country had "the right of auto-interpretation."

Moreover, the pact did not provide for judgment of violations by international courts or other international institutions. Great Britain, for example, signed the pact only after making this reservation. And it further stipulated that counterattacks in response to attacks on areas that involved crucial national interests were wars of self-defense. This included not only its own territory and that of its colonies, but even areas such as the Suez Canal.

The problem addressed by the Tokyo trial was whether Japan's war was essentially an offensive war rather than a war of self-defense. And those of us who study international law must ponder two issues: was this a war that was not defensive? And was a nondefensive war actually an international criminal act in the international law of that period?

Therefore, in terms of the understanding of the word *aggressive war* by average Japanese, I have grave doubts about the use of the term *shinryaku*, with its weighted nuances of "forceful" entry into another country, "stealing," "plundering," and so on. Moreover, I have the strong feeling that legal scholars, historians, and political scientists are carrying on their discussion without clearing up the misunderstanding. I was greatly impressed by Professor Ipsen's speech, and this led me to make these remarks about the need for greater precision in our use of terminology. Thank you. [Applause.]

CHAIR: Mr. Okuhara, I believe you have a related comment.

The Meaning of *Conspiracy*: Much Broader than *Plot*

PROFESSOR OKUHARA: Yes, my comment also has to do with terminology. In the discussion this afternoon of the historical problems presented by the Tokyo trial, as well as in the discussion this morning, the word *conspiracy* has been used a number of times. In understanding the Tokyo trial, I think this concept of a conspiracy is very important. In the case of Nuremberg, only eight of the defendants were convicted of conspiracy. But in Tokyo all but two of the defendants were found guilty on this charge (excluding Ōkawa, whose case was dismissed due to his mental illness, and Matsuoka and Nagano, both of whom died during the course of the trial). When the average person hears the word *conspiracy*—and before I began doing research on the two trials, I understood it in the same vague sense as other Japanese—it usually suggests something like a plot. For someone who knows a little more about criminal law, it is probably closer to *kyōbō-kyōdō seihan*—that is, collusion to commit a crime in which those whose do not actually take part in executing the crime are held equally responsible.

Yesterday, in fact, I attended a preview showing of the film *The Tokyo Trial*. The narration for the film suggested that it was strange that people who did not even know each other by sight should be prosecuted on the charge of conspiracy. However, as conspiracy is defined in Anglo-American law, there is no need for the defendants to know each other by sight or even by name. It is the theory of conspiracy in Anglo-American law that people utterly unknown to each other can be lumped together in one and the same crime. Confusion on this point can lead to extremely serious problems.

The legal definition of *conspiracy* helps to explain the different results of

Nuremberg and Tokyo. The Nuremberg tribunal dealt with the issue by combining the Continental legal theories of principal offense and complicity. This is an important point, and here I would like to quote my study of the differences between the Tokyo and Nuremberg trials: "On the charge of conspiracy, the Nuremberg judgment convicted only those who had attended one of the secret meetings chaired by Hitler in 1937, 1938, and 1939, those who had been advised of the content of those meetings or a limited number of other secret meetings, and those in positions that made it certain that they had accurate knowledge of the meetings."

Proof of a Conspiracy: The Writings of Ōkawa Shūmei

Neither the pronouncements of the Nazi Party's program in the "twenty-five points," published in 1920, nor the political doctrine outlined in Hitler's *Mein Kampf* was sufficient as evidence for the first requirement in establishing a conspiracy, that is, a common aim. To be specific, the decisions to carry out given actions and the actions themselves had to be fairly close in time; there had to be a specific purpose; and further, the alleged conspirators had to have attended meetings that took the form of conferences or have had positive knowledge of the proceedings and results of such meetings.

In the case of the Tokyo trial, however, the prosecution asserted that the plan for the entire conspiracy was to be found in the so-called political thought of Ōkawa Shūmei. In fact, the works cited by the majority opinion as proof of conspiracy were three of Ōkawa's books. As to when the conspiracy came into being, the majority judgment stated that it occurred during that period of time when unspecified numbers of unnamed staff officers had frequented Ōkawa's residence. What I want to emphasize here is this very difference between Tokyo and Nuremberg.

It was suggested earlier that the term *conspiracy* could be applied in the case of China. I tend to agree. However, while there were such charges against defendants in the Tokyo trial, they were all eliminated in the final majority judgment. The judgment concluded that everything from China to the Pacific War constituted a single conspiracy and therefore took up only the charge of an overall conspiracy. Precisely for that reason, the tribunal's judgment on events in China is extremely vague. [Applause.]

CHAIR: Thank you very much. Historians have a tendency to be sloppy in their use of such terms as *aggression* and *conspiracy*, and are often scolded by their colleagues in the field of law. In any case, I doubt that any Japanese historian—and there are many historians present today—still accepts the interpretation of conspiracy, or of an overall common plan, put forward in the Tokyo trial's view of history. That view has already been overturned by historical documents that have emerged since the trial and by subsequent examination of the evidence presented at the trial itself.

As to which Japanese word to use for *aggression*, historians are not of one mind. And, of course, the same thing is true of whether it was Japan that initiated hostilities in China. As to the issue of conspiracy, it is a well-known fact that there existed limited conspiracies; for example, the conspiracy among a small group of officers in the Manchurian Incident. However, I doubt that there is a single researcher in Japan who accepts completely the tribunal's view of history.

Pardon me for not sticking to my role as chairman. Are there other comments on the history of the period from 1928 to 1945?

QUESTION: I would like to speak from a standpoint quite different from that the rest of the participants. I speak as someone who fought in the front lines as a platoon leader and later as a low-ranking field officer. My position has nothing to do with arguments about peace and whatnot. I want to ask Professor Yu this question: When we were fighting in the course of the Manchurian Incident, isn't it true that China built a great wall between itself and Manchuria and said, "That isn't our country"? Wasn't that the position China took? And I also believe that the slogan in China when the Manchu [Qing (Ch'ing)] Empire was overthrown was "Up with the Han [Chinese], down with the Manchus [Manchurians]."

When we went to Manchuria, the Manchurians were being oppressed by the Han Chinese, who had poured into the area and chased them deep into the mountains of Jilin [Chi-lin]. It does no good to speak of this now, because already by the time the Han Chinese poured into Manchuria it was no longer feasible, but couldn't this have been an area where five races could live together in peace and harmony? Japan had checked Russia at the time of the Russo-Japanese War, and if we could have checked the Han Chinese at that time, Manchurians, Koreans, Mongolians, and other races could have formed such a state for co-prosperity. So when the Han came pouring in, Japan's plans for conquering the area fell into disarray. We fought in the front lines under those conditions.

When I saw the oppression of Manchurians by the Han Chinese in Jilin and other places, this is how I felt. That is my first point.

One Aspect of the Nanjing Massacre

My second point is that when you think about laws, international law and the like, please keep in mind the actual conditions on the battlefield. If you don't, it isn't fair to those who were charged with Class B and C war crimes. I would like to give as an example something that happened at the time of the Nanjing [Nanking] Incident. On the battlefield, you're likely to get it any minute. If something moves—it doesn't matter if it's grass blowing in the wind, a cat running, a dog running—you think first of all that it's the enemy. You fire a quick shot and then take a slow look. You're hunched down with your jaw jammed into the butt of a rifle, eyes wide open looking for the enemy; your only movement is to swivel your head back and forth. That's why those on the battlefield . . .

CHAIR: Excuse me, but could you keep your comment as brief as possible? Are you asking a question, or stating an opinion?

QUESTION: I am trying to say something for everyone's benefit.

CHAIR: So you are stating an opinion. In that case, please limit your statement to another minute or so.

QUESTION: If you don't treat everything as if it were the enemy, you get it yourself. That's why you deal with anything left on the battlefield as the enemy—whether soldiers, civilians, or children. Particularly when things are hot and heavy and you're getting shot at, anyone still on the other side is the enemy. The commander of the other side should have evacuated the civilians and the children. If you are going to blame us for a massacre, I wish you would blame the general of the other side for not evacuating noncombatants. That is all I have to say.

CHAIR: Thank you. I believe Dr. Pritchard would like to respond to these remarks.

A Difference between Firing in Battle and Slaughter of Prisoners

DR. PRITCHARD: I think there's quite a difference between firing in response to a sudden movement on the battlefield and such things as the massacre of Chinese prisoners of war for bayonet practice, don't you? These are among the sorts of things—and that of machine guns firing for eight- to ten-hour periods on prisoners of war outside of Nanjing—that actually come up again and again in the evidentiary documents. And I don't think that it does justice to your own soldiers or any other soldiers to confuse war crimes with the unfortunate incidents that just happen as a necessary consequence of hostility.

CHAIR: Professor Hata?

In Connection with Economic Friction

PROFESSOR HATA: I would like to comment on the question of Chinese immigrants into Manchuria. As you stated, the immigration of large numbers of Chinese into Manchuria began around the time of the Russo-Japanese War, and so it was a relatively recent development. Subsequently, immigration proceeded steadily, at a pace of about one million people a year. At the time of the Manchurian Incident, about 80 percent of the total population of thirty million in Manchuria was composed of Han Chinese. The actual number of native Manchurians was in fact quite small.

Now, immediately after the Russo-Japanese War, there was a great deal of trouble over Japanese immigration to the American continent, and as a result of this Foreign Minister Komura devised a plan to focus Japanese emigration on the Korean peninsula and Manchuria. In fact, he established a program to send a million emigrants to these areas. In the end, however, almost no Japanese emigrants went to Manchuria.

Thus, at the time of the Manchurian Incident, there were only two hundred thousand Japanese residents there. Almost all of these were employees of Japanese government enterprises, such as the Manchurian Railway, or people parasitic on these enterprises.

Colonel Kōmoto Daisaku, who was responsible for the assassination of Zhang Zuolin [Chang Tso-lin], observed in 1928, just before the assassination, that Japanese immigrants in Manchuria could not possibly compete economically with the Chinese, because the Chinese operated at a much lower standard of living. If the Japanese attempted to compete economically, he argued, they would surely be defeated, so Japan should take Manchuria by force. This observation is what moved him to take action. I believe that this statement embodies the essential nature of the Manchurian Incident. That is, Japan could not dominate Manchuria through peaceful economic competition between Chinese and the Japanese emigrants, and therefore it resorted to armed force.

Presently, a great deal of attention is being given to economic friction, and I wonder if it is not necessary to consider this problem from the same perspective.

CHAIR: Mr. Okamoto?

The Problem of Korean and Taiwanese Class B and C War Crimes Suspects

MR. OKAMOTO AIHIKO (director of *Watakushi wa kai ni naritai* [I Want to Become a Shellfish], a prize-winning TV drama about a Class C war criminal): Thank you. I would like to say something about an issue that is extremely important, but has yet to enter very much into the discussion. Professor Ōnuma mentioned the problems of the Koreans and Taiwanese under Japanese colonial rule, and, just now, Professor Awaya touched on the fact that citizens of those countries were convicted of Class B and Class C war crimes. These brief comments have moved me to develop the issue more fully.

As you know, the number of Koreans and Taiwanese convicted of Class B or C war crimes was by no means small: 178 Taiwanese and 148 Koreans (of these, 29 of the former and 23 of the latter died in prison).

The case of Korea is especially tragic. More than three thousand Koreans were taken off to POW camps in Southeast Asia to serve as prison guards. And since a good amount of English was needed for this work, some of the best educated people in the country were forcibly mobilized at that time. There may be people who object to my use of the phrase *forcibly mobilized*, but the facts justify it. There was a case in which fifth-year middle school students were literally dragged from the paddies where they were working, loaded onto trucks, and taken to a kind of concentration camp in Pusan. From there, they were taken directly to the prison camps in Southeast Asia. Moreover, while officially they were given the status of paramilitary personnel with the rank of noncommissioned officer, their actual status was worse than that of a common soldier. And since they were forced to work as prison guards, the prisoners knew their names and their faces. That's why so many of them were convicted for Class B or C war crimes. Hence the numbers I mentioned above.

Those convicted were held at Sugamo prison before the signing of the peace treaty. In the case of the Koreans, a number of them were released at Sugamo. But this took place at the peak of the Korean War, and many of these people had no choice but to stay in Japan. There is a taxi company in Japan called Mutual Progress Transportation (Dōshin Kōtsū). Most Japanese in the audience will have seen their taxis. This is actually an abbreviation for the name of the company formed by these convicted war criminals after their release: The Mutual Progress Society of War Criminals of Korean Nationality [Kankoku Shusshin Senpansha Dōshinkai]. A number of people from this group are still confined today at the Chiba National Treatment Center, having lost their sanity as a result of their experience. Ms. Utsumi Aiko, who is in the audience today, has recently published an outstanding book on this subject. Those who have died in Japan have received very poor treatment from the Ministry of Health—their funeral urns have not even been sent back to Korea.

The introduction to my question has somehow become quite long, but my question is actually quite a simple one. Legally, shouldn't these people have been set free once Japan was defeated? I am speaking, of course, of the Koreans and Taiwanese charged with Class B or C war crimes. I am no legal specialist, but it seems to me that this should have been the case. Instead, they were punished in a number of Asian countries—178 Taiwanese and 148 Koreans. What were the legal grounds, or principles, for the punishment of these people? I am a rank amateur, and I apologize if this is a stupid question. But I would very much like to know the answer.

CHAIR: This is a question concerning the legal side of the trial and would probably have been more appropriate for the morning session, but I think Professor Ōnuma can give you a brief explanation.

Acts Defined as Crimes Against Humanity

PROFESSOR ŌNUMA: Setting aside the various problematic points of this issue, and speaking in a purely legal sense, I can answer your question most simply in this way: At that time, the people of Taiwan and Korea were Japanese citizens, and in carrying out the acts of the state of Japan as members of the Imperial Army or the Imperial Navy, these people committed war crimes. Given this fact—the commission of a war crime during that period—they would not automatically become immune from prosecution by changing their nationality at a later date. Speaking in a purely legal sense, this was the basis for their prosecution and conviction.

This question provides me with a perfect opportunity to comment on points raised by Professors Okuhara and Paik this morning. Professor Paik suggested that the Tokyo trial did not deal with the problem of crimes against humanity. There is room for various interpretations concerning this point, but basically I think it is correct. And Professor Okuhara would probably agree. However, Professor Paik also pointed out that in Korea and Taiwan, which were under Japanese rule, and in Manchuria, which in fact was a puppet state, acts were carried out that would seem to fall under the purview of crimes against humanity. And Professor Paik stated very strongly that this fact must not be forgotten.

On the other hand, the substance of Professor Okuhara's position was that the Tokyo and Nuremberg trials were carried out under very extraordinary circumstances—tribunals convened in the immediate aftermath of World War II, which was extraordinary in the extreme—and that it was doubtful how much significance they could have in regulating the actions of nations in the future.

I stand somewhere between Professor Paik and Professor Okuhara.

No Immunity from Responsibility for Acts of Atrocity

I do not deny that there were cases of acts amounting to crimes against humanity in the countries under Japan's rule, such as Korea and Taiwan, and in the puppet state of Manchuria. On the other hand, however, speaking in terms of the degree to which these acts were shocking—the degree to which they were violations of fundamental justice—there is a difference between these acts and the systematic, collective, mass atrocities committed by the Nazis in Europe. At least, that is my own evaluation of these cases.

In this sense, I agree with Professor Okuhara that the decisive fact that gave rise to the two trials was the extraordinary outrage of world opinion against the atrocities committed by Nazi Germany—I earlier called this outrage the people's simple sense of justice. And, also in this sense, he is quite right to say that the situation was extraordinary.

It is quite a different matter, however, to argue that because the trial took place in extraordinary circumstances, there is nothing to be learned from it. Take Mr. Kojima's paper and Professor Yu's comments this afternoon. Although on the surface they seem to be in opposition, there is something they hold in common, something we can learn from: that we should evaluate the Tokyo trial objectively within a broad framework, considering not only the acts of Japan, but also those of all the other countries involved, and on that basis use what we have learned as a steppingstone toward future world peace. These were the common themes running through both their positions. Moreover, problematic as they may be in some respects, the two concepts I stressed this morning—the concept of leaders' responsibility and that of the duty of non-obedience to illegal state orders—may hold potential, I think, for regulating the actions of states.

Finally, I want to comment on the problem of atrocities against minority peoples in countries under Japanese rule. This issue was raised by Professor Paik. My own opinion is that while there may have been atrocities that reached the level of the crimes against humanity committed by Nazi Germany, in most cases Japanese actions did not reach that level. However, that is a separate issue from the question of how the Japanese perceive and deal with the fact that atrocities did occur. The fact that the responsibility of Japanese leaders for such atrocities was not pursued in the form of indictments for crimes against humanity does not mean that Japan can escape responsibility for those crimes.

CHAIR: I believe Professor Okuhara wants to respond to these remarks.

Crimes Against Humanity and Conventional War Crimes

PROFESSOR OKUHARA: Professor Ōnuma has just commented on views I presented earlier, so I would like to elaborate on my previous statement.

Before doing so, however, I want to comment on the question directed to Professor Ōnuma at the beginning. I think the nationality of the accused at the time of the alleged crime—whether Japanese or not—is irrelevant. The problem is the flag that a soldier was fighting under. After all, soldiers often fight under the flags of foreign countries. And if war crimes are in fact committed by a soldier, he should be judged guilty even if he is fighting under the flag of a foreign country. Therefore, I feel that the problem raised by Mr. Okamoto should be dealt with in terms of whether or not the people found guilty and punished had actually committed crimes.

Now I would like to turn to the question of crimes against humanity. I think it is possible that the inhuman acts committed in Korea, Taiwan, and Manchuria might actually meet the definition of crimes against humanity in cases where they would have been seen as conventional war crimes had they been committed in occupied areas [not in colonies such as Korea and Taiwan]; that is, in cases where the legal situation was not one in which the laws of war could actually be applied but in which the substance of the act involved was the same as that defined as a war crime by the laws of war. If they met these conditions, such things as forced labor or forced migration could become objects of prosecution. However, under the conditions of war that existed at the time, even ordinary Japanese citizens and students performed various types of labor service. Therefore, if forced labor or forced migration are to be judged under the category of crimes against humanity, our conclusion will depend on whether or not a specific people or race is seen to have been singled out for such treatment.

Finally, I would like to explain further what I said earlier about crimes against peace, when I referred to the enormous scale of the war. Briefly stated, what I wanted to say is that under existing international law persons who were judged to have committed conventional war crimes could be punished if apprehended. In reality, of course, they could not be punished if they were not apprehended.

In short, as I suggested earlier, in the case of a military conflict that breaks out between states maintaining normal national sovereignty, the only way to decide which was guilty of aggression is to establish an international tribunal and have the nations in question accept its jurisdiction. In regard to the issue of pursuing responsibility for aggression domestically or to the necessity of pursuing responsibility by various other available means, I am in complete agreement with Professor Ōnuma.

CHAIR: Thank you very much. This is a very important problem, and I would like very much to continue the debate. However, we have gotten somewhat far afield from the main themes of this session, so I would like to return to our main theme by asking for opinions or questions on Dr. Pritchard's paper, concerning such problems as the fairness of the trial, the selection of judges, and so on. Following these, I will accept comments or questions on Professor Awaya's discussion of the conclusion of the trial. But first, I think Professor Awaya has a comment.

The Tribunal Documents as a Historical Treasure House

PROFESSOR AWAYA: I would like to comment on the use of trial documents. This subject has some relation to Professor Hata's statements and is connected also with the conclusion of the trial. Professor Hata pointed out that postwar research on modern Japanese history has made great strides and suggested that current research has gone beyond the level of the trial transcripts. I tend to disagree. In the case of Nuremberg, the transcripts of the trial were made public after its conclusion. The voluminous transcripts of the Tokyo trial, however, were left sitting there when the trial closed, and were never made public. E. H. Norman, among others, believed that the great significance of the Tokyo trial would be its contribution to history, but at least in Japan the trial ended without fulfilling that task. My own research is on the history of the Fifteen-Year War, and I believe that the documents of the trial can still make an enormous contribution to historical research. In my own publications, for example, I have introduced evidence from trial documents concerning bacteriological warfare in Central China. Also, in materials provided to the Prosecutor's Division of the tribunal, but not presented in the proceedings, I discovered a copy of a secret report on the assassination of Zhang Zuolin [Chang Tso-lin] presented to the emperor by Prime Minister Tanaka Gi'ichi.

I believe such examples are only the tip of the iceberg. Some of the documents of the tribunal are now entering Japan on microfilm, and I think there is still a great deal of material buried there that can shed light on the history of the Fifteen-Year War—not only in the documents presented to the court, but also in the huge volume of material that was never presented. So I think the trial materials are still a historical treasure house.

The fact that these documents have not yet been exploited is related closely to the manner in which the trial was concluded.

CHAIR: Thank you. I will now recognize Mr. Matsudaira.

A Military Trial by the Occupation Army

MR. MATSUDAIRA: I would like to make a statement. It will take only three minutes. Japan pursued a colonial policy like that carried out by other countries in the nineteenth century, and when it pursued an imperialist course on the Asian continent, it was simply imitating the actions of other countries. Is it not true that it is illogical to single out Japan for criticism? The Japanese representative in the US-Japan negotiations clearly enunciated this in formal meetings with President Roosevelt. In response, Roosevelt said that things would be different if it were the nineteenth century. In the twentieth century, he said, world opinion would no longer tolerate acts of aggression. Therefore, he said, if you had come to me with this proposition in the nineteenth century, I could have understood, but in the twentieth century it won't do.

What President Roosevelt said can be interpreted as follows. As Professor Ōnuma also said earlier, there had already emerged in world opinion a certain view of aggression that could provide a basis for customary international law. This emerging, this budding view should be nurtured, not plucked out. But isn't that exactly what Japan was trying to do, pluck it out? This is what was meant, I think.

And for your information, I state as my personal opinion that this has nothing to do with the earlier argument that because other countries were committing acts of aggression Japan could also do so. That is my first point.

The second point has to do with Professor Ipsen's paper. I was quite impressed with his analysis, and there are many points with which I agree.

However, if I may state my conclusion first, the Tokyo and Nuremberg trials were fundamentally different in character. Others have spoken of this difference, but the basic difference between the two trials undoubtedly concerns the question of jurisdiction. In the case of Japan, the Tokyo trial was a military trial. It was a military trial conducted by the Occupation army, and punishments were applied that were essential to the administration of the Occupation. This is the basic mentality that informed the proceedings. In short, as Mr. Hagiwara has pointed out, it was a trial that was an extension of the ideology of World War I. Therefore, there were of necessity limitations on the jurisdiction of the tribunal as a military court, limitations strictly stipulated in international law. Hence if these restrictions on the Tokyo trial were different from those on the Nuremberg trial, then of course the nature and types of crimes the Tokyo trial dealt with and the severity of the punishments it handed down also had to be different.

The Possibility of Retrials

As you know, however, the Occupation ended with the signing of the San Francisco Peace Treaty. This meant that the legal force of the Potsdam Declaration came to an end at the same time. That is, since the peace treaty replaced the Potsdam Declaration, embodying the declaration within the treaty, any provision that does not appear in the text of the peace treaty is not binding on Japan—because Japan had become a sovereign state. Thus, the Tokyo trial is today incorporated in the legal system established by the postwar Japanese constitution and must be considered from the standpoint of the system of constitutional law that now exists. This takes us back to an earlier question. In considering the problem of Class B and C war criminals, and in view of the difficulties of the surviving relatives of persons convicted by the tribunal, I think it is possible to conduct retrials based on the postwar constitution in cases in which the tribunal may have gone too far or not far enough. I want to emphasize that I raise this possibility as a legal issue—a problem of legal technicality—and not as a political one. I am by no means suggesting political action to stage such trials. But would it not be possible? If Tokyo differs from Nuremberg, there must also be differences in this area. That is my second point.

The Japan-Soviet Neutrality Pact

Finally, I want to point out that there was no answer to my question this morning concerning the problem of the Japan-Soviet neutrality pact. I take this as a silent acknowledgement that Japan did not violate the pact, and I want to ask the chairman to see that this is clearly recorded in the minutes of this session. [Laughter.]

CHAIR: Thank you very much, Mr. Matsudaira, for your valuable remarks. In passing, let me say that Mr. Matsudaira attended the negotiations at the Japanese embassy in Washington just before the beginning of war with the United States—indeed, on the eve of Pearl Harbor.

I would like to avoid further discussion of legal theory, but I wonder if Professor Lounev would not like to respond on the issue of the Soviet-Japan neutrality treaty, particularly in regard to the historical facts.

PROFESSOR LOUNEV: Since neither the Ambassador nor I have the text of the neutrality treaty at hand, we cannot say at this time which particular article was violated. If we can obtain a copy of this text, we can go through it article by article, and we will find something, I hope. [Laughter.]

CHAIR: A very politic answer. [Laughter.] Mr. Hagiwara, you have the floor.

The Japanese Leadership's Concept of War

MR. HAGIWARA: I would like to elaborate a bit on Ambassador Matsudaira's first point. As I said earlier, I think we can compare the Pacific War and World War I. What I meant by that is that the image of war that existed in the consciousness of Japanese policy-makers at the time of the Pacific War—or, perhaps, the "unconscious premises" they had concerning war—was informed not by their memories of World War I, but rather by those of the Russo-Japanese War. I have run into many actual examples in my research that reinforce this perception.

CHAIR: There is a great deal I would like to say about the problem just raised, and about the Japan-Soviet neutrality pact, and I long to say it; but in view of my role as chairman and the lack of time, I shall remain silent. Yes?

The Pacific War: An Extension of the War in Europe?

QUESTION: I am not a historian, and I have not done a great deal of work on the Tokyo trial. However, since my work is indirectly related to the trial, I would like to pose some questions. This afternoon's panel deals with the historical perspective, but if that perspective were changed slightly, our evaluation of the trial would also change. Therefore, I would like to explain the kind of perspective I am thinking of, and then ask for your comments and opinions.

Recently, the United States and Great Britain have declassified a new body of documentary material dating from the war period. I have obtained microfilm copies of such things as the "Magic Documents" and the "Ultra Documents." My own specialty is political communication, but, in reading through these documents, I have had the irresistible feeling that Japan entered the war against the will of the Japanese people. That question aside, I cannot help feeling that the Pacific War arose as an extension of the war in Europe.

That is, already before the outbreak of war, the United States and Great Britain were of a single mind. They were already exchanging software and information and were moving in exactly the same direction. In fact, it is said that Roosevelt had entered into the phase of "undeclared war." In this sense, the Pacific War was in fact an extension of the war in Europe, and I have the feeling that our evaluation of the Tokyo trial could be reconsidered from that point of view.

Briefly stated, I wonder if the time has not come to re-examine whether Japan should be made to bear sole responsibility for starting the war. I would like to hear your opinions on the proposition that Japan was dragged into the Pacific War in a manner completely different from what it intended.

CHAIR: To whom is your question directed?

QUESTION: To anyone—the Chairman, Mr. Hagiwara, Mr. Kojima . . .

The Essential Nature of the Pacific War

DR. PRITCHARD: As someone who has worked on exactly the opposite problem, of looking at the prelude to the European war in terms of the influence of Far Eastern tensions, I think it is fair to say that a great deal of the tension, a great deal of the whole thrust of British and French appeasement, for instance, toward Germany and Italy, is simply a reflection of the weakness felt by those powers in view of worldwide threats, but predominantly as a reflection of Far Eastern tensions. And so I think it may be difficult to separate the two. But I don't think one could say that the Pacific War is simply a consequence of European tensions. Perhaps it is the reverse.

CHAIR: There is that view. Indeed, Dr. Pritchard himself, for example, has studied the Tianjin [T'ien-chien; Tientsin] Incident and has written a paper on the influence of this incident on the war in Europe. There is also the theory that the Fifteen-Year War constitutes a single war. Opposed to that is the view that the Manchurian Incident, the Japan-China War, and then the Pacific War should be considered separately. Indeed, there are so many different approaches that we could continue this discussion for several hours. Recently, I myself have been writing and speaking about my hypothesis that the essence of the Pacific War was a war between Japan and Great Britain, so I should like to join the discussion. I am afraid, however, that we will have to wrap up this afternoon's session.

Before doing so, however, I would like to introduce the person who, in Japan, is most familiar with the documents of the Tokyo trial, Mr. Toyoda Kumao. Mr. Toyoda has been in the Justice Ministry for some time and he has been engaged in cataloging and indexing these documents. Before the war, he was the naval attaché of the Japanese embassy in Berlin.

Before introducing Mr. Toyoda, however, I would like to recognize Mr. Furness.

Contributions of the Japanese Defense Team

MR. FURNESS: I want to make just one comment. Dr. Pritchard said that the Japanese counsel took very little part in the trial. Actually, they advised us, who were making the speeches—I am not making a speech now, by the way—but they were a tremendous help to us indirectly in presenting the evidence and in advising us on what testimony the witnesses could provide. When witnesses were testifying for the prosecution, they could advise us on how to cross-examine them. [Applause.]

DR. PRITCHARD: I didn't say that they didn't take an important part. What I said was that they rarely spoke before the tribunal so that the actual handling of the defense case, in that sense, was principally the work of the American defense counsel. Undoubtedly, a great deal of work was done behind the scenes by the Japanese defense counsel and of course, at various times, the chief of the Japanese defense division was even thought to have some sort of authority over the American defense counsel. It is not actually true that he had power over the American defense counsel, but it is commonly thought in some circles that that was true.

CHAIR: Mr. Toyoda, you have the floor.

A Prayer for Eternal Peace

MR. TOYODA: Thank you, Mr. Chairman. It is somewhat outside the scope of this symposium, but I would like to take this opportunity to make an announcement.

You all know, I am sure, that there is a memorial in Hiroshima to the victims of the atomic bomb. As it happens, the building we are in now was once the site of Sugamo prison, and a great number of war criminals were held here. It was in the northeast section of this site that Tōjō and other convicted war criminals were held and executed. After the signing of the San Francisco Peace Treaty, the Japanese government donated approximately eight thousand square yards of this area to the city of Tokyo in order to preserve a reminder of all the war crimes trials. The city of Tokyo in turn entrusted the management of this property to the Toshima Ward Office. About three years ago, the officials of Toshima Ward planned and constructed a peace park called the Toshima Ward Central Park. The park is right next to this building, and I hope you will all take the opportunity to see it for yourselves.

It was designed by a very famous master of Japanese gardens who came from Osaka, and it is truly a beautiful example of traditional Japanese gardening. In one corner, there is a peace memorial constructed of a single large natural rock. Together with the Hiroshima peace memorial in western Japan, it is our peace memorial. On its face is written only this: "We Pray for Eternal Peace" [*eikyū heiwa o negau*]. Thank you.

CHAIR: Dr. Röling would like to say a word.

DR. RÖLING: Thank you, Mr. Chairman. There was discussion about the roles of the Japanese and the American counsels. I would like to take the opportunity, now that there are Japanese and American counsel present, to put to them a question. I remember, at the time, that we judges wondered what was the nature of their cooperation. Some of us got the impression that the aims of the Japanese counsel and those of the American counsel were different—that the Japanese counsel, before anything else, were intent on defending Japan, the honor of Japan, and that that was their primary aim. The aim of protecting the accused seemed to be secondary. With the American counsel, it was just the opposite—that they were first of all trying to protect their clients, and perhaps could not have cared less about the honor of Japan. I would like to ask if that was a correct impression, or if there was something else that made cooperation difficult.

MR. FURNESS: Mr. Yanai Hisao, my partner, and I were defending Mr. Shigemitsu. We were also working so far as we could to defend the position of Japan. The case was divided into phases: the Burma phase, the naval phase, the Russian phase, and so on. I was lucky enough to defend on the Russian phase with Mr. Blakeney. I think we worked together all the way through the trial. We were defending the Japanese position, and I think that was our duty—that was our obligation as lawyers. And I don't think there was any difference between the Japanese and the American counsel on this point.

Necessity for Rule of Law for the Survival of Humanity

MR. BROOKS: Early in the trial, I considered some of the problems of the prosecution. I also considered some of the problems of the Japanese defense counsel. There is a difference in the concept of "judges" in Anglo-Saxon jurisprudence, in which the judge sits quietly and decides between what the prosecution presents and the defense presents. I finally realized that the Japanese, and the Australian justice, had the same system. That the judge wanted to say what he wanted to hear and what he didn't want to hear. I didn't care one way or the other what he wanted to hear. All I wanted was to see the truth come out, if possible, concerning what was causing these wars, and all I cared about was that we were setting a precedent in international law by being there—whether it was right or wrong. And I hope that the future will see that this is the only way that mankind can live on this earth. We must take the law and write it so that he who runs things can read. We must not take up arms, but take up the law and find out just what is right and just between nations—whether in criminal law or civil law—and what will prevent what has happened in the past. We have had an awful history. It is time we started living like brothers. That is what I was interested in.

Mr. Koiso did not trust me for a long time, but finally he exclaimed, "I have decided. I have found a friend from the distant foreign land." He realized that I was fighting with Webb about things Webb did not want to hear. He wanted to try the emperor. I believed that the emperor had been a puppet in the hands of circumstances beyond his control.

CHAIR: Thank you. Due to my incompetence as a chairperson, the discussion has jumped from issue to issue. Nevertheless, thanks to your participation, I think it has been a lively and fruitful session. As one of the conference coordinators, I am delighted with the results of today's proceedings. Thank you all very much.

THE TOKYO TRIAL FROM THE PERSPECTIVE OF THE QUEST FOR PEACE

May 29
1983
(morning session)

INTRODUCTION TO THE SESSION

CHAIR (Ōnuma Yasuaki): I am pleased to open this morning's session, which will begin the second day of this international symposium on the Tokyo trial. Since I have been obliged to play the roles of organizer, reporter, and chair in this symposium, I have had almost no time to prepare for my role as chair of this session. I am afraid I will have to rely on the cooperation of the other participants.

I would like to begin today's proceedings by answering a question put to me yesterday by a member of the mass media: Why a symposium on the Tokyo trial now?

A Solid, Scholarly Reexamination

Until the latter half of the 1970s, research on the Tokyo trial had been sorely inadequate. But looking over the situation in the latter half of the 1970s, one found reliable, academically sound activities beginning among scholars in various countries; these activities were occurring at the same time, yet they were completely independent. For example, in the Netherlands, Dr. Röling, seated beside me, finished his collection of documents from the trial; and in England, Dr. Pritchard was completing his massive editing of the transcript of the proceedings. In Japan, Professor Awaya, who is one of our panelists, myself, and others organized a small research group of scholars, journalists, and librarians interested in the trial. What all of these different activities had in common was that thirty years after the end of the war, and of the trial itself, we were liberated from emotional bias and were able to evaluate the Tokyo trial from a position of relative calm. This is one of the reasons the time is ripe for a reexamination of the Tokyo trial.

In a sense, it is understandable that debate over the trial in the period immediately after Japan's defeat should have taken the form of total support or total rejection—on the one hand, those who took at face value the words "the judgment of civilization" and on the other, those who shrugged cynically and said, "Might makes right." But after thirty years had passed, in the late seventies, I felt that finally we were approaching a period in which a sounder, more scholarly investigation of the Tokyo trial would be possible.

When I met Dr. Röling and Dr. Pritchard in Europe, they agreed with this opinion. I remember saying to them at the time that, if possible, I would like to organize an international symposium on the trial in Japan and invite them to it. This encounter became one of the driving forces behind this symposium.

Hopes for Peace in the Future

There is a second reason for holding this symposium now. Thirty years have passed since the end of the war, and there is a growing number of people who have no direct experience of war. The Tokyo trial is suffering, so to speak, from the effects of weathering. This phenomenon contains within it the danger that the Tokyo trial will be dealt with only in an extremely abstract manner. We feared that if we did not conduct a scholarly, objective evaluation of the trial now, the chances of doing so in the future would steadily diminish.

Having listened to yesterday's discussion, I think one can say the following concerning my first point: while, to be sure, some of those who were directly involved in the trial have a deeply rooted feeling of identification with the trial or a resentment toward it, still a certain perception of the trial is now held in common by most of the specialists. They recognize that although the trial had the defects characteristic of victors' justice, it nevertheless may hold one key to peace in the future.

Yesterday, the discussion took place mainly among the panelists and special guests. We were not able to hear from the younger people in the audience. It is important that we do hear from them, for as I suggested earlier, one of the reasons for holding this symposium now is to learn what the younger generation of Japanese thinks. For this reason, in this morning's session, after the papers by Dr. Röling, Mr. Tsurumi, and Mr. Kinoshita, we will reverse yesterday's order and take questions first from members of the audience, thereby hearing, we hope, from the young people present here today. Dr. Röling's presentation will last about forty-five minutes, and Mr. Tsurumi and Mr. Kinoshita will speak for about twenty-five minutes each. The presentation of papers will be followed by a short recess, and then the discussion will be open to questions from the audience. Again, I will give precedence to younger members of the audience and to answers from the three speakers.

Finally, I would like to reemphasize a point made by the chair yesterday. This symposium was organized in the hope that it would make a contribution to future peace. Thus, while it is natural that there should be a wide range of opinions, partisan attacks are out of place. I ask for everybody's cooperation in this matter. As I said before, we want to accept as many questions as possible from the general audience, but questions should be relevant to the speakers' arguments. Long-winded statements of personal opinions will not be recognized. Again, I ask for your cooperation in keeping this morning's session on schedule. I will now turn the floor over to Dr. Röling.

THE TOKYO TRIAL AND THE QUEST FOR PEACE

B. V. A. Röling

The Prohibition of War

Thank you, Mr. Chairman, ladies, and gentlemen. This symposium seeks to evaluate the great postwar trials of Nuremberg and Tokyo, and will focus on the trial that took place in this city against the "major Japanese war criminals." Since the conclusion of the Tokyo trial, in which I participated as the Netherlands judge, I have devoted my life to peace research and, being a lawyer, to the question of whether international law can contribute to the maintenance of peace.

One conclusion of that research has been this: Modern weapons technology compels mankind to eliminate war, for in a nuclear war the survival of the human race may be at stake. Scientists realized this from the outset. Bertrand Russell represented their opinion when, in his famous address in the House of Lords on 28 November 1945, he said, "It is not enough to make war rare, great and serious war has got to be abolished."

It is therefore necessary, in the first place, to have a strict legal prohibition of war, the prohibition against starting war. And that is precisely the present legal situation according to the UN charter. Article 2 (4) prohibits the threat and use of force. Only in one case may a state take up arms on its own decision—in case of an armed attack (art. 51). But many governments and scholars do not share this strict interpretation of the charter provisions. This interpretation, however, was reaffirmed by the General Assembly in 1974, in its resolution defining aggression. The most important provision of this large document is article 5: "No consideration of whatever nature, whether political, economic, military or otherwise, may serve as a justification of aggression."

The San Francisco Conference, which drew up the UN charter, ended on 26 June 1945. On that same day in London, the discussions began that led to the charter of Nuremberg, which in turn served as the model for the Tokyo charter, the legal basis of the Tokyo trial. These charters take as their starting point the theses that only defensive wars are allowed and that aggressive wars are not only illegal but criminal. One of the innovations of the charters of Nuremberg and Tokyo was the concept of the crime against peace: individual criminal responsibility for having brought about an aggressive war.

This was a new idea with a remarkable history. In the first years of the war, the crime against peace was hardly mentioned. Concern focused entirely on the atrocities committed during the war by the Germans. The Three Power Declaration [Moscow Declaration] of 1 November [or 31 October, depending on the time zone] 1943 envisioned the imminent punishment of those who had committed atrocities.

Stalin's Proposal

The initiative to bring aggression itself into postwar trial adjudication came from

Stalin. A few days after the joint "Declaration on Atrocities," and during the commemoration of the "Great October Socialist Revolution" on 6 November 1943, Marshall Stalin made a speech in which he declared: "In conjunction with our Allies we shall have to . . . take measures to ensure that all the fascist criminals who are responsible for this war and the suffering the peoples have endured shall meet with stern punishment and retribution for all the crimes they have committed, no matter in what country they may hide."

This suggestion aroused quite a bit of commotion in Allied governments and in the legal committee that was preparing for the postwar trials. There was a great difference of opinion about whether individual responsibility for initiating and waging an aggressive war could be deduced from international law.

The Role of Attorney General Jackson

This symposium is not the place to relate all the discussions which took place prior to the establishment of the charter. In his book *The Road to Nuremberg*, Bradley Smith revealed how the Allies finally agreed to try the Nazi leaders— rather than summarily shoot them, and how, particularly in the United States, the opinion took hold that the German leaders should also be tried for the crime against peace. It is curious to read that Biddle, as the American judge at Nuremberg, as well as Cramer, the American judge at Tokyo, originally believed that international law did not recognize the crime against peace. And yet both signed the judgments which held that the crime against peace had already existed at the time of the creation of the charter of Nuremberg.

Notable, too, is the diverging opinion of several nations after the first and second world wars. In 1919 France and England proposed to try the German emperor for waging an aggressive war. The United States prevented this, however, because such a criminal trial was considered to be in conflict with existing international law. In 1945 the positions were reversed. The United States now wished to prosecute those considered guilty of the crime against peace, the crime of aggression. France and England were opposed for legal reasons, the Soviet Union because of the fear that embarrassing things, such as the secret clauses of the Stalin-Ribbentrop agreement [German-Soviet Nonaggression Pact], would be disclosed. The United States, however, persisted under the fierce direction of Jackson, who had accepted the function of American delegate to the Conference of London. He is said to have gone to London "with fire in the belly."

The exceptional role that Jackson played shows how "the demands of the time" often make use of chance circumstances. In 1935 the United States adopted a "Neutrality Act," which gave the actual *coup de grace* to the Kellogg-Briand Pact of 1928. In September 1939, following the eruption of the war in Europe, America declared itself "on terms of amity with the contending Powers."

American Policy and the Crime of Aggressive War

Public opinion shifted, however, after the capitulation of France, and American policy was reversed. The laws of neutrality were now violated by the delivery of fifty destroyers, Lend-Lease, and many other actions. As attorney general, Jackson had defended the reversal with the argument that the German attack had been one of illegal and criminal aggression, and he wanted to endorse that theory. "Throughout the efforts to extend aid to the peoples that were under attack, the justification was made by the Secretary of State, by the Secretary of War, Mr. Stimson, by myself as Attorney General, that this war was illegal from the outset and hence we were not doing an illegal thing in extending aid to peoples who were unjustly and unlawfully attacked. . . . Now we come to the end and have crushed her aggression, and we do want to show that this war was an illegal plan of aggression. We want this group of nations to stand up and say, as we have said to our people, and President Roosevelt said to the people, as members of the Cabinet said to the people, that launching a war of aggression is a crime and that no political or economic situation can justify it. If that is wrong, then we have been wrong in a good many things in the policy of the United States which helped the countries under attack before we entered the war."

Hence the recommendation to have a criminal trial and to have a hearing "as dispassionate as the times and the horrors we deal with permit." The indictment should include "the crime which comprehends all lesser crimes," namely, "the crime of making unjustifiable war." These principles were laid down for the most part in the treaty of 8 August 1945 [London Agreement], the "agreement" in which the charter of Nuremberg was defined, later to be used as a model by General MacArthur for the Tokyo trial.

International Law and Aggressive War

The question is this: what was the position of international law in regard to aggressive war?

It is indisputable that the freedom of states to wage war was recognized at the beginning of this century. This is clear from the Convention for the Pacific Settlement of International Disputes of 1907, article 2 of which reads: "In case of a serious disagreement or dispute, before an appeal to arms, the contracting powers agree to have recourse, as far as circumstances allow, to the good offices or mediation of one or more friendly powers."

The Porter Convention of 1907 did not alter this. Neither did the stipulations of the covenant of the League of Nations, which in point of fact merely provided for a temporary postponement of war. The Kellogg-Briand Treaty of 1928 outlawed war as a means of national policy. But it left the question of the right to self-defense open, to be answered by the nations themselves. In any case, no mention was made of individual criminal responsibility. Kellogg and Borah explicitly declared in the Senate that a possible violation of the treaty could never be brought before an international court.

There was indeed a growing popular opinion in the interwar period that wars needed to be abolished. The Kellogg-Briand Treaty was an expression of this growing revulsion against war.

International law before World War II did not make aggressive war a crime. But Jackson—basing himself "on the common sense of justice"—was not prepared to let things be complicated or obscured "by sterile legalisms developed in the age of imperialism to make war respectable."

World War II followed, notwithstanding all the prewar expressions of longing for peace. But what occurred in that war, the German and Japanese atrocities, culminating in the German gas chambers, and the Allied violations of the laws of war, culminating in the dropping of atomic bombs on Hiroshima and Nagasaki, increased the repugnance against war and the outcry in favor of the maintenance of peace.

Prosecution of the Crime against Peace

The horrors of World War II intensified the emotional aversion to war. Rationally, the atomic bombs made the maintenance of peace a vital necessity. It is an irony of history that the illegal and criminal American atomic bombs probably contributed to the conviction that Japanese aggression had been criminal. War must be brought to an end, and starting a war is illegal, yes, criminal: those opinions were strengthened when, after the capitulation, the atrocities committed were fully exposed.

Jackson understood this exceptional situation, in which the prevailing emotional opinion cried out for that which the world in fact needed: a prohibition of war. In his report of 6 June 1945, he wrote to the American president: "Now we stand at one of those rare moments when the thoughts and institutions and habits of the world have been shaken by the impact of world war on the lives of countless millions. Such occasions rarely come and quickly pass."

Hence his insistence that the crime against peace should be included in the charter of Nuremberg: it was a law that the world needed and that would mature because of the prosecution and punishment of the crime against peace.

The Tokyo charter followed the Nuremberg example. The trial was to be conducted based on an indictment that included the three categories of crime: crimes against peace, conventional war crimes, and crimes against humanity. Not everyone was a proponent of such a trial. In the United States, the wish prevailed to prosecute and punish only those who were responsible for the attack on Pearl Harbor. That surprise attack had to be avenged.

During a conversation I had with MacArthur, the general told me explicitly that he had not at all wanted the Tokyo trial as it was now conceived. He had been in favor of a short court-martial concerning Pearl Harbor, a treacherous attack in an undeclared war.

American Political Reasons for the Crime against Peace

There were many emotional and political reasons in the United States for having a trial concerning Pearl Harbor. However, since the precedent of Nuremberg was set, it was hardly possible to avoid prosecuting Japanese leaders for the crime against peace. Restricting the Japanese indictment to the undeclared attack on Pearl Harbor would have amounted to a repudiation of the Nuremberg principles. The Nuremberg trial made it necessary to hold a similar process in Tokyo, even though the situation in Asia was so different, so much more complex, and legally so much more difficult.

The crucial question for both tribunals was this: what is the position of the tribunal with respect to the charters? It was quite clear that the jurisdiction of these tribunals was restricted by the provisions in the charters: there was no jurisdiction that was not based on the charters. But did the jurisdiction which the charters granted have to be adopted without further questioning? Were the judges bound merely to applying the charter? Or was it their task to test the charter provisions against existing international law?

The Potsdam Declaration contained the statement: "stern justice shall be meted out to all war criminals." Stern justice, but justice! Did this mean that the victors in the war were entitled to create new international law, to declare as crimes acts that were not considered crimes at the time they were committed? Moreover, through Jackson, the United States had insisted that international tribunals should be established by which the world would confirm that wars of aggression were illegal and criminal, thereby vindicating the American violation of the neutrality laws. Could that goal be reached if the judges were called upon merely to apply the charter provisions?

New International Criminal Law Created by the Victors?

The Nuremberg tribunal indeed decided that it was not its task to examine the legality of the charter provisions. This was also the conclusion of the majority judgment at the Tokyo trial. Nevertheless, both verdicts considered the question of whether or not existing international law declared aggressive war illegal and criminal. Nuremberg concluded that the charter was "in conformity with international law at the time of its creation," and Tokyo adhered to this.

My personal conviction was that the victors had no authority to create new criminal laws and punish the vanquished on the basis of those new laws. Moreover, to claim this license would create a hazardous precedent and later provide an opportunity, after a successful war, to eliminate hated opponents as war criminals.

Thus the question was this: what was the position of international law? And not only the text of treaties should come under scrutiny here, but the practice of nations as well. After the Napoleonic wars, voices were heard demanding that the French emperor be simply killed. The German poet Kleist expressed those feelings in his poem "Germania an ihre Kinder": "Schlagt ihn tot! Das Weltgericht / Fragt euch nach den Gründen nicht."

However, the action taken against Napoleon was restricted to political measures. The emperor was removed from the political scene as a source of future danger to peace, "comme ennemi et pertubateur du repos du monde." Measures were taken "les mesures de précaution, que le repos et le salut public peuvent exiger à son égard."

There was a serious movement after World War I to try the German emperor. England and France urged this, but the stand of the United States against it led to article 227 of the Treaty of Versailles. The emperor was to be tried on account of the "violation of international morality (not legality) and the sanctity of treaties." The trial was to be conducted "according to the highest motives of international policy (not justice)." (The parenthetical insertions are mine.) Apparently, the intention was to cast the desired political measures into a judicial mold.

The Crime against Peace *in statu nascendi*

These aspects played a role as well after World War II. Political measures were needed to protect the fragile peace against potential leaders who might provide a nucleus for groups bent on revenge. There was also a growing aversion to war which was fueled by the war crimes and atrocities committed by both sides. The form of a criminal trial might contribute to the progressive development of international law in such a way that it would no longer recognize the freedom of a state to wage war, but would completely reject it and would regard aggressors as criminals and outlaws.

This idea of putting potentially dangerous persons out of the way had been present ever since prosecution and punishment began to be considered. Stalin expressed ideas of this nature, and in the Tokyo trial this aspect became exceedingly obvious.

The Potsdam Declaration had already emphasized the need to eliminate former political leaders: "There must be eliminated for all time the authority and influence of those who have deceived and misled the people of Japan into embarking on world conquest, for we insist that a new order of peace, security and justice will be impossible until irresponsible militarism is driven from the world."

In his "Opening Statement," Chief Prosecutor Keenan referred to this aspect: "For the accused in the dock are no contrite penitents. If we are to believe their claims as already asserted in this trial, they acknowledge no wrong and imply that if they were set free they would repeat their aggression again and again. So that from the sheer necessity for security they should be forever restrained." The Soviet prosecutor spoke in the same vein.

It can be seen as a new element that, after World War II, a criminal trial was chosen as the means of deciding who had been—and who still were—the dangerous, aggressive leaders. Another new element was the rhetoric which surrounded this political action. It was a rhetoric that harmonized with the existing emotions and opinions.

International law was *en route* to banning war and rendering it a criminal offense. The crime against peace was *in statu nascendi*, so to speak.

Various Types of Crimes against Peace

The concept "crime" may include many different kinds of acts, varying from deeds that are punished as intolerable examples of repulsive immorality and injustice to "political crimes," where the actual situation of power and authority determines which acts are lawful and which are criminal.

Hence it is possible and, I think, permissible to speak of the crime against peace with the understanding that we are concerned with a kind of crime (and here I quote from my dissenting opinion, II, p. 1060) "where the decisive element is the danger rather than the guilt, where the criminal is regarded an enemy rather than a villain, and where the punishment emphasizes the political measure rather than the judicial retribution."

This interpretation is not so much a break with existing international law. Nevertheless, it sustains the movement of international law in the direction of making aggressive war a real crime. Naturally, this opinion also has consequences in regard to the quantity and quality of the "guilty" and to the punishment to be imposed. When we consider the punishments inflicted, it seems to me that a clear discrepancy is discernible between the terminology of "the crime against peace" as "the supreme international crime" and the punishments imposed. Shigemitsu was found guilty of this "supreme crime" and also of conventional war crimes, and for that he was sentenced to seven years imprisonment. No one who was found guilty only of aggression received the death sentence. Only those who were judged guilty of grave violations of the laws of war or of crimes against humanity were sentenced to the supreme penalty of death. Stimson remarked rightly: "Certainly, then, the charge of aggressive war has not been established in international law at the expense of any innocent lives."

This mildness of the judgments has been attributed to all kinds of motives, such as the novelty of the offense and the uncertainty of its contents. But is it daring to assume that the sentences arose from a different viewpoint than one might suspect from the given motives? Could it be that here, as so often with judgments which create new law, the sentences were superior to their motivation?

American Deal on Biological Weapons Research

We now come to the conclusion and the general evaluation of the trial. It is possible to express criticism founded on the unfair features of the proceedings. The trial was not adjusted to the obviously disparate power positions: the prosecutor had the archives at his disposal and derived his refusal to allow "fishing expeditions" from established Anglo-Saxon trial rules. There was indeed unfairness at times. But not to such an extent that, as a judge, one felt compelled to resign.

Grave errors were committed. It is my firm belief that some men were sentenced who should have received praise instead. In my dissenting opinion, I argued for the acquittal of Shigemitsu, Hirota, Tōgō, Kido, and Hata. Since then I have become less certain about the last one, because of later revelations of criminal Japanese military practices in Manchuria involving biological weapons research. It is possible that Hata was connected with this atrocious behavior of the Japanese army. But this, the most heinous of Japanese war crimes—bacteriological experiments on prisoners of war—remained concealed from the tribunal. As has become clear from now-disclosed official American documents, the United States wanted, in a cheap way, to get hold of the results of these criminal experiments, experiments which, as the documents show, had cost great amounts of money and thousands of human lives. The results of the experiments were secured by the United States with a promise of nonprosecution, and thus this criminality was kept from the court.

"Asia for the Asians" and the "Liberation" of Colonies

Tokyo was more complicated, factually and legally, than Nuremberg. In Germany the defendants were the leaders of a thoroughly criminal government, which in cold blood had organized the murder of millions of Jews, and which aimed, by violent means, at a domineering position in the European *Grossraum*. And in Japan? Here aspirations for the extension of power to the north and the south had been prevalent for a long time. Those tendencies were fed and strengthened on the one hand by the fear of the Communist danger in China, and, on the other hand, by the concern for the oil supply. Those motives did not justify armed aggression. But since the cold war we have become, perhaps, a bit more accustomed to state misbehavior arising out of fear of Communism, and since the Club of Rome drew attention to the scarcity of raw materials, the concept of "economic security" has received quite a lot of attention in national policy. We have witnessed since 1945 quite a few illegal military interventions by both of the superpowers with the aim of providing for "ideological" or "economic" security.

The possibility of expelling the colonial powers from Southeast Asia motivated certain groups in Japan. This task was regarded by them more or less as Japan's "manifest destiny." In the course of its history Japan had learned to mistrust ideological aggression and to fear its effectiveness, first that of Christianity, later that of Communism. Now it was considered Japan's turn to employ this weapon, with the cry, "Asia for the Asians." Hirota and Konoe were supporters of this ideal and thought to realize Japan's historical summons via ideological subversion and economic penetration. That, however, would have taken time.

The military did not grant this time and "liberated" the colonies by direct military action. Yet when this had been accomplished and the European powers had capitulated, the military did not seem equal to this "great historic mission." After they came to power, it became clear that they wanted Japan to take over the position of the former colonial authorities.

Atomic Weapons and the Prohibition of War

Considering the aspects and motives of Japan's actions mentioned above, to judge Japan's aggression according to the legal opinions of that time was all but simple. Opinion underwent a change thereafter, and not only with respect to colonial relations. Mankind became aware, more and more, that the hard fact of the existence of atomic weapons demanded a strict observance of the legal prohibition of the use of force in international relations; demanded, too, that violation of the rule forbidding the initiation of a war should be an international crime.

In the Tokyo judgment, as well as in that of Nuremberg with regard to Germany, the victor's authority had already imposed this new law on Japan and applied it to the Japanese leaders. And even though this cannot be called in a legal sense totally correct, it does not diminish the law-creating effect. New law can rise from solidarity and mutual benevolence; it can also originate from coercion and power.

Notwithstanding several negative aspects of the verdicts of Nuremberg and Tokyo, they did undeniably contribute to a legal development that mankind urgently needed. The United Nations adopted the principles laid down at Nuremberg and Tokyo. The crime against peace has become an accepted component of international law. It makes the legal prohibition of war to *jus cogens*. It is a logical consequence of the factual situation: war between nuclear powers may eliminate life on earth. It also is a consequence of the legal situation existing today: the UN charter now clearly recognizes the prohibition against starting a war. Dramatically stated, the prohibition against war and the concept of the crime against peace are conditions for peace and human survival.

The judgments are a "landmark in law." One might add, a landmark raised by a revolutionary action. This action is still in progress and now turns against the nations still prepared to react with military means against adverse ideological developments and economic measures.

An International Duty Transcending State Obligations

In our time, when nationalism and militarism flourish unashamedly and show the governments to be slaves to their instruments of power, peace may well depend on public opinion against war, and thus on the peace movement, the mass action of citizens who demand a different and peaceful kind of international behavior.

To these peace activists, the condemnation of the leaders guilty of initiating and conducting an aggressive war is a landmark. It may provide the legal basis for their protests against an aggressive government policy. It can also contribute to the understanding that the citizen has the right to refuse to cooperate with government policy which under international law is branded as criminal. It is not only a right, but even a duty.

For perhaps most revolutionary is the consideration in the judgment of Nuremberg—and Tokyo concurred with its judicial conclusions—that the essence of the applied law is that individuals have international duties which transcend the national obligations of obedience imposed by the individual state.

Now that governments seem to be entangled in irresponsible militarism— now that it becomes ever more clear that only the collective will of the people can save humanity from extinction—the judgments of Nuremberg and Tokyo have become an indictment against the present behavior of the superpowers.

Jackson stated rightly at the time: "We are not prepared to lay down a rule of criminal conduct against others which we would not be willing to have invoked against us." If we are able to keep that thought alive, the postwar tribunals can be considered to have really contributed to the quest for peace.

Mr. Chairman, having listened to the various discussions here, I wish to make one additional remark. I think the most important question concerning the Tokyo trial might be whether we will continue to concentrate on its negative, unfair aspects, or whether we will focus on its positive aspects, that is, the aspects which have significance for the future, that reinforce the general opinion that resorting to war as a means of resolving disputes is no longer a viable choice in our times. Thank you. [Applause.]

A Summary of Dr. Röling's Paper

CHAIR: Thank you, Dr. Röling, for an eloquent and moving presentation.

Dr. Röling spoke quite slowly in a manner that was easy to understand, and I doubt that there is any need for repetition. However, I would like to summarize two or three of his main points.

First, he argued that the crime against peace had not been established in international law at the time of the outbreak of World War II, that its introduction into the trial was a result of American national interests, and that in this sense the crime against peace was a political crime.

He also suggested that while there were undeniable procedural problems in the trial, it nevertheless maintained an acceptable degree of fairness.

Dr. Röling also stated that, as a judge on the tribunal, he argued that Shigemitsu Mamoru, Hirota Kōki, Tōgō Shigenori, Kido Kōichi, and Hata Shunroku should have been acquitted. Today, however, he has some doubts concerning Hata, because of new evidence concerning the latter's involvement in bacteriological warfare. In this connection, he also referred to the fact that the United States had made deals with the Japanese involved in bacteriological warfare experiments in order to obtain the results of the experiments, and that as a result this evidence was concealed from the tribunal.

After touching on the fact that the superpowers have engaged in illegal military activity since World War II for various ideological and economic reasons, Dr. Röling argued that even though there are legal problems concerning the Tokyo trial, these problems do not diminish its law-creating effect— that, in fact, in today's world the prohibition of war and the concept of crimes against peace are conditions of peace and human survival. Specifically, the condemnation of the leaders guilty of initiating and conducting an aggressive war can provide the legal basis for the peace movement's protests against individual governments; it also contains within it the concept of the individual citizen's duty under international law to refuse to obey illegal orders of the state. This, he argues, is the most revolutionary significance of the law created at Nuremberg and Tokyo.

Dr. Röling concluded his paper by recalling Jackson's statement that laws applied to others must also be applied to ourselves. He added the comment that while listening to the discussions yesterday it had occurred to him that the ultimate question was whether we would pay more attention to the negative aspects of the trial or to its positive significance—whether we would use it as a steppingstone in our quest for peace. If we choose the latter, the trial can indeed become a means toward future peace.

Dr. Röling has provided a universal perspective on the Tokyo trial. Our next speaker this morning, Mr. Tsurumi Shunsuke, approaches the trial from a somewhat different viewpoint. His paper focuses on perceptions of the trial in Japan, on the point of view and the reactions of the Japanese masses, and on the prehistory of these perceptions. I will now turn the floor over to him.

WHAT THE WAR TRIALS LEFT
TO THE JAPANESE PEOPLE
Tsurumi Shunsuke

I want to consider the question of what the war trials have left in the minds of the Japanese people.

Popular thought, you see, inevitably has a "prehistory." The famous ethnographer Yanagida Kunio [1875–1962] describes the relation between history and prehistory in a manner reminiscent of Japanese oral history: "In the old days, it was like this. Now . . ." He rarely speaks of specific dates or even periods. In thinking about the history of popular thought, this manner of speaking is extremely apt, for you really can't divide this kind of history into neat chunks of time. Behind the question I have posed for myself—how the Japanese people feel about the war trials now—is the additional question of how they felt while the war was going on. We can't really separate the two.

A War Chopped Up into "Incidents"

So, first of all, I would like to consider how the Japanese looked at the war while it was still going on, before war trials had come into existence. From the time the Japanese army began waging a war of aggression against China in 1931, when the "Manchurian Incident" occurred, until the country's final defeat, the Japanese had a period of fifteen years to think about the war. Especially at the beginning, when the fighting was not that intense, people thought Japan could always turn back. What blurred the situation—what convinced so many people that Japan could turn back—was the impression created by the government that each episode in the long war was in fact a discrete "incident," that each of these incidents was the last.

With each small war—the "Manchurian Incident," the "Shanghai Incident," the "China Incident"—the people were given the impression it had been quickly disposed of. So even today, people who grew up during that period still have that same vague impression. A good many people in that age bracket still perceive these "small wars" as a series of "incidents" that occurred prior to, and completely separate from, the Greater East Asia War [Pacific War], which began with the first clear declaration of war in 1941. If they are honest about their subjective perceptions, I think many people fifty and over would have to agree that this is an accurate reconstruction of their sense of history at the time.

"Responsibility for Defeat" and "Responsibility for Starting the War"

In terms of this consciousness of those alive at the time, these incidents—since they were cleared up almost as soon as they had begun—seemed not to be interconnected. Some people thought it would be bad to involve the nation in a war that might be lost. And this thought is linked to the idea of responsibility for losing the war, an idea which emerged after the war. There was another way of thinking, one which asked whether it was permissible to begin such a war. This, you see, is a matter of responsibility for starting the war. I think it is very important that we distinguish between the two: responsibility for losing the war and responsibility for starting it. Even as I separate the two, however, I want to say that they overlap in many respects, and that this fact becomes an important pivot.

Take, for instance, modern Japanese intellectuals and their way of thinking about antiwar movements. They tend to reject anyone whose motives for participating in the movement are not, fundamentally, the same as their own. I think this is a mistake. You are not going to have a movement at all with that kind of thinking. This is a key point I want us all to consider.

Now, most Japanese before the war thought that China was militarily weak. In fact, that was highly doubtful, but people did not have the kind of information that would have led them to question it. As it turns out, precisely this view of China led many elementary school students to ask whether it was not somehow wrong to wage war on such a weak country. Actually, this was quite commonplace among children in this age group. It was this view that provided the prehistory for the concept of "responsibility for starting the war," which appeared in the immediate postwar period. In this sense, you see, the concept of responsibility for starting the war already existed among first- and second-graders in 1931 and 1932.

Based on this, I think that there already existed in the period between 1931 and 1941 both a position that raised the possibility of defeat and a position that questioned the moral pros and cons of starting the war in the first place. But because the individual episodes of the war in China were isolated as discrete "incidents" that "ended" one after the other, the movements that might have developed from either of these positions sputtered out. So neither of them ever emerged in any clear form.

Of course, given the nature of the Japanese state at that time, any public statement that raised the possibility of defeat or questioned the morality of starting the war was subjected to suppression, as represented in the words, "You don't believe in our certain victory." [It was quite a different thing to have this said of you in that period from what the words themselves may suggest to us today.] This had the power to prevent either of these ways of thinking from developing into something more.

It is also possible to consider this chopping up of Japanese aggression in China into a number of isolated "incidents" to have been a deliberate stratagem devised by the leadership of the time. Naturally, it is possible to consider it in the opposite light. This is related, you see, to the problem of conspiracy under consideration here. Fujimura Michio has argued, for example, that Japan was essentially under military occupation by the army during this period. This theory sparked a controversy that is still raging today. It is certainly true that the military, as one part of the ruling elite, consistently took the position that the war (which was made to appear to the public as nothing more than a series of isolated incidents quickly taken care of) should be continued. It must be kept in mind, however, that this is only true of that one small part of the leadership. I think one's view on whether or not there was a common plan or conspiracy changes according to how one defines the parent body of the conspiracy. And that fact itself demonstrates that the consciousness of the ruling elite (and the military as one part of that elite) of responsibility for the defeat and for starting the war was clearly different from the people's consciousness of responsibility for defeat and for starting the war.

The Occupation: A Starving People's View of the Tokyo Trial

On 8 December 1941 (Japan time), the Japanese government issued a declaration of war, officially beginning the "Greater East Asia War." This war ended on 15 August 1945. On 11 September of the same year, GHQ issued the first orders to arrest suspected war criminals, and the Tokyo trial was in session from 1946 into 1948.

The second problem I want to address today is that of popular perceptions while the trial was going on. Very little remains from that period that approaches a public opinion survey, so one must draw conclusions from reactions to various events surrounding the trial.

In this period, popular views of the war were clouded by new factors other than the earlier perception of the war as chopped-up fragments labeled "incidents." One of these was the existence of the American army of occupation. The Occupation propounded its own "correct" view of the war and backed it up, in a way different from the Japanese military, with GHQ's power to enforce it. Another was hunger. There were areas in which hunger sharpened people's thinking. This mainly took the form of questioning the ruling elite's responsibility for defeat—"who drove us into this state of hunger?" But this questioning was not directed toward responsibility for starting the war, which was the direction that the prosecutors representing the victors at the trial were attempting to focus on. Here lay the disparity between the intentions of the leaders of the victor nations and the perceptions of the masses of the defeated country. That is to say, the main thrust of the people's attack on Japan's wartime leadership was directed not at their responsibility for starting the war but at their responsibility for losing it.

If the Japanese people had conducted war trials at that time with a certain degree of autonomy, I think the leaders' responsibility for the defeat would have been the central issue, not (as in the case of the Tokyo trial) the question of their responsibility for starting an aggressive war. And I think it was natural at that time for people to question their leaders' responsibility for defeat. Given this situation, it is hard to imagine that something similar to the Tokyo trial would have arisen independently from the Japanese masses.

The Overall Picture of the Fifteen-Year War

When the Tokyo trial ended, and it was announced that death sentences had been pronounced on seven leaders, there was no strong reaction from the Japanese masses. Here, I would like to pick out something from a newspaper article that I believe is typical of popular responses to the trial in this period.

> I hope that a trial like this will never be held again in any country of the world. To that end, the equality of races, freedom of commerce, and freedom of migration must be established. I believe that unless these three principles are established, aggressive war will occur again. (Kimura Gorō, physician, forty-eight years old, *Yomiuri Shinbun*, 13 November 1948)

This opinion is well thought out, and I believe it represents the thinking of most people in the period immediately after the trial. It also has much in common with the minority opinion written by Judge Radhabinod Pal of India. In the period after the defeat, the Japanese people were living in conditions that made them part of the Third World, so it is natural that the thinking that came out of these conditions should have been of this nature.

However, there is still another reason the Japanese did not express clear-cut criticism of the conclusion of the Tokyo trial: the fact that they could not yet see the war as a whole. (What passed for newspapers at that time consisted of only one tabloid page. There was no television. And there weren't even that many books.) Moreover, the publication of reports on the atomic bomb damage in Hiroshima and Nagasaki was suppressed on SCAP orders. Neither were the Japanese told that there had been subtle differences of opinion over the necessity of dropping the atomic bombs at this late stage of the war. Had they known these things, the Japanese people would have had a very different overall picture of the Fifteen-Year War. Popular thought is based on *images*, and if the overall picture of the war—the image of the war—had changed, popular judgments of the war would have changed too.

Admiral Leahy, who was chairman of the Joint Chiefs of Staff under Roosevelt, was opposed to dropping the atomic bombs. He was no mere admiral in the navy, no mere fleet admiral, but the chairman of the Joint Chiefs, and he left exact memoranda. In fact, they are cited by the English historian Liddell Hart in his history of World War II—that kind of record.

Popular Images of the War

Knowledge of this negative evaluation of the decision to use the atomic bombs, written by a leading figure in the American military itself, would have changed popular images of the war, and this in turn would have given a different coloration to their evaluation of the results of the war trial. We're talking here about overall images.

SCAP censorship ended when the San Francisco Peace Treaty was signed on 28 April 1952, and soon afterward the *Asahi gurafu* [Asahi Graph] published a special issue on atomic bomb victims in Hiroshima and Nagasaki, making the facts widely known among the Japanese. Thus, it was just after the end of the occupation in 1952 that the Japanese people finally learned the facts concerning the damage inflicted by the two bombs. While the more recently released information concerning the biological warfare units in the Japanese army had a big impact, the facts about the atomic bombings had an even bigger impact. Legally, it can perhaps be said that these facts have nothing to do with the issue of responsibility for starting the war. But that is not the way the history of popular thought is structured. If the trial had been convened after these revelations, a much different response would have emerged from the Japanese masses.

Perceptions of the Trial in 1983

The third issue I want to take up today is that of perceptions of the trial in 1983. By raising this issue, I certainly do not intend to suggest that there is any single viewpoint held by the Japanese people as a whole. There are substantial differences of opinion among the Japanese attending this symposium, as was quite evident in the discussions yesterday. Rather, what I want to do today is single out for discussion those areas in which the popular view of the trial differs from the conclusions reached by the Tokyo trial and, in doing so, to suggest that those areas of disagreement fall into a number of currents.

Since 1948, when the Tokyo trial handed down its judgment, the Japanese people have witnessed the Korean War and the war in Vietnam. This has led them to assume a stance of ironic skepticism toward the confident pronouncement of Japan's guilt handed down by the Allied powers in Tokyo. There is an expression for this: *mayu ni tsuba o tsukete kiku*. Literally translated, it means "listening with spit-moistened eyebrows." What it really means is this: "listening with frank skepticism." In short, the image of the war trials has changed. Images run together, and as they run together they are re-formed.

In addition, the Japanese economy has grown with incredible speed since the Korean War, and the Japanese are no longer hungry. This too gives a different color to the image.

The Defense that "We Don't Want to Fight for a Lost Cause"

A while ago I proposed a distinction between responsibility for defeat and responsibility for starting the war—first, then, responsibility for defeat. Popular perceptions of the responsibility for losing the war have become even hazier today than they were in the immediate aftermath of defeat. But they still exist. They survive in the feeling that "next time I don't want to fight in a losing war." Until 1945, there were many Japanese who believed that there were wars that had to be fought, even if Japan lost. Today, their numbers clearly have become smaller. This is due to basic changes in the structure of the Japanese masses. It is because of these changes that people who were born before 1945 are given such labels as the "wartime generation" [*senchūha*], and ridiculed by younger generations. The belief that one should sacrifice himself or herself for the sake of Japan is now quite old-fashioned.

Moreover, most Japanese believe that our present prosperity has come about thanks to help from the United States; so even now they think that the Tokyo trial, though it may have been unfair, was a *quid pro quo* for bread and butter. However, this is not to say that they accept the judgment of the Tokyo trial. Indeed, quite the opposite. To take only the issue of the fairness of the trial, that Japanese do not believe the Tokyo trial was fair is amply demonstrated by the nationwide popularity of Shiroyama Saburō's documentary novel *Rakujitsu moyu* [English trans. 1977: War Criminal: The Life and Death of Hirota Kōki], both as a best-selling novel and as a popular television drama. Most Japanese think of the Tokyo trial as a display of power—indeed, a flaunting of power—by the victor nations for the benefit of a defeated one. It does not remain in the hearts and minds of average Japanese as the sort of moral influence that the foreign prosecutors intended it to be. This is absolutely clear. I think it *should* remain as a kind of moral influence, but that I think so personally is irrelevant.

What the war trial did leave in the minds of the Japanese people was the desire not to take part in a losing war. This is the philosophy that might makes right. And it was confirmed. Well, would a winning war be all right, then? Feelings are divided on this question. Some say there is no alternative but to take part if it's a winnable war, or if it's a war for survival. Others say they want no part in any war whatsoever.

The Judgment of "Civilization"?

Next, with regard to responsibility for starting the war. In the immediate postwar period, when Japanese said "the war" they meant the war that lasted from 1931 to 1945. If the person who used the term was young, this was obvious, and people understood what was meant. Today, people have come to think of that war as just one of many wars that have been fought in the world. This is a tremendously important change in popular thought. In this context, the hope shared by both the American prosecutors and the Japanese who read the newspaper articles about the trial has, unfortunately, faded. At that time, both sides hoped to make the war fought from 1931 to 1945 the last war, not only for the Japanese but for all of humanity. But then came Korea, and then Vietnam. Later, in the postwar educational system that had been a "gift" of the Occupation, the Japanese learned not only about the postwar misdeeds of the former Allied powers, but also about wars that had been started in the past by the United States, England, the Netherlands, and other Western countries. And while the Japanese share the hope that human society can be remade from scratch so that war will end, the doubt now clearly exists whether prewar civilization was so morally superior, as the chief prosecutor for the United States claimed in his opening address, that it had the right to sit in judgment on the war.

Was "civilization" as claimed by Mr. Keenan really so splendid? Even before the war, the civilization that the Allied prosecutors held up for adulation at the trial had committed innumerable acts of aggression. And at the end of that war, the United States had dropped two atomic bombs on Japan, acts that a number of military historians—including Liddell Hart and even Admiral Leahy, the chairman of the Joint Chiefs at the time—consider to have been militarily unnecessary. Subsequently, the United States fought an undeclared war in Vietnam, similar in a great many respects to Japan's war of aggression in China. All these facts contributed to the popular belief now current that "civilization" was unqualified to take a high and mighty moral stance toward a defeated Japan.

From a different angle this way of thinking was reinforced by the fact that the United States rescinded the purges of important wartime leaders who had been directly involved in the prosecution of the war. These orders were issued immediately after the executions of the seven men condemned by the Tokyo tribunal, and the United States later supported the return of these figures to positions of power in Japanese politics. Indirectly, this way of thinking was also reinforced by a feeling of confidence among the Japanese when Japanese industry became able to compete with the United States in the manufacture of automobiles—that most typical of American industries. These were different factors but both of them played an extremely important role. In short, the Japanese masses today do not feel the same sense of inferiority toward the United States and Europe, or the same sense of shame for Japan's responsibility in starting World War II that they felt in the immediate postwar period.

Perceptions of the Trials of Class B and C War Criminals

I would like to expand the discussion beyond the Tokyo trial itself to include the other war trials conducted in the immediate postwar period. As I said earlier, people think in terms of images, and images expand. In the popular thought of Japanese today, the Tokyo trial is not a special case. It is tied up, as if in a single unbroken chain, with all of the trials of so-called Class B and Class C war criminals that were conducted by various countries throughout the world. Legally, these trials may be different from Class A war crimes trials, but popular thought does not see the breaks in the chain. It sees all of the postwar trials as forming a single pattern. That's why, as a matter of course, if the image of the other trials changes, so does the evaluation of the Tokyo trial.

The Tokyo trial ended with the execution of seven wartime leaders. But trials of alleged Japanese war criminals were conducted on a much wider scale. Accounts of these trials have been published one after the other, and gradually the story of the postwar trials has spread. The number of such publications written in the last thirty-eight years is extraordinary, and they are not read solely by academics. They are read by average Japanese and then passed on by word of mouth. I think that this has created a certain "fact" in popular opinion. It has created a modern myth, one that has spread in a way much different from that of the ancient myths of the *Kojiki* [Japan's first written history].

When you spoke of war trials in the period from 1946 to 1948, you were speaking of the Tokyo war crimes trial, the trial of important and visible wartime leaders such as Tōjō Hideki. But today, nearly forty years after the end of the war, the Tokyo trial remains in people's minds as one of the many war crimes trials that were conducted in various places in the immediate postwar period. Thus, for example, *Seiki no isho* [Testaments of the Century], an exhaustive collection of writings compiled by the families of people executed as war criminals, includes writings of people who were executed as war criminals, regardless of the distinction between those convicted of Class A war crimes and those accused of Class B and C war crimes. There are Koreans and Taiwanese among them.

The view that all these people can be grouped together as war criminals does have a weak point, however: it blurs the distinction between those who had power and those who did not. It does not provide the politically expedient possibility of prosecuting wartime power elites for failures in leadership, both in terms of responsibility for defeat and in terms of responsibility for starting the war. However, the publication of this collection performed a function quite different from the political effect I just mentioned; it recorded the testimony of people who had been designated as war criminals by the various victorious powers. Indeed, this testimony is one of the subjects that I want to discuss today. It would be untrue to say that this publication is completely apolitical.

Were the People Executed Simply Unlucky?

Okamoto Aihiko's production of Hashimoto Shinobu's *Watakushi wa kai ni naritai* [I Want to Become a Shellfish], broadcast on television in 1958, aroused great sympathy for those who had been executed after the war as Class B and Class C war criminals (those not at the highest levels of the government). Nonfiction books based on research into these cases were widely read. Among them are Kamisaka Fuyuko's *Sugamo purizun 13-go tetsutobira* [The Iron Door to Cell #13, Sugamo Prison] and her *Nokosareta tsuma—Yokohama saiban BC-kyū senpan hiroku* [Wives Left Behind—The Secret Records of the Yokohama Trials of Class B and C War Criminals] and Utsumi Aiko's *Chosenjin BC-kyū senpan kiroku* [Records of Korean Class B and C War Criminals]. This last book records the cases of Koreans—Korea was then a Japanese colony—who were forced to become prison guards in Japanese POW camps and were then punished by the victor nations as war criminals. Also published were a great number of records concerning people who were sentenced to death and executed by tribunals conducted without a show of evidence. In many cases it seems that these people were wrongly accused.

Ishiwara Yoshirō, Uchimura Gōsuke, and others have published moving accounts of their experiences in the Soviet Union, where they were tried for war crimes and sentenced to long terms of hard labor in Siberia. There are also books by Japanese who were tried for war crimes in China. The record of Japanese atrocities in China covers a long time and a lot of territory, and it is hard to make excuses. Some of those imprisoned for war crimes have recanted their confessions after returning to Japan; but many of those who have written about their experiences in China acknowledge their guilt. In general, however, it would be difficult to say that the trials, particularly those of Class B and Class C war criminals, were conducted with fairness. Very few of those who were punished feel that their punishments were just, and Japanese popular opinion agrees with this assessment.

Thus, more than a reaction against the Tokyo trial itself, the basis for criticizing the postwar trials arises from viewing that trial within the context of the popular perception of all these trials together, a perception that makes no distinction between the International Military Tribunal for the Far East and all the other postwar trials. The Tokyo trial and the other trials are seen to be connected in an unbroken chain. In a word, there is a widespread feeling that the people executed as war criminals in the postwar trials were simply unlucky. This is not quite the same thing as a looking at the Tokyo trial alone and concluding that Tōjō Hideki was unlucky. Rather, seen in the context of the thousand or more [920?] who were executed after trials that are perceived to have been unfair, Tōjō Hideki also begins, somehow, to appear unlucky. From the viewpoint of the prosecutors and judges in these trials, this way of thinking would no doubt seem quite preposterous. But it is something that cannot be wrapped up in the neat packages presented by these trials, and it is by no means exceptional.

A Moral Deficiency

Why did this happen? Why this cynicism in popular perceptions of the war trials? I finally understood the answer to this question as I was listening to the discussions yesterday. It happened because the war trials, including the Tokyo trial, defined war criminals as a group of people that did not include the accusers themselves.

Yesterday, two of the discussants used the model that I am about to propose today. One of them was Professor Ōnuma. The other was Mr. Matsudaira. That's surprising, isn't it? Two people in opposing ideological camps making use of the same model. The model itself is from C. L. Stevenson's *Ethics and Language*. I will read it once slowly, and I think we will get a good idea of the framework of the war trials after World War II.

A: It is wrong to steal.
B: You stole too, didn't you?

This is the whole dialog. It is a simple model. A is taken aback by B's retort. Rhetorically, his argument is weakened. That is, his imperious accusatory attitude is weakened. However, logically and ethically, that is completely irrelevant. That is what I want you to see. In terms of logic, B has in no way refuted A's initial statement. Logically, there is no reason at all for A to back down. A can reply to B's retort by saying this: "Yes, I stole. Still, it is wrong to steal."

A can respond in this way, and when he does his statement possesses a higher morality than his original accusation. Any other ethical position is phony. There is no morality in shouting out that people who have stolen are bad. And to see morality in such a pronouncement is nothing more than a reflection of our cheap, worldly philosophy—that is, it is extremely low on the ethical scale. [Laughter.]

The war trials—Keenan's indictment of the Japanese leaders at the Tokyo trial, for instance—did not possess this kind of high morality. In the courtroom and before the Japanese people, the victor nations proudly held up the standard of Western civilization, a civilization that was supposedly perfect, and found the Japanese guilty. Morally speaking, I think there is something lacking here.

A Courtesan Is in the Dark without a Lover

The Tokyo trial had something of the aspect of a sideshow. And there was something in the dramatic poses struck by the actors in this show that was lacking ethically. On television recently, I watched a performance of a representative Kabuki play, *A Courtesan Is in the Dark without a Lover*. It's really a fine play— deeply ethical. Watching it on television, I was greatly moved. [Laughter.] It has a very deep ethics and a strong human appeal, because it depicts the life of a character many Japanese identify with strongly.

However, the Allies' condemnation of Japan in the name of civilization never had such high morality as displayed in Tamasaburō's performance. I say this with all the conviction of my own ethics and my entire existence.

By contrast, however, the Japanese people at the time did not make any clear protest against the Tokyo trial. Rather, an attitude that the war trials cannot be accepted at face value has gradually made its appearance in the forty years since then—via the publication and popularity of accounts that call into question the postwar trials.

Before explaining this attitude, I must comment briefly on some smaller currents of opinion—by no means the mainstream—that are nevertheless significant in postwar Japan. One of these is a current that would see the war crimes trials from the viewpoint of the victims of Japan's aggression—Korea, Taiwan, China, the Philippines, Burma, Singapore, Malaysia, and the other Asian countries. This current is by no means strong. I would very much like to strengthen it, but I fear that it is a hopeless dream. Certainly it does not command a significant following yet among the Japanese public.

Another way of thinking accepts the Japanese convicted as war criminals as simply being unlucky, and looks upon what is happening around them with a feeling that they themselves could also be unlucky. Intellectuals will think that this view of war criminals as simply unlucky is hardly worth considering. I disagree. The perception that people executed as war criminals were unlucky means that some Japanese are looking at their own lives, and at the things that are happening around them, with a feeling that they could be unlucky too. This view lacks the power to lead people to pursue the responsibility of their leaders for war based on a clear distinction between those in power and the masses, who have no real power of their own. In this sense, it is politically defective. But it is also free from the excesses and the vulnerability to mistakes inherent in a pursuit of responsibility of that kind. I think that this is enormously important. And I also think that this kind of popular sentiment possesses a high morality, far superior to that of the usual movements led by intellectuals.

One Force in the Quest for Peace

The judgment of the Tokyo trial held up the "universal principle of humanity" in its condemnation of Japanese war criminals. If proclaiming such universal principles does not encompass everyone—including the criminals—in a call for their future realization, it tends to become a pronouncement from a position having both power and authority, like that of a philosopher-king. In contrast, individuals wrongly accused by the philosopher-king—or even rightly accused— slowly begin to give testimony, in stumbling, murmuring voices, concerning their own actions. This testimony is not intended as an attempt to replace the power and authority of the philosopher-king by brandishing different universal principles. But when one tries to make out the overtones of the various voices raised in this sporadic murmuring, pleading special circumstances based on self-interest, the modest doubts they express amount to this: "Are you god?" Or in the case of the philosopher-king who does not believe in gods: "Are you the law of world history?" If, in this way, the individual testimonies, the voices of Japanese punished by the various war crimes trials, are given a careful reading, they can become a force in our present quest for world peace.

The "Testimony" of Yoshida Mitsuru

I would like to conclude my paper by examining ideas for independent trials to be conducted by the Japanese, ideas that are almost meaningless in a strictly legal sense.

Yoshida Mitsuru survived the sinking of the battleship *Yamato*. Later he served as a director of the Bank of Japan, entering, as it were, one of the gun turrets of the battleship of Japan's business world, that is, of today's economic superpower Japan. It was after rising to the position of director that he suggested that every person now over fifty had an obligation to set down a "testimony" explaining how it was he had been dragged into the war. Everyone—cabinet minister, military officer, student—had this duty. What was important was the accumulation of such testimonies. Everyone was at fault. Each person had responsibility proportional to his status. He said this a year before his death. I thought at the time, the Establishment can't be all bad.

He didn't need to say what he said, but he did say it, in *Shokun!* [a popular magazine published by Bungei Shunju]. Indeed, he came there precisely to say it. I was really impressed. He had such tenacity of purpose.

Evaluating the Trial in a Spirit That Transcends It

Ishiwara Yoshirō was sentenced by a war crimes tribunal in Siberia, and he speaks of the trial he received: "I will not accuse; I will only testify." This happens to have the same logical structure that I just talked about.

The act of testifying is quite different from making an accusation under the banner of some great universal principle, and people wonder whether it is the correct path to universality. But I believe that it does not close off the path to universality. In fact, I think it has something special.

Take Chief Judge Webb's comment to former prime minister Yonai Mitsumasa: "The Prime Minister is the most stupid witness I have ever listened to." Yonai's mumbling, his claim to have forgotten things he had seen or heard, no doubt made him look stupid. But I think Yonai's behavior at the tribunal was something quite different from the European way of doing things. And so long as we Westernized Japanese intellectuals see it as something deviating from the path to universality—as something retrograde—it creates a gulf between Japanese intellectuals and the masses.

The war trials did play a role, I think—though in an extremely distorted manner—in creating a repository for the accumulation of this kind of testimony. In a sense, the kind of movement envisioned by Yoshida Mitsuru has occurred on a mass scale; I don't think it would have occurred without the war trials. This is an irony of history—or perhaps I should call it the cunning of history. The war trials, the Tokyo trial among them, have appeared in popular thought as a strange historical trick.

These testimonies are a call for independent trials by the Japanese people themselves, of a different nature from the war trials carried out by the victor nations of World War II. Perhaps they should be called anti-trials.

As Dr. Röling suggested earlier, the goal of both the Tokyo trial and the Nuremberg trial was the creation of legal norms to stop war. I completely agree with him that we must not lose sight of that goal. These norms are revolutionary in the history of mankind. And precisely because they are revolutionary, there were a great number of unfortunate, wronged victims, just as there were in the French Revolution. I am attempting to shed light on this darker side—on the shadows of the war trials. This does not mean that I reject the goal of the trials. But if a trial does not leave something in the hearts and minds of people that transcends the trial itself, it loses its humanity. [Applause.]

CHAIR: Thank you for a most stimulating talk.

[Recess]

CHAIR: I will now reconvene this morning's session. First, we will have Mr. Kinoshita's presentation, and then I will open the floor to questions.

WHAT THE TOKYO TRIAL
MADE ME THINK ABOUT
Kinoshita Junji

Mr. Tsurumi's presentation was very impressive. The interpreters must have had a terrible time with the title of a certain Kabuki play. [Laughter.] I'll try to make their work easier by sticking to the text you have before you.

Personal Reflections on the Tribunal

How have the average Japanese perceived the Tokyo trial? The introduction to the program of this symposium suggests that there are two opposing stances. One of these stands on the side of the prosecution and the majority opinion judgment, accepting the conclusions of the tribunal without question. This stance, for example, attributes total responsibility for the war to militarist cliques in the army and the zaibatsu. The other stance, represented by the argument that the tribunal was victors' justice, stands on the side of the defense and totally rejects the tribunal. I agree that these two mutually contradictory viewpoints have existed, and I also approve of the statement in the program introduction that "the confrontation between these two positions is barren and unproductive." Given the truth of these statements, however, could there have been a "Japanese position" that stood between these two extreme positions, or indeed even one virtually unrelated to them? Indeed, can there be such a position today?

Other papers presented in this symposium consider this problem from a broad perspective. Mr. Tsurumi has given us an excellent analysis of the concrete facts of public opinion, both in the immediate postwar period and in the present. In this paper, however, I want to state some personal feelings based on my own experience. Because they are personal, these feelings may seem out of place in a symposium devoted specifically to a reexamination of the Tokyo trial, and I may appear to be barking up the wrong tree at times. However, I firmly believe that if all of you here today will take it upon yourself to judge to what extent these personal feelings can have universal meaning—even if you conclude that they can have none at all—that process will, in itself, pose universal problems that transcend my own feelings.

Why Did I Fail to Pursue War Responsibility?

What I have in mind to begin with is something like the following.

One of the great differences between Japan and Germany, both of which were subjected to international military tribunals, is the fact that the German people themselves pursued responsibility for the war outside the context of the international tribunal and are still doing so today. In Japan, on the other hand, there have been almost no prosecutions of Japanese for war responsibility by the Japanese themselves. As other speakers have pointed out, this does not mean that there was no movement at all to hold war crimes trials conducted by Japanese. But the movement for Japanese trials was merely an idea concocted by the leadership to deal with the matter by the Japanese government rather than leaving it to the Allies, and of course it never materialized. It can easily be imagined that even if these trials had materialized, they would have been little more than farces of political opportunism. On this point I learned much from Professor Awaya's presentation yesterday. But what I am talking about here is a movement for trials from below, trials from within, trials carried out by the Japanese masses.

This does not mean that sporadic attempts to pursue war guilt have not taken place in politics, academia, the arts, and other fields. But these attempts, taken individually, were extremely weak, in a sense that I wish to consider below. And what is even more important, they never coalesced into a single movement strong enough to effect changes in postwar Japan. True, the circumstances in Japan were different from those in Germany, where there were clear criteria, such as membership in the Nazi Party, by which the commitment of individuals to state policies could be judged. But Germany is not the issue now. Nor is any general theory based on Japanese character or Japanese sentiment. My question today is this: Why did I fail to pursue the responsibility of the Japanese for the war, and what are the implications of this failure?

"If Only"

Just once, in 1946, when the Tokyo trial opened, I had a chance to attend the proceedings. A young playwright, I had just published my first play and had gotten a job as a lecturer at one of the private universities. In short, it was the year I had finally managed to achieve a degree of status in life, one that entitled me to speak out. But having achieved that status, I did not pursue the war guilt of the Japanese. Why?

Looking back on myself in that year, I can plead a number of extenuating circumstances. For one thing, I did not yet have the ability to identify the problem. Mr. Tsurumi spoke a while ago of hunger, and it is certainly true that hunger, and the social turmoil right before my eyes, forced my entire attention to the problem of how I was going to make it through each day. There are many other reasons I could give. But what I am left with is the fact that I failed to pursue the problem.

What is important for me today, after the passage of more than thirty years, is not simply to recall myself as I was then. Rather, it is what "myself as I was then" makes me think about today. I have two feelings about this.

I can explain the first in this way. Looking back on my own past, there are many things I regret not having done differently. There are some things I recall not just with regret, but with feelings of bitter remorse—things about which I feel that *if only* I had done things differently . . . And yet I didn't do things differently, and that is the real source of my remorse. If there are "degrees of remorse," I feel the greatest remorse for my failure to pursue the responsibility of war collaborators, and especially that I failed to do so in the period immediately after the war, when it could have had real effect. *If only* a large number of people had joined hands at that time, we might have prevented a suspected Class A war criminal from becoming prime minister of Japan less than ten years after the judgment of the Tokyo tribunal. We might have been able to put the issue of a Japanese republic on the political agenda. Even if it were impossible to accomplish any of this under the American Occupation, wouldn't it have been possible at least to raise these as social issues?

I have used the words *if only* a number of times. Of course, common sense tells us that speculations—the "if only's"—are meaningless in history. And since my own past is history, you may think that it is equally meaningless for me to speculate about the "if only's" in my personal history. But I believe these "if only's" do have meaning, and I think I can explain why in the following way.

"If Only" and the Immediate Past

Postwar Japan has seen the rise of an interesting phenomenon, what Japanese call "the history boom" or "the historical literature boom." Whether ordinary Japanese people find history entertaining as a tale of days gone by, unrelated to the modern realities they are living through, or whether they view it as illustrations of precepts that will enable them to understand the modern world, in either case it is taken for granted—indeed it is a basic premise of which they are not even aware—that "if only's" are meaningless in history. It follows naturally that it is meaningless to wonder, for instance, what would have happened *if only* Oda Nobunaga had not died in 1582. However, unlike the events of the distant past, I believe it is both possible and necessary—that is, meaningful—to consider the "if only's" in one's own personal history. Why should this be? Because the act of looking back at one's own past with a sense of remorse that things might have been different *if only* I had done this instead of that has the power to make us examine and reflect upon our present position and to propel us along our future course.

Therefore, I want to make a distinction between the distant past, in which "if only's" concerning the death of Nobunaga in 1582 really don't have much significance, and the past that is directly linked to our own lives. I would like to call this past the immediate past. I believe that inserting "if only's" into this immediate past—that is, looking back at the past with bitter sorrow—is enormously meaningful.

"The Original Sins of Japanese Modernization"

I think it is also possible, indeed necessary, to extend this "immediate past" a little beyond the limits of one's personal history. What I mean by this is that we Japanese can trace our immediate past back to 1868, the starting point of Japanese modernization. Again, I feel that this is not only possible, but necessary.

At the root of this idea, what made it conceivable for me, were some words used more than twenty years ago by the poet and critic Fujishima Unaki, who is here today. The words are: "The original sins of Japanese modernization."

Mr. Fujishima, I recall, identified the three original sins of Japanese modernization as the plunder of Okinawa, the colonization of Korea, and the aggression in China. By "original sins" he meant that we modern Japanese must continue to carry the burden of those "original sins." This is to say that the modern history of Japan since 1868 is our "immediate past." The distinquished Hungarian literary theorist György Lukács, in his *Geschichtsphilosophischer Versuch* [Theory of the Novel], has written that genuine historical literature "resurrects the past as the prehistory of the present." His "prehistory of the present" is nothing other than my "immediate past."

There are still other "original sins" in Japan's modern history besides the three identified by Mr. Fujishima. Japanese aggression against China was the origin of the Fifteen-Year War, which was the object of judgment at the Tokyo trial. But what made that aggression possible, the very source from which it sprang, was the contempt with which the Japanese Empire, and the people of that empire, viewed other Asian peoples. This, I think, was the greatest original sin of all. Even after Japan was defeated and forced to relinquish its colonial empire, this contempt remained deeply rooted. How deeply rooted can be appreciated, I think, if one considers that even today an extremely large number of Japanese fail completely to grasp the meaning of the loss of Japan's former colonies. Despite what may appear on the surface, they have inherited this ideology of contempt for other Asian peoples without the slightest fundamental change.

In this way, the problem of pursuing the responsibility for the war, raised by the Tokyo trial, has made me think about the various related problems I have outlined, perhaps in a different dimension from the one in which they were dealt with at the trial.

Our Stance toward War Guilt

Earlier I said that my failure to pursue the responsibility of Japanese for the war is the greatest regret of my life. The second feeling concerns the stance I took when I finally began to pursue responsibility for the war. My thinking used to go like this: I had earned a position from which I could speak out on social issues only immediately after the end of the war, and I had not collaborated with the war either before or during the war. In short, I had entered society in the immediate postwar period with my hands clean. For that very reason, I should take the lead in pursuing the war guilt of others!

It seems strange to me now that so much time passed before I realized that this way of thinking was wrong. The change came about only after I had seen a great many things as several years passed following the defeat. A considerable number of Japanese, reflecting on their own acts of collaboration during the war, tried to denounce themselves. Leaving aside a small number of truly splendid cases I know of personally—and there may have been a suprising number that never came to light—these self-accusations were often quite laughable. There were cases of people in what we Japanese call the "sincere faction," people who respond with complete sincerity but also total naivete to the currents of the times, who carried out self-criticism uncritically, based on the new postwar ethos, and became completely different people from what they had been during the war. There were others, to put it somewhat cynically, who seemed to be falling all over themselves to do some good in an attempt to forget what they had done during the war, precisely because what they had done was so clearly wrong. The most grotesque were the reactionary figures who calmly remained in their former positions in politics, perhaps truly thinking that this was a kind of atonement. In these cases, the pursuit of ultimate responsibility for the war became even more ambiguous. And meanwhile, many people who bore clear responsibility for the war returned to Japanese society and steadily regained their former positions in society, some of them complacently, others obsequiously.

The Sting of Guilt

As I watched all this happening in the immediate postwar years, I began to be troubled by a nagging doubt: What if I had had the right to speak out publicly during the war? What would I have done? What if I'd *had* to speak out: Could I really say that I would not have collaborated with the war effort?

As I said earlier, it was true that I entered society after the war with my hands clean. But wasn't this in fact nothing more than a result of not yet having a voice in matters during the war? There is absolutely no guarantee that I would not have supported the war if my age and social position had forced me to do so.

The West German playwright Martin Walser has written a play called *Der Schwarze Schwann* [The Black Swan], which takes as its theme the persecution of the Jews. Walser, who is more than ten years younger than I am, has said that it was purely an accident that he did not become one of the perpetrators of Auschwitz. I cannot help having precisely the same feeling toward myself. Iwabuchi Tatsuji, the noted specialist in German theater who introduced these words of Walser's to Japan, has written the following about the German writers who are pursuing the responsibility of other Germans for the war:

> They are not simply denouncing the people who were committed to the Nazis. They are also addressing those people who would remove from the records and consign to oblivion an inexpedient past, and they are saying simply that they want them to dig up that painful past instead of repressing it, just as they themselves are doing. ("'Mikeisan no kako' no Shomondai" ["Various Problems of 'The Past as an Unsettled Account'"], *Teatoro* [Theater], January 1975)

In other words, those who would pursue reponsibility for a war, who would criticize or accuse others, are unqualified to do so unless they are painfully aware that they too, as human beings, contain within themselves the potential for acts that would expose them to criticism and accusation. Perhaps, therefore, it is precisely criticism and accusation of this kind, based on a hard self-awareness, that can have meaning and, having meaning, be effective. In short, I believe that only those who are capable of feeling the pain of guilt that stings themselves can sting others.

A Contradiction: The Essence of Things Is Finally Grasped
Only When It is Impossible to Do Anything about Them

As I have said repeatedly, what I regret most bitterly in my own immediate past is the fact that I did not pursue the guilt of war collaborators in the period immediately after defeat, when doing so could have had a real effect. But thinking about it now, even assuming that I had been able to pursue the question of war guilt in that period, undistracted by the hunger and disorder of the period, the manner in which I did so might well have amounted to little more than a self-righteous denunciation of others. Indeed, I am quite sure that the most I could have done in that naive period of my life would have been to accuse others because I thought my own hands were clean. By the time I began to understand the shape of the kind of criticism and accusation that could have meaning, and therefore be effective, the period in which criticism and accusation could have a real impact was somehow over. Why did this happen? Because it was only by observing the conditions of Japanese society in that same period, and by watching that period pass, that I finally arrived at a proper understanding of the situation. And I suspect that it was the same for many Japanese of my generation. However, I don't think we can discuss this situation with such flippant phrases as "the irony of history."

This contradiction in history—that it is often precisely at the point in time when it has become virtually impossible to do anything that we are finally able to grasp the fundamental and ideological basis for doing it in the first place—is an important key, I think, in considering the problem of historical progress. In the present context, however, it would be a digression to go into this problem further.

Thinking Directed at the Past and the Future

The themes of the Tokyo trial are numerous and varied. I have considered only one of them, though I think it is the core issue; namely, the problem of responsibility for the war. I have stated feelings about this issue that are completely personal, and in place of a conclusion I would like to explain briefly the reasons why I cling so tenaciously to this single issue.

Actually, more than stating reasons, what I will do is present two propositions. One is that of thought directed toward the past. The other, as you might expect, is thought directed to the future.

First, consider thought directed toward the past. Ibuchi Tatsuji, who I have already quoted, introduced in Japanese the German phrase "unbewältigte Vergangenheit," which he translated as "the past upon which accounts have yet to be settled." The past as an unsettled account. This reminded me that the East German playwright Bertolt Brecht, who died in 1956, had also used this expression. I don't remember where it was, so I will try to express what he said in my own words: Man hurries too much toward the future, leaving too much of the past behind as an unsettled account.

This is not the distant past, but the past that is directly linked to us, in which there are things that are inconvenient for us to acknowledge, that we desperately want to say never happened. What Brecht wanted to say is that we have to bring these things out—that we have to bring them out and settle accounts before we proceed further, or, conversely, that we cannot proceed further without settling accounts. I don't think I have to say that this is a positive philosophy, and one that has nothing to do with such things as mere confession and penitence.

Finally, the question of thought directed toward the future. There is an international convention that was adopted in the twenty-third session of the UN General Assembly and that came into effect in 1970. It has yet to be ratified by Japan. Its title is the Convention on Non-Applicability of Statutory Limitations to War Crimes and Crimes Against Humanity. This title suggests that the evidence is so convincing that these crimes will never be effaced. Certainly there are crimes that one may forget. But people seem to forget all too quickly even those crimes that must never be forgotten. Especially we Japanese.

When we think about the Tokyo trial from the standpoint of our common quest for peace, I think these two propositions are basic. It is certainly true that the complete realization of either is impossible. But isn't it true that the period we call "modern" is a period that forces us to accomplish the impossible? Thank you. [Applause.]

QUESTION-AND-ANSWER PERIOD

CHAIR: Thank you, Mr. Kinoshita, for a most moving presentation. Any attempt by me to summarize this paper would only lessen its impact, so I will not do so. I will now open the floor to discussion. As I promised earlier, I will first recognize questions or comments from the younger members of the audience. In fact, I received written questions from three members of the audience during the recess. I will begin with the youngest person's question, which is directed to Dr. Röling. It reads as follows: "I was deeply impressed with Dr. Röling's paper. Judge Pal also wrote a minority opinion. I had occasion recently to read his opinion, and given the situation at the time, I was impressed with the dispassionate objectivity that informed his quest for peace. I would like to ask Dr. Röling for his views on its current significance."

DR. RÖLING: Justice Pal's attitude, from the very beginning, was that the war fought by Japan was a war for the liberation of Asia and that therefore it should not be regarded as an aggressive war. It was a more or less belated reaction against the [Western] aggressive wars by which the [Western] colonial system was established centuries ago. That was his opinion in respect to crimes against peace. In regard to conventional war crimes, Pal's opinion was that every party in every war will commit war crimes, and that it was unfair in principle to punish only the war crimes committed by defeated nations. His attitude can easily be understood, and I have respect for the opinions of my friend Pal.

But I regretted very much that his attitude prevented him from seeing the Tokyo trial as an expression of the belief that redressing the injustices of the world by war is now a thing of the past. In former times, such wars were fought, and they were tolerated. But that time is over, for our history of wars has left behind weapons of destruction that no longer permit war for any cause.

Therefore, I think Pal's judgment is understandable if we look at the past, but not when we look at the future. It takes away from the Tokyo trial the important aspect that the judgment contributes to the opinion, which is an essential condition for survival, that wars are no longer possible, and that we should learn other ways of conducting international relations and maintaining peace.

CHAIR: I think Dr. Röling's answer is quite clear in the simultaneous translation. To summarize briefly, however, he believes that the essential points of Judge Pal's position were that Japan's war was fought for the liberation of Asia, and that all parties to war commit conventional war crimes, not only the defeated countries. Dr. Röling feels that this position is worthy of respect. However, he thinks it is unfortunate that Pal's position led him to believe that it was still permissible to redress injustice by waging war in a period when war for any reason is no longer permissible.

The Reasons for Prime Minister Hirota's Death Sentence

I will now move to the next question, which is also directed to Dr. Röling. "Based on all the evidence, former Prime Minister Hirota was an advocate of peace, and I cannot agree with the imposition of death sentences on civilian officials. Moreover, the tribunal did not take into account the Hakone conference just before the end of the war, in which Hirota sought the Soviet ambassador's cooperation in bringing the war to an end. What were the real reasons that he was given the death penalty?"

DR. RÖLING: I agree with the man who raised this question. In my dissenting opinion, I tried to explain why I considered Hirota not guilty. I find it one of the great errors of the Tokyo judgment that a man like Hirota was condemned, and even condemned to death. It is to my utter regret that I was not able to persuade my brethren at the time that Hirota should have been acquitted.

CHAIR: I am now prepared to recognize questions from the floor. Yes, Mr. Tanaka.

MR. TANAKA MASAAKI (Japanese translator of Judge Pal's dissenting opinion): I have questions for Dr. Röling and Mr. Furness. I understand that Dr. Röling has paid a visit to the Kōa Kannon on Mount Izu in Atami. As you know, the Kōa Kannon is dedicated to the seven executed war criminals and the war victims of both Japan and China. Following Judge Pal, he is the second of the judges to do so, and I want to offer him my sincere thanks and deepest respect.

My first question has to do with the accusation contained in Justice Bernard's minority opinion that a clique was formed by seven of the judges, the so-called "majority judgment faction," and that this clique essentially controlled all of the proceedings of the trial. The other four judges—Dr. Röling,

Judge Pal, Judge Bernard, and even Chief Judge Webb—were, let us say, discriminated against. When we look at this situation at the stage of the judgment itself, we are left with the impression that the entire trial was nothing but a farce. I would like to ask Dr. Röling and Mr. Furness about these points. That is my first question . . .

CHAIR: I would like to limit everyone to one question. There are many other people waiting their turn.

MR. TANAKA: But this is even more important.

CHAIR: I am sorry, but I cannot recognize another question.

MR. TANAKA: Well, then, it can't be helped. Very well, I would like an answer to my first question then.

CHAIR: Dr. Röling, would you like to respond first?

The Majority and Minority Opinions

DR. RÖLING: In the dissenting opinion of Judge Bernard, he protests the way in which the majority judgment was honored. And I think he is to be believed. I personally was not in favor of disclosing the way in which the majority judgment was prepared, but there it is. It was one of the unfair happenings in the Tokyo trial. The majority drew up the judgment. Every chapter was communicated to the other judges for their comment. I remember having put my criticism in writing. Sometimes it was taken into account, and sometimes not. It was a procedure that was not correct. Thus, I agree with the man who posed the question, and I am strongly convinced that when eleven judges must deliver judgment, they must communicate with all the eleven in the decision-making process that leads to the judgment. So, I agree with what Bernard writes, and it is very regrettable that things happened in that way. And therefore I think one shouldn't take the judgment at face value. One should consider it very critically, and take into account the dissenting opinions that belong to the overall result of the trial.

CHAIR: Thank you. Dr. Röling agrees with Judge Bernard's allegations, and feels that it is very regrettable that these things occurred. And, in this sense, he thinks it is important that the judgment be read as a whole, including the dissenting opinions.

This question concerns disagreements among the judges, but since it was also directed to Mr. Furness, I wonder if he would like to comment briefly.

MR. FURNESS: Yes. I think this is one of the examples of the bad conduct of the trial. I understood that even the president of the tribunal, Sir William Webb, was more or less excluded from the discussions. He did not file what could be called exactly a dissenting opinion, but he did file an opinion in which he said that he did not agree with the findings of the tribunal.

Of course, I had nothing to do with rendering an opinion. But since I was there, I must say that I agree completely and am most pleased with the opinion of Judge Röling. I thought the court was very strange. Some of the judgments, I understood, were rendered on the concurrence of only six of the judges. It could be otherwise. I don't know anything about it, but I heard that the rumors might be true. Questions concerning that should be referred to Judge Röling, and he should have the right to say that he doesn't want to comment.

CHAIR: As Mr. Furness has suggested, I believe Dr. Röling has a very strict view of professional ethics, and that may prevent him from responding. Dr. Röling, would you like to comment further?

DR. RÖLING: Well, I think from several facts that are known one can figure out that some death penalties were delivered by a bare majority. It is a bit difficult to talk about what happened in chambers, but I remember quite well the astonishing effect of one particular event. It was when the voting had taken place about the sentences, and the possibility arose of judges protesting the fact that a bare majority was leading to a death sentence. Any protest was prevented, however, by the closing of the session in chambers by the president.

MR. FURNESS: I know about Mr. Shigemitsu, of course. I thought he should have been acquitted. But he came to me and said, "I don't like the sentence against me, but I have to bear it, and of course it's very mild when compared with the others. What I am indignant about is the sentencing to death of Hirota, which is absolutely undeserved. So don't waste your time trying to do anything for me, but do what you can for Mr. Hirota." I firmly believe that the death sentence on Hirota was unjust.

CHAIR: Thank you. I would like to leave this question, and turn to other issues. A number of other people in the audience seem to have questions.

QUESTION: I have a question for Dr. Röling. The number of judges and prosecutors from countries that had suffered during the war was extremely small. Why weren't judges and prosecutors called from such countries as Indonesia, Malaya, Burma, and Korea? I assume that there were various political reasons, but I wonder if you could tell us more on this point.

A Trial by Judges Only from the Victor Nations

DR. RÖLING: We as judges had no power to determine which countries would participate in the trial. It was a political decision, and only the independent nations, the sovereign nations, that had been at war with Japan were chosen to have representatives on the bench. That was precisely the reason that Pal and Jaranilla came later, a couple of months after the trial had started.

Personally, I regretted that the bench consisted only of representatives of the victorious, sovereign nations. In my later publications, I had in mind not so much the fact that there were no representatives of the colonial peoples, but the fact that I would have preferred the cooperation of the representative of a neutral country, and even a representative of Japan. Time and time again, I got the feeling that if a Japanese judge had been present, he could have informed the court of internal relations within Japan that were difficult for us to grasp from the documents that were before us. One might conclude that, in the future, if ever such a trial is held again, one could learn from this that it is desirable to have also neutral judges and judges from the defeated nations.

That was my opinion at the time. Now, however, I am convinced that if ever another world war occurs, there would be no people left to sit as accused or as judges.

CHAIR: Thank you. There seem to be a number of other questions. Yes, you have the floor.

Webb Opposed All of the Death Sentences

QUESTION: I have a question for Dr. Röling, based on his presentation. Defense counsel had plans to introduce a large volume of evidence to the tribunal, and in fact attempted to do so, but the tribunal rejected almost all of this evidence. On what grounds was the evidence rejected? And also, within the bounds of what he can say, I would like to ask Dr. Röling to explain whether these decisions to reject evidence were based on deliberations in meetings of the judges, and to speak in general about deliberations among the judges up to the judgment itself.

DR. RÖLING: It is difficult for me to know the reasons why a majority of the court often rejected evidence, but if you look at the transcripts, you will see that the president, returning to open court, announced that the rejection was decided by a majority opinion, and in several cases it was my personal wish [that he make that announcement].

CHAIR: Thank you. I will recognize another question. Yes, go ahead.

QUESTION: I would like to ask Dr. Röling about just one fact. The charter of the IMT states: "All decisions and judgments of this Tribunal, including convictions and sentences, shall be by a majority vote of those members of the Tribunal present. In case the votes are evenly divided, the vote of the President shall be decisive." What I would like to know is this: In the case of Prime Minister Hirota, was the decision to impose the death sentence six to five—that is, five to five before President Webb cast the deciding vote? According to Webb's separate opinion, he was not necessarily in favor of the death penalty in any of the cases before the tribunal. He wonders if imprisonment, life sentences, or even exile would not be more appropriate, and if it was not cruel to impose death sentences on old men. And yet, if he did in fact cast the deciding vote in Hirota's case, how are we to interpret the contradiction?

DR. RÖLING: You can read in the dissenting opinion of Sir William Webb that he was opposed to every death penalty because of the fact that the emperor had not been tried. He said that he found it unfair that subjects who obeyed his [the emperor's] orders (calling him sovereign) should be punished by death when the principal culprit was not accused or tried. You can conclude from this that Sir William did not play a role in condemning Hirota to death.

CHAIR: If there are no further questions from the floor . . . Yes, but I trust you will stay within the time limit, and please make it a follow-up question.

Educational Problems Surrounding the Tribunal

QUESTION: I would like to pose a question to Mr. Tsurumi. Listening to the presentations yesterday and today, and especially to Mr. Tsurumi's paper, I think it is generally recognized that the proceedings of the tribunal were not fair. Mr. Tsurumi stated that the Japanese masses do not believe today that it was a fair trial, that they perceive the trial as a display of power by the Occupation, and that no moral influence from the trial remains in popular thinking. He also pointed out that the trial itself is inseparably linked in popular thinking with the trials of Class B and C war crimes throughout Asia. I quite agree with these observations.

However, as a person who studies international law, and as a teacher who lectures to university students, I have many opportunities to hear their opinions. As I said yesterday, the younger generation tends to believe that Japan conducted an extremely bad war. The Japanese translation of "aggression" for example . . .

CHAIR: I would prefer that you didn't continue that argument today . . .

QUESTION: Yes, I won't go into a detailed discussion today. But what I would like to point out is that there is a view among some international legal experts that war was recognized by international law. Moreover, it is now widely recognized that the legal foundations for the jurisdiction of the tribunal were shaky, and that the proceedings of the tribunal were unfair. However, the younger generation has been taught throughout elementary, junior, and senior high school that the trial was conducted properly, that a just judgment was rendered, and that Japan actually waged a criminal war of aggression—that the dropping of atomic bombs on Japan was, in the words of one of the Allied commanders, the "punishment of God," and must be endured. Therefore, Japan must always maintain a low profile—must always be aware of the crimes of its past.

They believe that if we go to China or anywhere else, we must apologize for Japan's past. And they don't know the real history. I think it would be more correct to take the position that even while Japanese should reflect seriously on their country's past history, the peoples of the former Allied powers should reflect on their histories.

As Mr. Tsurumi pointed out, the Tokyo trial is inseparably linked in popular thinking to the unfair trials of Class B and C war crimes, and accounts of these trials are gradually coming out and being circulated. But there still remain, in the historical awareness of young people, and in their view of Japan, the historical inaccuracies. I fear that the influence of these views will be an obstacle for them in terms of fulfilling their responsibilities in today's world as citizens of Japan. Mr. Tsurumi did not mention the fact that this consciousness of the Tokyo trial, and by extension the Allied powers, as having been totally correct—that Japan was completely wrong—still exists. I would like to ask for his opinion on this subject.

CHAIR: Mr. Tsurumi, would you care to comment?

MR. TSURUMI: I certainly feel that elementary and secondary school textbooks should deal with the Tokyo trial in more depth. Dr. Röling suggested, for example, that the express intention of the trial was to stop aggressive war. But that aspect of the tribunal has become quite blurred. The direct logical implication of this aspect of the trial, that when a country's leaders launch an aggressive war, the rights of individual citizens to reject the war and to refuse to participate in it are protected by international law, simply has not been grasped by the Japanese masses.

Taking myself as an example, I participated in efforts to aid Vietnam War deserters throughout that war, but until today it had never occurred to me that these efforts were directly linked to the Tokyo trial. That is, this interpretation of the Tokyo trial was unknown to us who were actually carrying out the movement on a day-to-day basis. I really feel I've had my eyes opened today. I quite agree, therefore, that we must make greater efforts to enhance and promote discussion and consideration of the Tokyo trial in textbooks and classroom situations at the junior and senior high school levels.

CHAIR: Thank you very much, Mr. Tsurumi.

Unfortunately, we have run out of time. Additional questions and comments have been posed by the panelists and the special guests. These questions and comments will be accepted during the open discussion this afternoon. Thank you all for your cooperation this morning.

THE CONTEMPORARY SIGNIFICANCE OF THE TOKYO TRIAL

April 29
1983
(afternoon session)

INTRODUCTION TO THE SESSION

CHAIR (Hosoya Chihiro): I will now open the afternoon session. Our discussions this afternoon will be organized somewhat differently than the other sessions. The topic of this session is the contemporary significance of the Tokyo trial, and it will be the final session of the symposium. Therefore, after hearing two papers on the topic of the session, we will conclude with a general discussion of all the issues that have been raised during the two days of the symposium.

Our first speaker today will be Professor Richard Minear of the University of Massachusetts, who was the first person to publish an extended critique of the Tokyo trial in English. The other is the distinguished historian Ienaga Saburō, who I am sure requires no introduction. As many of you may know, there was a Minear-Ienaga debate on the Tokyo trial a few years ago. It is not in my power to say whether this debate will be reenacted today. Professor Minear, you have the floor.

THE INDIVIDUAL, THE STATE,
AND THE TOKYO TRIAL
Richard H. Minear

Thank you, Mr. Chairman. I think the friendly discussion to which the Chairman referred, the friendly disagreement, will not be so much in evidence today. And I look forward to hearing Mr. Ienaga's comments as well. By way of introduction, let me say a few words first. Because of the weaknesses of the Tokyo trial, there is a great temptation to dismiss the trial and the ideals behind the trial. I hope it is possible to salvage some of the ideals. I fear that my book on the Tokyo trial was sometimes misinterpreted, both in Japan and in America. I did not suggest that Japan was without blame. Several speakers have mentioned already the medical experiments, and this week I had the privilege of visiting the Maruki Gallery to see its depictions of the Nanjing [Nanking] Incident. There were crimes on Japan's part. The Tokyo trial was a flawed trial, but Japan was not without guilt. Now let me turn to my prepared remarks.

Historians and Implications

The Tokyo trial was—or purported to be—a legal proceeding; but its purpose was as much historical as legal: to establish once and for all the record of Japanese misdeeds in the Pacific. Even as it looked to the past, it looked also—or tried to look—into the future: to establish norms of international conduct. Thus the authors of the Tokyo trial tried to live history both backward and forward.

Now Professor Ienaga and I—both of us historians—have been asked to deal with the implications for the present of the Tokyo trial, and to do so before a group including a great number of lawyers. One might think that it would be easier for historians in 1983 to deal with the implications of an event thirty-five years old than for Robert Jackson at the London Conference and Sir William Webb and Justice Röling at Tokyo—none of them historians—to live history backward and forward. But such, I think, is not the case. Despite the saying that hindsight gives us all 20:20 vision, Professor Ienaga and I are at no distinct advantage over the others.

This is so because, as Charles A. Beard wrote in 1934, to write history is to engage in "an act of faith." The historian, he wrote, "consciously or unconsciously performs an act of faith. . . . for certainty . . . is denied to him. . . . He is thus in the position of a statesman dealing with public affairs; in writing he acts and in acting he makes choices, large or small, timid or bold, with respect to some conception of the nature of things." The historian as statesman—this is not, perhaps, a conception with which many of us are comfortable. But Beard's statement is a wise statement nonetheless. Writing history is not primarily a matter of getting one's facts straight, although that is always an important and laudable undertaking. It is primarily a matter of taking a stand—as Professor Ienaga has done so forthrightly and eloquently in his book on the Pacific War and in his long court battle with the Ministry of Education over textbook censorship.

This morning Professor Ōnuma said he hoped to hear from the younger generation. I hope that, despite my graying hair, I may qualify in some sense as younger. I first encountered the Tokyo trial in the early 1960s. I was then a beginning graduate student in Japanese history; and for some reason I have since forgotten, I poked around in the Tokyo trial documents at the Harvard Law Library's Rare Book Room. But I had no driving motivation, no statesmanlike vision into which to fit the trial. Five years later, the American war in Indochina suggested a context; and my book was the result. That context was one restricted quite narrowly to American concerns, to my belief that American policies and actions in Indochina were morally insupportable and politically counterproductive. I argued further that there was a direct link between the ideology behind the Tokyo trial and American policy in Indochina. If that is the case, the Tokyo trial was not merely a travesty of justice; for all the reasons mentioned by Professor Ōnuma and others here, it also deceived the American public, validating a parochial, ethnocentric, self-serving, chauvinistic view of the Pacific War and preparing the way for mistakes twenty years later in Indochina.

There is much in that view which I still find compelling; but I am no longer sure that that context is the most important one. So what I want to do today is to examine two alternative contexts, contexts which are both broader and ultimately more significant than bilateral relations between Japan and America or even than postwar American policy itself. The first context is that of the conduct today of sovereign nation-states; it is a partly legal, partly moral, partly political context. The second context is that of the conduct today of individuals in a world where chaos rules.

Sovereign Nation-States Today

What can we say of the conduct today of nation-states? Is it not true that most of them appeal to high ideals even while subverting those ideals at every step? Does that indicate that we all recognize certain standards of international behavior, that there exists a common law basis upon which to build legal prohibition? Or does it indicate that national self-interest will always come first, that no matter what they say, nations will always act selfishly?

Soon after the Tokyo trial, Joseph B. Keenan, the chief prosecutor, wrote in these terms: "The situation of the defendants was comparable to that of American soldiers about to take a beachhead; that is, the lives of morally and legally innocent men may be sacrificed in the achievement of the common purpose, but the common good requires the taking of the beachhead." Keenan is one of the less admirable characters of the Tokyo trial; and his immediate reference was likely confined to defendant Shigemitsu. Still, his logic applies to all twenty-five defendants, to those sentenced to death as well as those sentenced to lesser terms. It applies perhaps to the trial itself. In the years since 1948, has the beachhead been taken? If the common purpose has been achieved, we can answer, yes. The beachhead was taken; lives were not sacrificed in vain. But if the common purpose has not been forwarded, then what of the Tokyo trial?

In terms more elevated than those of Keenan, Richard Falk has described the Tokyo trial as "a world order promise by the allies to the future." Tokyo and Nuremberg together were one part of a crusade "to save succeeding generations from the scourge of war." That phrase, of course, comes from the preamble to the charter of the United Nations, and it is the United Nations which was intended to be the second part of the crusade. But the fundamental question is the same: has Falk's promise to the future been kept? Have we lessened the scourge of war?

Is the world today qualitatively different from what it was in 1941 or 1930? The level of violence has surely undergone significant escalation; but otherwise? Technology changes; but do people and politics? At the London Conference establishing the charter for the Nuremberg trial, the two chief ideological partners were the Soviet Union and the United States. In many ways their positions were mirror-images, and representatives of each used the adjective "peace-loving" with confidence and frequency. Today one of them is fighting a war in Afghanistan; and the other is engaged quite openly in "destabilizing" the government of Nicaragua. The world can look to them for statesmanship in the pursuit of peace only when their own interests are not directly affected. Given their own definitions of those interests, there are few disputes which do not affect them directly. And can we say that other powers, less powerful, are qualitatively different?

To be sure, the view from the year 2000—if there *is* a year 2000—may be markedly different from the view today. Should nation-states cease to exist, should the resort to force become illegal except as authorized by a world government, then Tokyo would loom as a major landmark. Then we could say that the beachhead had been taken. But until such time will not Tokyo remain a beachhead in an invasion that was called off?

Individuals in a Chaotic World

The level of violence has escalated thanks to technological "advances." And many look to technology for the answer. But the real problems, of course, are political, not technological, and they must be dealt with politically. In *this* campaign, the technocrats are at a distinct disadvantage. E. P. Thompson's definition of "defense expert" is relevant here: "a person with a hole in the head where politics and morality ought to be, who can then get along all the better with moving around the acronyms. . . ."

If politics, not technology, is the key, where do we look for help? If nation-states are more the problem than the answer, to whom can we turn? In 1972, when the American war in Indochina was still going on, Richard Falk wrote that "the Nuremberg idea lives on as an instrument of individual resistance to governments engaged in aggressive warfare. In this respect, the vitality of the war crimes idea has to do with the great historic struggle of the people to place moral and legal limits on governments." He continues: "The great efforts of law are anti-governmental in character, limiting and discrediting the pretensions, abuses, and excesses of governmental power." Is Falk correct? Is there room for significant nongovernmental action? If so, what are the implications for our judgment of Tokyo? Is the Tokyo trial in this context a beachhead in a different cause?

Since 1948 there have been two tribunals which merit discussion alongside Nuremberg and Tokyo. In 1961 the state of Israel prosecuted Adolf Eichmann, convicted him and executed him. But there are real problems with that trial: it was not international; its defendant had been kidnapped; and the political entity convening the trial had not existed at the time of Eichmann's misdeeds. For these reasons, I think, the Eichmann trial did not add to the force of Nuremberg and Tokyo; it may have weakened their force.

The second tribunal may not strike some here as a tribunal at all. I refer to the panel of notables summoned by Lord Bertrand Russell to accuse the American government of war crimes in Indochina. But in our second context the Russell tribunal may have great significance.

First of all, the Russell tribunal took Nuremberg and Tokyo as its precedents. In the words of Jean-Paul Sartre, "The judgment of Nuremberg necessitated the existence of an institution to inquire into war crimes and, of necessity, to sit in judgment''; the Russell tribunal, he remarked at another point, was ''formed out of a void and for a real need.'' Without Nuremberg, without Tokyo, would that ''void'' have been so apparent?

Second, the Russell tribunal had no official status. That is, as far as the world of sovereign nation-states was concerned, it was completely unauthorized, extralegal. In Russell's own words: ''Our tribunal . . . commands no State power. It rests on no victorious army. It claims no other than a moral authority.'' Indeed, Russell was so bold as to claim: ''I believe that these apparent limitations are, in fact, virtues.'' The tribunal was free, he suggested, to be ''a tribunal of conscience.'' Is this mere self-serving rhetoric? Or is there more to it? If our context is not state action but the actions of individuals in a chaotic world, then we cannot dismiss the claims of Falk and Russell out of hand.

Once again, I think, our judgment of Tokyo and its implications depends upon our politics, our statesmanship. My own perspective owes much to my interpretation of the American war in Indochina and the role of popular protest in ending it. The protesters, I think, had a clearer grasp of reality than did the ''defense experts.'' In passing, let me say that parts of yesterday's discussion reminded me more of the Vietnam war than the Pacific War.

That experience has seemed to repeat itself in more recent times. As a local official of the town of Amherst, Massachusetts, I had to consider plans put forward by the federal government for relocating vast numbers of citizens in the event of the threat of nuclear war. In the case of Amherst, these plans called for our town of 30,000 to play host to 185,000 people. My fellow Selectmen and I found the plans preposterous, deluded. We rejected the proposal. Once again, the view from outside Washington was far more sound than the view from within Washington.

The nuclear freeze presents a similar situation. So also, I submit, does the recent statement by the American Catholic Bishops, speaking with great force on nuclear arms. In E. P. Thompson's words, I think we must ''protest and survive.''

I have drawn these examples from my own experience in order to suggest the reasons for my judgment of the Tokyo trial. But I do not want to leave the impression that my experience is unique, or uniquely American. I suggest that the fundamental dilemma is universal, not specifically American; that ''reasons of state'' increasingly stand revealed in their danger for us all. Indeed, it is this grim perspective on the acts of nation-states which leads me to the conclusion that Tokyo has meaning today for its role in strengthening individuals in this campaign against the acts of our political leaders.

Guilt and Innocence: Some Reflections

There is a side of any such moral argument which we seldom examine, though examine it we must: I refer to the dangers of moralism and self-righteousness. Writing in 1941, long before Nuremberg and Tokyo, the American revolutionary pacifist A. J. Muste urged that no attempt be made after the war ''to fasten sole war-guilt on any nation.'' Yesterday there was talk of soul searching. I agree wholeheartedly that we need soul searching. At Tokyo, I think, there was very little soul searching, particularly not on the American side. Writing during the war in Indochina, Muste quoted the words of an unidentified Italian: "The problem after a war is with the victor. He thinks he has just proved that war and violence pay. Who will now teach him a lesson?"

Muste's reasoning is reinforced with great eloquence by the South African writer Laurens van der Post, who was himself a prisoner of war of the Japanese and who witnessed a number of Japanese atrocities. Yet after the war he refused to cooperate in war crimes prosecutions against his former captors. Writing in 1970, he explained why: "I myself was utterly opposed to any form of war trials. . . . There seemed to me something unreal, if not utterly false, about a process that made men like the War Crimes Investigators from Europe, who had not suffered under the Japanese, more bitter and vengeful about our suffering than we were ourselves. There seemed in this to be the seeds of the great, classic and fateful evasions in the human spirit which, I believe, both in the collective and in the individual sense, have been responsible for most of the major tragedies of recorded life and time . . . the tendencies in men to blame their own misfortunes and those of their cultures on others; to exercise judgment they need for themselves on the lives of others; to search for a villain to explain everything that goes wrong in their private and collective courses. . . . As I saw it we had no moral surplus in our own lives for the lives of others. We needed all our moral energies for ourselves and our own societies." Later in the same essay, van der Post wrote: "I had learnt to fear the Pharisee more than the sinner; judgment and justice almost more than human error." In a sense Muste and van der Post are both elaborating on the adage that to judge someone else guilty is to find ourselves innocent. In this connection, I found Mr. Kinoshita's comments this morning particularly moving.

In our context, not of sovereign states, but of individual action in opposition to acts of state, the issue of timing is crucial. It is relatively easy to criticize after the fact; it is much more difficult to speak out before or during the commission of dubious acts. But the protest against war crimes by individuals within the nation at fault is most necessary when and where it is most difficult, not when it is easiest.

Conclusion

I began with Charles Beard's statement that historians are like statesmen, that in writing we act and in acting we make choices "with respect to some conception of the nature of things." I have described my own "conception of the nature of things" and suggested how the Tokyo trial fits into that "problem consciousness." In the narrower contexts—of judicial procedure, of law, of American and European images of the Pacific War and of Japan—the trial remains for me a travesty. So also in the context of regulating the conduct of sovereign nation-states. It is in the broader context of individual or popular resistance to unwise acts of state that for me the case against the Tokyo trial is not yet closed. Thank you. [Applause.]

CHAIR: Thank you for an extremely insightful presentation. I found Professor Minear's conclusion, that the case against the Tokyo trial is not yet closed, particularly thought-provoking.

The major points of the paper may be summarized as follows. Professor Minear engages the issues of the Tokyo trial in terms of the experience of Vietnam, which he views as an extension of the Pacific War and of the Tokyo trial itself, and concludes that Vietnam happened because Americans failed to grasp the true lessons of history. He also suggests that we must consider this problem within the framework of the nation-state system we have today, that within this framework there exists the ideology of "reasons of state," and that we should consider the issues against that background. He concludes his analysis by challenging us to consider how the individual should exist in a world order based on nation-states, that is, a chaotic world.

I will now turn the floor over to Professor Ienaga.

THE HISTORICAL SIGNIFICANCE OF THE TOKYO TRIAL
Ienaga Saburō

On the Compatibility of Patriotism and the Universal Principle of Mankind

I would like to begin with my own view of how we Japanese should evaluate the Tokyo trial in the historical context of modern Japan.

I am convinced that patriotism must not be inconsistent with the "universal principle of mankind"* and that they can coexist with no inconsistency. Humanity—whether at the level of the individual, the race, the nation-state, or all humankind—is finite and relative. And historical progress that follows the universal principle of mankind becomes possible only through actual practice grounded in an infinite repetition of self-negation, in which the finite nature and the relativity of the self are set in sharp contraposition to the absolute and the infinite. In this sense, a short essay written in English by Uchimura Kanzō in 1897 still has great relevance today. It is entitled "National Repentance," and I would like to quote part of it here:

> A Nation needs repentance as much as an individual. Repentance is humble acknowledgement of the supremacy of the Eternal Law of

---

*Preamble to the Japanese Constitution: ". . . Government is a sacred trust of the people, the authority for which is derived from the people, the powers of which are exercised by the representatives of the people, and the benefits of which are enjoyed by the people. This is a universal principle of mankind upon which this Constitution is founded. . . ."

Justice, from which no man or nation—not even Japan—can be exempt. . . . Nothing can buy off the just penalties of sins by whomsoever committed, but contrite and broken hearts. No glories of war can cover up the innocent blood that is shed in connection therewith. The sooner we own our evils *as evils*, the better.[1]

I support this view as a legitimate proposition, independent of Uchimura's Christianity.

Given the fact that the Fifteen-Year War began with Japan's aggression against China in 1931, and that the war expanded with the fighting in China as its nucleus, it is impossible to deny Japan's "sin." And yet, as I shall suggest later, it is a fact that the justice administered by the Tokyo trial was in some respects "victors' justice," and it is hard to say that the entire process of the trial was carried out solely according to the "Eternal Law of Justice."

The Failure to Prosecute War Crimes Ourselves

Be that as it may, we must not fail to consider the fact that the Japanese people failed to pursue the issue of responsibility for the war and to punish Japanese war criminals with their own hands. The Italian people overthrew the Fascist regime with their own hands. And the Germans are still punishing Nazi war criminals today. I feel deeply ashamed when I read the biography of the German theologian Dietrich Bonhoeffer, who fought against the Nazis and was killed by them, or the Japanese translation of writings left behind by the martyrs of the Italian resistance movement, for it is virtually impossible to find Japanese who gave up their lives in the struggle against their own corrupt government.

Kimura Tōru has recently made public an incident which bears on this issue. Toward the end of the war, Hosokawa Karoku was framed and thrown into jail for alleged misdeeds of the Communist movement in the so-called Yokohama Incident.[2] Immediately after the war, while still in prison and before his liberation, Hosokawa showed his "Precepts for Starting Again" to Kimura, who was in the same prison on the same charge. This essay included a list of the urgent tasks that should be completed immediately, and one of the items on this list was the following: "The trial and punishment by the Japanese people themselves of those responsible for the war."

Kimura shared this view and tried to persuade the editors of his newspaper to support it. In January 1946, just after Kimura's release from jail, an editorial meeting was called to discuss the question of how the paper should handle the problem of war crimes. At this meeting, Kimura made the following statement:

Shouldn't the pursuit of responsibility for the war and the prosecution of war crimes be carried out by a people's tribunal established by our own hands? Shouldn't we expose the crimes of the war criminals before all the people and judge them openly through our own people's tribunal?

This idea is completely different in nature from the idea of autonomous trials put forward by the Japanese government. As Professor Awaya pointed out yesterday, the government's proposal called for trials conducted from above. Kimura's idea, inspired by Hosokawa, called for the prosecution of war crimes from below—by the Japanese people themselves.

In the end, however, the Japanese people themselves never pursued the responsibility of Japanese war criminals. In view of this grave historical failing, we must view with great doubt any wholesale repudiation of the Tokyo trial as "victors' justice." Here, it is well worth recalling another of Uchimura Kanzō's essays, published in English in 1897. A satirical piece, it is entitled "The Savage Deed of the Savage Cabinet":

> The voice of their own countrymen they have suppressed (in the name of Loyalty and Patriotism, as hypocrites and scoundrels always do, says Dr. Samuel Johnson), but the voice of the world they can never suppress. And because they oppress the poor powerless people, Nature employs, now, as of old, Nebuchadnezzars and Sennacheribs to bring these minor despots to justice. Because Freedom suffers violence in Japan, there float round that Island Empire alien fleets to guard it from the hand of the oppressors. What the Japanese people fail to do because of their powerlessness, these foreign fleets may accomplish by their pressure upon the tyrants.[3]

Japan's acceptance of the Potsdam Declaration in August 1945, and the various measures subsequently imposed on Japan by the Allied powers based on that acceptance—one of them being the Tokyo trial—may truly be seen as literal realizations of Uchimura's prophecies. Indeed, I wonder if it cannot be said that this is a manifestation of Hegel's *List der Vernunft*.

Schemes Aimed at Rehabilitating the Greater East Asia War

I lay particular stress on this perspective because we must not overlook the fact that in postwar Japan down to the present day there has been a tendency to reject the Tokyo trial *in toto* as unfair, and that this tendency is linked inseparably with a second tendency: to assert the legitimacy of the war waged by Japan and to suppress or obliterate the aggressive nature of that war and the inhuman criminal activity that took place in the course of waging that war, and on the other hand, to elevate to martyrdom the individuals executed at the Tokyo trial. Further, we cannot overlook the fact that it is invariably the case that the minority opinion of Judge Pal is used as a powerful reinforcement for this position, and that this tendency is linked to the policy of political forces that seek to revive Japanese militarism.

The ideas underlying this tendency are in every way identical to the concepts employed by those who affirm the "Greater East Asia War." One of the most naked expressions of these ideas is the inscription on a monument erected on 3 May 1982 by the Fukuoka Prefectural Society for Honoring the War Dead of the Greater East Asia War. It reads as follows:

> Seen in retrospect, this last great war was a holy war in which Japan risked everything for existence and self-defense, hoping to liberate oppressed peoples and to live in prosperity with all nations. Although Japan ultimately sank in bitter defeat, the peoples of Asia have won

the glory of independence and freedom one after the other: this is a sublime historical achievement unprecedented in world history.

Schemes to rehabilitate the "Greater East Asia War" also appear undisguised in the policies of public institutions. The Ministry of Education's policy in examining textbooks for official approval, which evoked international criticism last year, is only one of many instances that could be cited.

We need only look at the Ministry of Education's request for revisions in my own textbook on Japanese history in 1964 to see that it is the government's policy to force public educational institutions to deal with the war in terms of a set relationship: rehabilitation of the "Greater East Asia War" on the one hand, and total repudiation of the Tokyo trial on the other. The Ministry demanded that I delete the phrase "the reckless war," used in reference to the Fifteen-Year War, on the following grounds: "Considered from a world perspective, is it not unfair to censure only Japan?" Similarly, concerning the Tokyo trial, I was told this: "We want you to add somewhere the fact that the trials held at the time were one-sided trials by the victor nations."[4]

In light of the situation now prevailing in Japan, I cannot help feeling the urgent need for a just evaluation of the Tokyo trial based on sound scholarship.

The War in China: An Aggressive War

It cannot be denied that in some respects the Tokyo trial was an example of "victors' justice." That the illegal and criminal acts of the Allied powers were not included in the tribunal's deliberations—and especially that acts of indiscriminate slaughter, such as the atomic bombing of Hiroshima and Nagasaki, were not considered—is precisely as Pal's minority opinion pointed out. Even apart from the atomic bombs, the United States cannot escape responsibility for the massive slaughter of noncombatants with conventional weapons in air raids on Japanese cities. Nor can the Soviet Union be absolved of responsibility for atrocities against Japanese noncombatants in Manchuria and Northeastern China, which included murder, looting, and rape. I am convinced that Japan violated the neutrality pact first, so I believe that Japan has no moral right to criticize the Soviet Union on that issue. But just as the United States should not escape judgment, the atrocities committed by the Soviet Union in Manchuria should not be exempt from censure. To ignore the fact that these war crimes had also been committed by the Allied powers too was not fair and just.

Moreover, as defense counsel Takayanagi Kenzō argued in court, the trial was legally defective because it did away with the fundamental principle of modern criminal jurisprudence that prohibits retroactive application of penal laws. Even Yokota Kisaburō and Dandō Shigemitsu, eminent Japanese legal scholars who generally supported the trial, and who went on to become supreme court justices, were forced to acknowledge this legal defect.

Thus, it would be difficult to deny that there were significant problems with the trial. However, it does not follow that all of the acts for which the defendants were punished should have been exempt from prosecution. It is clear even in the minority opinions of Chief Justice Webb and Justice Röling, who is here today, that opinion was divided on some of the tribunal's actions, beginning with the prosecution's selection of those to be indicted and extending to the factual grounds of the court's findings on individual defendants, to the recognition of criminal responsibility for certain acts, and to the weighing of the sentences to be handed down. But at the very least, I believe that it is impossible to deny, without resorting to sophistry, that taken as a whole the war waged by Japan from September 1931 to August 1945, the war that became the object of the Tokyo tribunal, was a war of aggression.

It is so obvious that Japan's war with China was one of aggression that even the minister of education and the prime minister have been forced to acknowledge that fact publicly in the National Diet. And I think it is impossible to judge Japan's war with the United States, England, and the Netherlands in isolation from its aggression against China, for that war began precisely because Japan rejected demands for a total withdrawal of its forces from China in order to continue its aggression there.

Gandhi's Letter to the Japanese People

The famous opening statement of defense counsel Kiyose Ichirō at the trial rests fundamentally on the same kind of thinking as the contemporary movement to affirm the "Greater East Asia War," and it is utterly impossible to support. And as for Judge Pal's minority opinion, though, as I have said, it contains a number of sound arguments, his justification of Japan's aggression against China reeks of the prejudices of his vehement anti-Communist ideology. This had already been shown in 1949, or earlier, in William Costello's critique of the Pal opinion.[5] Even if some of Pal's arguments are absolutely just, I must raise my voice to protest the danger of his minority opinion being used as strong evidence of the illegality of the Tokyo trial.

I have no knowledge whatsoever of conditions in India at the time. However, in an open letter entitled "To Every Japanese," which is dated September 1942, Mahatma Gandhi, the leader of the Indian independence movement, stated that if the Japanese army were to attack India, "we will not fail in resisting you with all the might that our country can muster." Moreover, medical teams were organized in India to help China, and one team of doctors was sent to China. Three of these doctors went to the front lines with the Eighth Route Army, and one of them, Dr. Kotnis, was killed in the performance of his duty. Indeed, solidarity between the peoples of China and India was established on the basis of their shared purpose of resisting Japanese aggression.[6] In view of these historical facts, it is difficult for me to understand how to situate Judge Pal's minority opinion in the political thought of the Indian people at that time. I would be quite interested in hearing the opinion of a specialist on this point.

If I seem obsessed with the Pal's opinion, it is because I cannot dismiss the fact that it is inextricably linked to the movement to assert the injustice of the Tokyo trial and to affirm the "Greater East Asia War," and that it is being used ultimately in the service of a wholesale negation of Japan's postwar pacifism and democracy. When I consider the fact that the Japanese people were not able themselves to prosecute those responsible for the war—a war that was accompanied by a great number of atrocities committed by Japanese—I cannot help worrying about the dangerous effects of totally repudiating the Tokyo trial by ignoring its positive significance and dealing only with its flaws. Even if the tribunal was flawed, it was nevertheless the only public attempt to establish the illegality of the Fifteen-Year War. Again, I can only see in that Hegel's *List der Vernunft*.

Humble ''Repentance'' for Past Mistakes

Today, the Tokyo trial has already shrunk to the realm of bygone fact, so what we Japanese must do now and into the future is rigorously to pursue the legal, political, and moral responsibility for the Fifteen-Year War in some form that is without flaws. Such a pursuit is nothing other than a process of ''National Repentance,'' in which the facts of the matter, as established by rigorous scholarship, are seen in light of the ''supremacy of the Eternal Law of Justice.'' Unlike the Tokyo trial, it will not have the coercive or executory powers of political authority. It will be supported only by our intelligence, our sense of right, and our conscience. But precisely for this reason, its spiritual authority will be greater. Here, I would like to express my total support for the similar argument in the opening statement made by Sartre at the Russell tribunal in 1967, convened to inquire into the criminality of the Vietnam War. This matches the earlier citation of Professor Minear, but that is a coincidence. I am not plagiarizing him. [Laughter.]

We can prosecute as well the innumerable acts of atrocity committed by the state against the Japanese people, and we can also investigate the numerous violations of Japanese domestic law by the state during the war. Yet at the same time, the Japanese people must also censure themselves for their failure to prevent these violations of law and criminal acts by the state. I am convinced that the manifestation of this kind of determination would win the approval of the people of the former Allied powers, who organized the International Tribunal for the Far East. And, at the same time, I would like to think that this kind of determination on the part of the Japanese people would evoke a similar process of self-criticism within the countries of the former Allied powers for the war crimes committed by their own countries. Humble repentance for the mistakes of the past, I believe, is an indispensable precondition for avoiding World War III, the threat of which we confront at this very moment. [Applause.]

GENERAL DISCUSSION

CHAIR: Thank you, Professor Ienaga. The central points of Professor Ienaga's paper are quite clear, as is his political position, and I don't think there is any need for me to summarize his presentation or add anything to it.

The Ienaga-Minear debate centered, I think, on the minority opinion of Judge Pal, but even on that point their differences in viewpoint seem to have narrowed considerably.

Now, several participants have indicated that they have comments on this morning's presentations. At the risk of throwing cold water on this heightened atmosphere, I would like to recognize those questions first. I will then accept questions on the papers of Professor Minear and Professor Ienaga, and then open the floor to free debate.

Professor Ōnuma and Professor Pritchard have questions for Mr. Tsurumi.

Concerning Logical Propositions

PROFESSOR ŌNUMA: In his presentation this morning, Mr. Tsurumi cited the model that former Ambassador Matsudaira and I had used earlier. This model goes as follows. A argues: "It is wrong to steal." B refutes this argument by saying: "You stole too, didn't you?" This diminishes the force of A's argument. Mr. Tsurumi argues that, logically, there is no reason for this to happen, and suggests that it is quite possible for A to reply: "Yes, I stole. Nevertheless, it is wrong to steal." He also suggests that this rebuttal has a higher ethical value than A's original statement. I have discussed this point with some of the other panelists, and a number of them have said that they really did not understand it very well. I must confess that I don't quite get the point either, and I wonder if Mr. Tsurumi would not elaborate a little further. That is my first point.

A related point concerns the fact that Mr. Tsurumi's argument is based on a question of logical premises. To this extent, I wonder how it is connected to popular thought, which Mr. Tsurumi himself argues is a mode of thought that moves according to images and not necessarily according to logic. In fact, he suggests that popular thought is different from the thought of intellectuals like those seated here on the podium, and that intellectuals are not always reliable as human beings. I would like to ask how the logic he employs is linked to popular thought.

The Fairness of Class B and C War Crimes Trials Conducted by the British

DR. PRITCHARD: First and foremost, I would like to express my own admiration for Professor Röling's paper this morning. But in regard to the two Japanese papers this morning, I'd like to say that I'm not only entirely in agreement and sympathy with the views of Kinoshita-san, but I am extremely disturbed by Tsurumi-san's presentation, which was echoed by several of the subsequent questions from the floor this morning. I am profoundly disturbed by the tendency of many Japanese today to glide away from the misconduct that indeed occurred, or to doubt the genuine revulsion which any such acts inspired in the hearts of Allied prosecutors and judges, many of whom had known a lifetime of military service (I am speaking now of the Class B and C trials).

Having, quite apart from my Tokyo trial work, studied in detail every single word of some nine hundred trials of Japanese accused of war crimes by the British, I can say that at least the Anglo-Saxon trials were conducted, with a few exceptions, in broad compliance with the codified military laws and regulations which would have bound their own soldiers.

Now, I think if one actually doubts the existence of the evidence, or of the crimes themselves, one should, in the first instance, forget the emotion and go back to the records themselves. They are available. Make no mistake. The vast majority—the *vast* majority of those trials—concerning conventional war crimes, were conducted with scrupulous fairness. And, in fact, it was only due to the limitations on the part of the prosecutions' investigating teams that countless war criminals, through luck or mischance, were returned to Japan as ordinary prisoners of war and therefore escaped the military jurisdiction—the area of military jurisdiction—of relevant courts.

So don't throw out the baby with the bathwater. The great majority of those convicted for minor war crimes offenses were very, very guilty. That's all.

Problems of Rhetoric and Logic

MR. TSURUMI: First, I want to respond to Professor Ōnuma. In response to A's argument that "it is wrong to steal," B says, "You stole too, didn't you?" The effect of B's statement is to weaken A's accusation. Since it has the effect of weakening A's attitude toward B, it is effective in terms of rhetorical technique. Logically, however, it does not refute A's argument. It in no way fulfills that function.

Nevertheless, A is taken aback. But if A, despite his dismay—or, perhaps, because of it—can clearly say, "Yes, I stole. Nevertheless, it is wrong to steal," that statement has even more weight than his initial accusation.

I thought of this during the war. Somehow, I knew that I did not want to "kill," and I resorted to all sorts of means to avoid doing so. But I was gripped by the fear that I might not be able to hold out to the very end if voices arose all around me saying, "They are going to kill us, so kill them!" I was saved by chance, and somehow managed to come through the war without killing anyone. Ultimately, however, at the very extremes of human behavior, I think that people can continue to cry out, even if their own hands are covered with blood, "Yes, I killed. Nevertheless, it is wrong to kill." I believe that statement has weight in terms of human morality in its most ordinary form.

Earlier, I mentioned a Kabuki play. The play is about a prostitute, and in terms of our ordinary sense of morality, she would be considered a sordid creature. But this character's statements have a certain kind of weight, and the fact that they have been passed down through the generations as a part of Japanese culture shows that they have something the Japanese masses empathize with, the power to evoke a response. In other words, the masses see in them a collectivity of people of which they feel a part.

I do not know who deserves to be called an intellectual, but if intellectuals are considered to be a group of people who have been selected from the masses by some method, formal education for instance, it becomes easy for those selected in this way, when looking at others, to see them as forming a group that does not include themselves. And if intellectuals do not fight against this danger, the thought of intellectuals will become a reified system that even they themselves can no longer change or influence. My own way of thinking is based on the bias that unless they themselves are party to some form of mass thought, even intellectuals will end up no longer being able to change themselves.

Returning to our model with this view in mind, I think you can see how A can respond to B's rebuttal by saying, "Yes, I stole. Nevertheless, it is wrong to steal." It is an ideal, you see: if we can actually say this, then and only then does the statement that "it is wrong" have logical weight. That's what I was trying to say. Does that answer your question?

CHAIR: How about it, Professor Ōnuma?

MR. TSURUMI: Still not good enough? [Laughter.]

In other words, there are groups that include oneself and those that do not. Those who wish to affix responsibility for the war often create "people responsible for the war" as a group that does not include themselves. That has no weight. That is what I wanted to say.

Can One Criticize War Criminals?

In regard to Mr. Pritchard's comment—I'm not sure whether it was a question or a rebuttal—I would like to say this. In practical terms, we would have to investigate more than a thousand cases to learn the whole story of the Class B and C war trials. I based my own conclusions on information from people in the Justice Ministry of the Japanese government, people who have had access to these records all along. I have not reinvestigated all of the primary documents myself. However, I want to point out that what I say in my paper is that there are cases in which the law was applied correctly and cases in which it was applied incorrectly. I do not wish to argue that there were great numbers of defendants in these trials who were innocent. That is my first point.

Even in the play *Watakushi wa kai ni naritai*, to which I referred earlier, the central character is not innocent. But we must look at the circumstances—even though he is not innocent, he has been driven to do what he does. I managed to get through the war without killing anyone, but that was due in large part to chance. That feeling remains with me today, and I cannot bring myself to accuse those who did kill people. I think that same feeling exists among the Japanese masses today.

It would be difficult, I think, to refute Mr. Pritchard by searching through his evidence and finding innocent people who were punished. But that is not essential to the points I wanted to make in my paper. The logical structure of my argument is different.

Still, in the case of Mr. Kimura, for example, who wrote out his last will and testament in the back of Tanabe Hajime's *Tetsugaku tsūron* [General Theory of Philosophy], I think it is quite clear that he was innocent. Kimura records how he was framed by his superiors, and I think there were many similar cases. That is, when superior officers colluded to frame someone else for a crime, there was no escape. This was especially true in the case of Korean and Taiwanese residents of Japan, whose personal relationships with superior officers were slight, and who also had language problems. It was easy for superiors to use them as scapegoats. Moreover, I think there were times when, because they were Koreans, they were forced to beat and kill people in order to prove their loyalty. One case I know of personally is that of a man who was half-Caucasian. He was an extremely cowardly man, and his fear of be-ing bullied became his motive for participating in atrocities ordered by his superiors. One has to look at these kinds of circumstances.

Language Barriers

Mr. Pritchard's assertion that scrupulously fair trials were conducted in the case of Class B and C war crimes differs sharply from the impression that Japanese have. I would like Mr. Pritchard to survey the documentary material available to Japanese and see whether or not it changes his opinion.

Ms. Utsumi Aiko is here today, and I have been able to read her materials, those of Ms. Kamisaka Fuyuko, and material written by Mr. Tsukuba Hisaharu. One's strongest feeling when looking at these documents is that of sympathy for the accused. The same may be said of the materials in the collection of the Justice Ministry. It is quite impossible to say that these were fair trials.

The principal reason may be found in the problem of language. Few Japanese can function in any language other than Japanese. They can't even speak English very well. When testimony is given not in English but in Dutch or Malay, the situation is extremely difficult. Dreadful mistakes increase in number. When you're actually in the courtroom, the language barrier is enormous.

I have had the experience of participating in a court-martial myself. Held at Iwakuni, it was the court-martial of an American deserter whom I had helped. Halfway through the proceedings, the interpreter appointed by the US Army began to hesitate, and finally lost track of what was being said completely. He came to me, a witness for the defense, to ask whether the En-glish and Japanese matched. The judge, a colonel, sat there with a look of complete exasperation on his face. Incidentally, the sentence was relatively light.

This is my only experience with courts-martial, and it was this way even though it involved only Japanese and English. But the Tokyo trial and the other war trials were held immediately after the war. They involved going from Japanese into English, Malay, or Dutch; and when trials had to be conducted in a short time, many mistakes were made: that can be inferred as a matter of course from my own experience, limited though it was.

CHAIR: Thank you. Mr. Furness, you have the floor.

MR. FURNESS: Mr. Tsurumi said that in that television play, "I Want to Become a Shellfish," a crime had been committed. The man that was accused was a private, and he was assigned to a firing squad. He was ordered to execute an American prisoner. He resisted. He ran away. And then he was brought back and threatened to be hurt unless he fired the shot, or one of the shots, to kill the man. Now, he finally did it. I know that because I read the scenario of that particular drama. Do you really think that he committed a crime? You said that he committed a crime. Do you really think so?

MR. TSURUMI: In the play, it is concluded that he did. Actually, the producer is here today. Why don't you ask his opinion?

CHAIR: Thank you very much, Mr. Furness.

QUESTION: Could Dr. Pritchard perhaps be given the opportunity to reply to Mr. Tsurumi, because I feel his integrity has perhaps been seriously challenged. He might like to take this opportunity to say just a few words.

Courts-Martial of Japanese and of Allied Soldiers Compared

DR. PRITCHARD: I haven't actually had the opportunity to see those particular files in the Ministry of Justice to which he has referred. What I read instead were the complete transcripts, plus all the proceedings on review. I saw the documents in evidence, and I saw also what happened to the various appeals which went forward. So those documents comprise perhaps a hundred thousand or more pages. It took me about a year simply to read the material, let alone actually begin to digest it.

I may say also that the files on which I based my conclusions had not been opened to public scrutiny before. In fact, I had to get special permission to use them. But no restrictions were placed upon my use of the records. Now, I think that it's always possible to find a feeling of dissatisfaction with the findings of courts, and to find testimonials and the like which go through your own Japanese system. But I think that this is a separate issue from the integrity of the legal proceedings themselves.

As far as the specifications for the trials were concerned, there really was no difference at all between the proceedings conducted against Japanese and the military courts-martial which might have been considered against British or other Allied soldiers. There was a special army ordinance which said that only Japanese citizens would be tried under these particular courts-martial, and also some wider ranges of evidence might be considered. Partly, that was a reflection of the fact that in atrocity cases the victims are often no longer available for testimony, and therefore some classes of hearsay evidence may be admitted for whatever value they may have. But that is not to say that such wider terms of reference would not be subjected to very close scrutiny by the judges concerned.

Many of the judgments, in the case of the British trials, were reasoned judgments, and the sentences which were pronounced do show very clearly that the circumstances of the defendants in the commission of their crimes were taken very seriously into consideration. So I don't think it's possible to say that simply because someone was perhaps forced to commit a particular crime, that was not taken into consideration. It was in every case taken into consideration. In many cases, people were acquitted by some tribunals for simply obeying orders where there was no chance of their escaping the authority of their superior officers. In other cases, they were given very small sentences, even cases where the crimes committed were very horrific. I think perhaps that's about as far as I ought to go at this stage.

The Possibility of New Collaborative Research

MR. TSURUMI: One thing occurs to me. I think it would be extremely profitable if Japanese and non-Japanese specialists could work together on the Class

B and C war crimes, pooling the materials that exist in Japan and those that exist in foreign countries. I just now realized that this possibility exists.

I also want to point out again that I am not saying that all of the Japanese defendants, or even a majority of them, were innocent. Some were innocent; some were not. What I'm saying applies regardless.

My opinion that the trials were marked by fairly dubious procedure appears to conflict somewhat with Dr. Pritchard's position. At the end of the war, even translation from Japanese into English or vice-versa was terrifically difficult, and there were very few people who could handle both Japanese and the non-English languages easily. The quality of interpreting in the case of the Tokyo trial was fairly high. But still it wasn't easy, and there were a number of extremely difficult problems. There are any number of cases, and although I won't go into detail, there are accounts of trials in which numbers were painted on the defendants' chests and witnesses were instructed: "Say that #3 harmed you."

Dr. Pritchard says that the British trials were fair. Mr. Kimura, the man I referred to earlier, was tried for an incident that occurred in the Nicobar Islands, a small group of islands in the Indian Ocean. From what he has written, I feel that he is one of the convicted war criminals that was innocent. Therefore, this kind of injustice could occur even in British territory.

In any case, at the very least, I want to insist that new international research is possible, and that it is a pretty crude form of justice that finds someone guilty using an interpreter from a different language and a different culture in what is not only literally but also experientially a very short period of time.

CHAIR: I wonder if the discussion is not becoming too specialized. In fact, several participants have indicated that they have questions for Professor Röling, and I expect considerable debate on the presentations by Professors Minear and Ienaga, and then questions from the floor and the panel. I hesitate to interrupt this discussion, but I think we should move on to other issues. I would like to turn first to discussion of Professor Röling's paper. Professors Okuhara and Ipsen both have questions.

The Possibility of Revolutionary Action Creating Law and the Opposite Possibility

PROFESSOR OKUHARA: I have a question for Professor Röling. The problem I would like to raise is that of the effectiveness of the General Assembly resolution affirming the principles of Nuremberg. Professor Röling acknowledges that the principles of the Nuremberg trial had not become customary international law at the time of the trial itself, but he suggests that the adoption of the General Assembly resolution has made them part of customary international law. Professor Ipsen, on the other hand, takes the opposite position.

For my part, I feel that one of the most important proposals regarding the UN resolution was eliminated in the process of drafting it for consideration by the General Assembly. This, of course, is the vital clause that would have given the resolution binding force on all countries. In the process of drafting the resolution, there was opposition to this clause, and it was eliminated. Indeed, I recall that the Netherlands, Professor Röling's own country, was formally opposed to this clause. I would like Professor Röling to comment on that and to explain a little more fully the grounds upon which he considers the principles of Nuremberg to have become international law at that point in time.

PROFESSOR IPSEN: With your kind permission, I should like to refer to the statements made by Dr. Röling, and to the statements of Professor Minear, both of which deeply impressed me.

Professor Röling has tried, as few other international lawyers have done, to build a bridge between the international law in force at the time of the Nuremberg and Tokyo trials and the international law urgently needed for a peaceful international community. As Professor Röling has said, this bridge was built, as far as the Nuremberg and Tokyo law is concerned, by a revolutionary action. The fascinating appeal of this idea, however, should not lead us to neglect the very basic element of law—the hard core of law. The basic element of law, of national as well as international law, is its character and function an an obligatory model of behavior for individuals and for state organs in the case of national law, and for states in the case of international law.

The peace-securing function of law is intimately connected with this basic element. A revolutionary creation of new law may increase the peace-securing function of law, but at the same time it risks destroying that function completely. I should like to refer at this point to the image of a beachhead that was used by Professor Minear. Perhaps, in some cases, such a beachhead may be assaulted without any success.

The IMT Laws: No Contribution to the Prevention of War

As to the question of whether the revolutionary action of creating the Nuremberg and Tokyo laws increased the peace-securing function of law, the answer in my opinion cannot be completely affirmative. On this point, I am unfortunately in disagreement with my distinguished colleague Professor Röling. He has stated, "The crime against peace has become an accepted component of international law." Since the two trials, there has been no international legal instrument in which the crime against peace has been laid down a second time. Consider for instance the Convention on the Non-Applicability of Statutory Limitations to War Crimes and Crimes Against Humanity, on which we had a discussion yesterday. This convention only refers to war crimes and crimes against humanity—not to crimes against peace.

Since Nuremberg and Tokyo, there have been more than eighty international armed conflicts, in which more than sixty states have been involved. Therefore, there must have been at least thirty aggressor states, for one state has been the aggressor in these cases. Presently, strategic nuclear doctrines are discussed not only in military circles, but also quite openly among political leaders. And in the execution of these nuclear strategies, which would cost not millions but hundreds of millions of lives, political and military leaders are apparently undeterred by Tokyo or Nuremberg. Professor Röling holds that the law of Nuremberg and Tokyo has been effective. Yes, it has been effective as a repressive law applied by victorious nations. However, it has failed up to now to be effective as a law preventing responsible leaders from resorting to war.

Thus, I have strong doubts that the Nuremberg or Tokyo law, at the stage it has reached today, can contribute significantly to the prevention of war. Other additional methods must be found. One might be the progressive development of international criminal law along the lines I suggested yesterday. Another may be the creation of regional collective security systems to endorse the general security system of the United Nations, which has, as we know, its deficiencies. A third may be a collective economic security system.

In this connection, I am reminded of the words of the first chancellor of the former German Reich, Otto von Bismarck, who said at the end of the Franco-German War of 1871: "Public opinion demands fervently that, in cases of wars, the victor shall, on the basis of the code of morality, have a trial of the defeated and punish him for all evil he has done, but punishment is not an instrument of politics. Politics do not have to take over the task of a judge. The aim of politics cannot be to take revenge for what has happened, but only to provide that the same doesn't happen again." Thank you, Mr. Chairman.

CHAIR: Dr. Röling, would you like to respond?

For the Preservation of Peace

DR. RÖLING: Yes, Mr. Chairman, but it is not very easy. I realize that, since World War II, more than a hundred wars have taken place, if we also count all the internal wars where military forces opposed each other. And so we can say that, up to now, the world has not lived up to the principles of Nuremberg and Tokyo. That is not to say that at present the situation of international law is such that it does not recognize crimes against peace. The trouble with international law is that it is so weak—that it makes misbehavior only a bit more difficult. But even for that we should be grateful.

I realize that if peace is to be maintained, a lot more has to happen than to prohibit war and to declare it to be illegal and criminal. It is only one aspect of numerous steps that have to be taken—adaptions that are demanded if the world is to know peace.

I have often expressed the opinion that the price of peace is severe, even harsh, and that it is very difficult to live up to the challenge of maintaining peace. Of course, there are always differences among lawyers as to the precise contents of international law. It is my sincere conviction that the United Nations has by several actions expressed the opinion that the current law is that aggressive war is illegal and criminal.

The Definition of Aggression as an Authoritative Interpretation of the UN Charter

You know that when the cold war was at a very high peak the United Nations tabled three issues: the codification of criminal international law, the definition of aggression, and the establishment of an international criminal court.

I believe that was in 1956. I had the opportunity in the United Nations to protest against this in the General Assembly. I said that if conflicts were very tense at the moment, there was all the more reason to go ahead with these measures.

In 1956, I was a member of the committee on defining aggression. There was the Suez military intervention. There was the military intervention in Hungary by the Russians. So if we had concluded any definition of aggression, we would have condemned by that definition the powers that were busy fighting at that very moment. Thus, it was politically impossible to go on.

Now we have this definition of aggression. It was said yesterday that it is only a resolution, and we all know that resolutions are only recommendations.

However, this recommendation was an authoritative interpretation of the charter provisions, a conclusion from the charter provisions, and it pointed out that no reason of economics or politics could justify the use of military force. The fact that the law is not applied is one that I recognize and deplore. That is not to say that the law is not there. It is not the purpose of recognizing the criminality of aggression to punish people in the future. If there is a nuclear war, there will perhaps be nobody left to sit in judgment or to be condemned.

The significance of the United Nations, or the existence of this law, is not in its application after such a war but the effects it will have in times of peace, the effect it will have in preventing war. It is only a small contribution. I know that the prohibition of war is less important than changes in international law that will provide for better relations between nations. In that area, much has been achieved already: decolonialization, the acceptance of human rights, the quest for a new law of the sea, the work toward a new international economic order. These are all conditions of peace. Important innovations are being brought about.

Protesting Policies of Aggression

But I would hope that lawyers would come to the conclusion that the law exists at this moment, and that it may guide all those protesting against their governments—against the aggressive policies they are pursuing today—that it may become a basis for demanding that governments take a more rational point of view.

To mention one government, the American government, I think it manifests the irresponsible militarism that was criticized and condemned in the Potsdam Declaration. When we compare its policies to the agreements achieved in 1979, the SALT II agreements, and not only the agreements that were reached, but also the agreement to proceed at once with negotiations as soon as SALT II had been ratified, then we see the agreement between Brezhnev and Carter as a means of negotiating so that the aggressive capabilities of both armies would be diminished. They would both take away from their armies the capabilities necessary for a surprise attack or for a disarming first strike. And I think this is the way we should go.

Of course, it is a consequence of the prohibition of war that it becomes a restriction not only on the right to use arms, but also on the right to possess arms. [In 1979,] the [two] governments were on the way to achieving that. That has now been lost. I agree, therefore, that at this moment we are in a very unfavorable time and a very unfavorable climate. But one very positive thing has come about from that unfavorable climate: the mass movements of the populations of Europe and America—almost everywhere in the world—to protest what is going on. It helps those people to know that they are protesting something that is, according to many scholars and lawyers, a crime.

CHAIR: Thank you very much, Dr. Röling.

The difference of opinion between Professors Ipsen and Röling reflects, I think, basic differences in their respective views of and approaches to international law. I also suspect that it reflects differing views of the contemporary world. On the latter point, I ask that there be further discussion after the recess.

A question for Dr. Röling has been raised from the floor by Mr. Tanaka, the Japanese translator of Judge Pal's minority opinion. However, Professor Ienaga's paper was extremely critical of Judge Pal's position, and I think it might be more fruitful after the recess, to direct this question to him.

[Recess]

CHAIR: I would now like to open the final discussion period, which will close the symposium. In the time remaining, I would like to direct discussion to a consideration of the contemporary significance of the trial, mainly focusing on the papers given by Professors Ienaga and Minear.

First, Mr. Kojima informs me that he has a brief question for Professor Minear.

Actions as an Individual and Feelings as a Citizen

MR. KOJIMA: Thank you. In his presentation, Professor Minear argued that the concept of "reasons of state" was both pointless and dangerous. He also suggested that there is a need to strengthen campaigns by individuals against their political leaders. The problem here lies in the word *individual*. Certainly, this is easy if we are talking, as Professor Minear does, about individual actions that transcend the barriers of country, race, religion, and culture—individual action as a member of mankind in general. However, it was true in the past as it is today, and will continue to be so for quite some time, that the individuals of every country are also citizens of nation-states; and considering the matter from the standpoint of a member of a nation-state, a citizen of a country, I think that every individual is likely to have other feelings as well.

In 1944, about one year before the end of the Pacific War, we had a welcoming party at my upper secondary school for new students. The foreign students from China who had come to my school mounted the dais and gave speeches. These students had been sent to Japan by the Wang Zhaoming [Wang Chaoming] government in Nanjing [Nanking], which was a Japanese puppet regime. Most of the speeches were long, and I still remember clearly only the words of the last speaker. I would like to quote them here:

We still cannot speak to each other as members of the human race. Unfortunately, we can speak only as the citizens of nations that are enemies or allies. When we graduate, we will not return to Nanjing. We will join the Jiang Jieshi [Chiang Kai-shek] government in Chongqing [Chunking] and fight. That is because we believe it is our duty to protect the people we love and to protect our country. Moreover, we think it is a proud duty. If we should meet on the battlefield, shall we not fight against each other proudly as fellow graduates of this school?

This Chinese student left the dais amid thunderous cheers and applause.

Perhaps that feeling was a manifestation of the kind of patriotism that Professor Ienaga discussed in his paper. And that is also one of the important factors that has enabled mankind to survive up to now, for its foundation is the readiness to offer oneself for something outside oneself—that is, the spirit of self-sacrifice. The meaning of what that Chinese student said was in complete accord with what we felt in our own hearts. And it was that spirit that brought us to our feet clapping and cheering.

As members of a nation-state, individuals have this kind of simple love for their own country, territory, and people, and they share the spirit of doing one's best in the service of one's country. The problem is the relation between the kind of individual action that Professor Minear advocates and this feeling of patriotism as a citizen of a nation-state.

CHAIR: Professor Minear, would you like to respond?

PROFESSOR MINEAR: Mr. Kojima said that his question was a simple one. Obviously, it is a very complicated one indeed. In fact, I think it goes to the heart of much of our discussion today. I have been impressed by the extent to which Professor Röling's comments and Professor Ienaga's comments and Mr. Kinoshita's comments and my comments speak to the issue of individual responsibility—the responsibility of individual citizens. I think we agree on the need to rethink our responsibilities as individuals and as members of groups. Obviously, that is a very difficult process, and we may not all wind up agreeing. It's very difficult in part because flag-waving patriotism—patriotism of the narrower sort—is often the easier path. But I do not think it is a hopeless situation. Yesterday, there was a complaint—and I think the complaint was justified—that one result of the Tokyo trial was to speak of Japan as a guilty nation. Certainly, for most Americans the result of the Tokyo trial was to reinforce the idea that the Japanese nation was guilty. But let me quote briefly from the German writer Friedrich Dürrenmatt, a novelist who wrote in 1961 a novel called *The Quarry*. The novel deals with the search for a German war criminal. At one point, the searcher had this to say: "I refuse to make a distinction between peoples and speak of good and bad nations. But a distinction between good and bad people I have to make. If there is a god, he will recognize not nations but only individuals, and he will judge each one by the measure of his crimes and acquit each one by the measure of his own justice." This is Dürrenmatt, a novelist, writing in 1961. It seems to me that what our discussion here today has called for, yesterday as well, is soul-searching on all our parts—on all sides of the Tokyo trial, on all sides of more recent political issues. We must each act in the way that Mr. Kinoshita this morning so eloquently spoke of. We must examine our own consciences, and work in the ways that our consciences most lead us to take.

CHAIR: Thank you. There are a great number of questions and comments concerning Professor Ienaga's paper. Professor Hata has a question about the degree to which the Fifteen-Year War was one continuous event.

Why "The Fifteen-Year War"?

PROFESSOR HATA: It seems to me that this afternoon's session has turned into something of a ceremony of confession and repentance. As a historian, I would like to shift the focus slightly and return to the question of how to view the period of history that came under the scrutiny of the Tokyo tribunal.

There is a good deal in Professor Ienaga's paper with which I am in agreement. However, I would like to ask him for a little more explanation of his repeated use of the term "the Fifteen-Year War." Mr. Tsurumi, who I hear is the inventor of this expression, is also here today, and I would like to ask him later about that.

Recently, the term has begun to be used frequently even in textbooks. Actually, it is quite a new term. Professor Ienaga said that the Fifteen-Year War began in September 1931 and ended in August 1945; but count it out and you'll see that it's thirteen years and eleven months. I have often wondered how this period ended up being called the "Fifteen-Year War." The "Thirteen-Year War," or the "Fourteen-Year War," would seem to be more appropriate. That is my first point.

Related to this is one of the viewpoints of the Tokyo trial, what I called yesterday the "Tokyo trial's view of history." This is a continuous view of history—a way of looking at history in terms of its continuity. At times this way of looking at history can be extremely dangerous. For example, the wartime leadership of Japan explained its policies by claiming that, for one hundred years, the imperialist nations of Europe had conspired in a common plan to commit aggression against Asia and Japan, and that Japan was now engaged in a war to resist that aggression. When did this begin? The accepted theory at the time was that it began when Admiral Perry came to Japan. A considerable number of Japanese still hold that view today. As this example shows, when it becomes difficult to legitimize one's position, all one has to do is carry the argument further back. Once one has done that, arguing that everything started here or there, at some point one comes up with a theory of history that substantiates one's position.

I think it is extremely dangerous to put forward a view of historical continuity in terms of a time scale that is too broad. I would agree with the idea of lumping the so-called Manchurian Incident and the so-called Japan-China War together in one package, in the sense that they were both wars between Japan and China. However, I wonder if the war that is called the Pacific War or the Greater East Asia War are not qualitatively different from these earlier conflicts. I consider the latter to be a new war, and I do not necessarily think that it was the inevitable product or result of the war between Japan and China.

As Mr. Tsurumi said this morning, the wartime leadership deliberately chopped up an ongoing war into increasingly smaller "incidents." Mr. Tsurumi suggested that this constituted one kind of conspiracy among the leadership. I do not know whether there was in fact a conspiracy in this sense, but I am concerned that if we take too broad a frame of reference, we may overlook some serious problems. My own opinion is that the Greater East Asia War was not a war between Japan and China, but principally a war between Japan and the United States. Moreover, I think that, essentially, it resulted from the spread of the European war, which centered on Nazi Germany, to Japan. If possible, I would like to hear Mr. Tsurumi's view, too.

Japan's Main War Theater: China

PROFESSOR IENAGA: I do not think that war is always a matter of government against government. In the case of China, the elements of a people's war were quite pronounced. For example, the war that was called the Manchurian Incident cannot be limited to the fighting between the army of Zhang Xueliang [Chang Hsüeh-liang] and the Japanese army. The war of resistance against Japan in the puppet state of Manchukuo began at this time and continued without interruption afterward. Even if there were temporary compromises between Japan and the government of Jiang Jieshi [Chiang Kai-shek], the Chinese people's war of resistance in Manchukuo continued throughout. Therefore, we must recognize the historical continuity of the conflict.

Moreover, while Japan and China were at war, the countries that would later become the Allied powers first gave material aid to Japan's aggression against China, in fact materially supported Japan's war. Later, when the situation changed, they stopped exporting strategic materials to Japan, and it became very difficult for Japan to continue the war. In short, it was a question of oil. Without oil you can't wage a war. The problem for Japan quickly became a question of swallowing American demands or not swallowing them. Of course, there was also the problem that the Tripartite Pact had lost any real substance, but the crux of Japan's strategic dilemma was the lack of oil. Japan's rejection of the Hull Note, which incorporated the demands of the Chinese government and called for total withdrawal of Japanese forces from China, became the reason for the outbreak of war between Japan and the United States. Therefore, the ongoing war in China and the subsequent war with the United States, Great Britain, and the Netherlands are inextricably linked.

Most important is the fact that the war in China continued right up to August 1945. For people like me, who consider China to have been the principal theater of World War II as it relates to Japan, it is here that the continuity of the Fifteen-Year War can be discovered. I have discussed this in more detail in my book *Taiheiyō sensō* [The Pacific War], but I think what I have just said responds to the question.

The Problem of Continuity

MR. TSURUMI: I created the phrase "Fifteen-Year War" by accident. The "Manchurian Incident" occurred when I was in the third grade. We were told soon after that it was over, and then the "Shanghai Incident" occurred. Again we were told that it was over, and this time it was the "Japan-China Incident." I was a second-year student in junior high school at the time, and thought of all these incidents as separate events. It was not until after the war that I realized that it was wrong to think of them separately, that it made more sense to see them as a single chain.

So, speaking from my own subjective experience, they were indeed separate incidents. If you are going to write subjectively, it's okay to treat them that way. However, viewing them in a larger historical perspective, you learn more by considering the fifteen years as a unit. With this as a hypothesis, you can see more than before. That's the way it should be, isn't it? A concept is meaningless if it doesn't serve that function.

Professor Hata also pointed out that if you count carefully, from 1931 to 1945, we should call it the "Thirteen-Year War" or the "Fourteen-Year War." Indeed, that's the way we count when we calculate our own age, and yes, calculating precisely, it is thirteen years from 1931 to 1945; and academics no doubt feel that it is important to be precise, but I'm not a scholar. I'm a dilettante. And I made up that phrase thinking that the "Fifteen-Year War" was easier to grasp.

Speaking of precision, when you talk about how far you walked, do you say 1,970.75 meters? After all, you're taller in the morning than you are in the evening. Does anyone specify to the exact second, or the precise millimeter? It's that kind of problem. [Laughter.]

CHAIR: Thank you. I wonder if there is a question or a comment from the floor concerning this problem of the continuity of the Fifteen-Year War. Yes, go ahead.

The Point of No Return

QUESTION: Thank you. I would like to direct my question either to Mr. Tsurumi or to Professor Hata. It is related to the Fifteen-Year War.

If we call the war that began with the Manchurian Incident the Fifteen-Year War, and if there was a chance to end the war before it reached that point, when was the last chance to do so?

In my own opinion, once the Manchurian Incident had begun, the newspapers became thoroughly jingoistic, and it would have been very difficult to check the reckless escalation of the war in China by the Guandong [Kwan-tung] Army. In 1927 and 1928, at the time of troop deployments to Shandong [Shan-tung] and the assassination of Zhang Zuolin [Chang Tso-lin], there was still a non-intervention movement, and after the assassination, when the Guandong Army began to advance into Jinzhou [Ching-chou], the central government did not issue an imperial rescript [to allow the advance].

However, the Japanese people were not told until after the war that Zhang's assassination had been a plot organized by Kōmoto Daisaku. If they had been told at the time, there might have been a chance to stop the war. I am convinced that it would have been possible to prevent the war only at a stage before the Manchurian Incident. Therefore, if we are to question responsibility for the war, I think we should question it at that stage in history, when there was still the possibility of options. At the level of the Japanese people, we should ask about their inability to mount full opposition; or question the responsibility of the political parties, or the responsibility of the highest levels of the political world.

Once the Manchurian Incident had begun, it would have been difficult to turn back the wheels of history. If one accepts this proposition, I think it is best to view the war as a single chain of events. Even though it may have been divided into separate incidents, such as the Manchurian Incident, the China Incident, or the Shanghai Incident, the overall movement was in the direction of war and fascism (though there may be problems with this word). The question is completely hypothetical, but in what period would you place the last chance to prevent the war?

CHAIR: When was the last chance to prevent the war? Changing the wording slightly, we might ask when was "the point of no return." This question can become highly academic, and I don't want to go into it too deeply. I would like to ask Professor Hata or Professor Ienaga for a general response.

PROFESSOR HATA: This "point of no return" is an extremely difficult question. Of course, there was always a "last chance" to prevent the war, right up to the very end. But chances gradually became slimmer. Generally speaking, and on a very commonsense level, I would say that the last real chance to avert the war was in September 1940, when the Tripartite Pact was concluded.

Saionji Kinmochi, the last of the great genrō, was still alive at that time, and there is an anecdote about him that symbolizes, I think, the significance of the Tripartite Pact. Upon hearing of the agreement, he is said to have remarked to his maids, "This means none of you will die natural deaths." Saionji had given up hope, and I think this was Japan's point of no return.

MR. HAGIWARA: I wonder if we can't push the point of no return much further ahead. In fact, I think we can take it right up to the final Japan-US negotiations in November 1941. I am referring, of course, to the two Japanese proposals, A and B, that called for a *modus vivendi* with the United States.

One indication that there was still a chance to avert the war is Hull's famous remark that if Japan was smart it would watch the developing situation in the European theater a little longer. That is, war between Germany and the Soviet Union began on 22 June, and, as you know, the world watched the unfolding of the war with only one question in mind—when would Moscow fall? Ambassador Ōshima tended to swallow almost whole the German propaganda announcements, even when they pushed the date of Moscow's fall up to September, and then to October. By late November, when Hull made the statement, it was obvious to him that Japan, if it were smart, would wait a few months to see the outcome of the war on the eastern front. Of course, Japan did not wait. Hull's statement was made after the so-called Hull Note in November, and was followed by the second proposal by Japan for a *modus vivendi*. This discussion becomes very specialized, so I will omit the details, but basically I think we can push the point of no return further than Professor Hata, up to the American handling of the final Japanese proposal in the negotiations that were going on in November 1941.

CHAIR: Thank you very much. Mr. Tanaka has a comment concerning the Pal judgment.

Mistakes in the Majority Judgment

MR. TANAKA: There are a number of statements in Professor Ienaga's paper concerning Judge Pal's minority opinion. I am quite sure that he has studied it carefully, but I think his interpretation is mistaken in some respects.

There are in all six majority and minority judgments—six statements of judgment; but only one—Pal's—takes up the extremely important issue of the atomic bombing of Hiroshima and Nagasaki and asks, in very strong and unmistakable terms, why the tribunal did not address this issue. This has now become a serious problem. I think Professor Ienaga may have overlooked it.

Furthermore, Pal was by no means suggesting that Japan was right. He did not say that. He questioned whether it was right to impose such a trial on Japan one-sidedly. He said it was a political trial, and that if this political trial were permitted, it would be as if so-called international law did not exist. And he said that the foremost victim of World War II was the truth of law. He viewed the Tokyo trial from that standpoint. And I think he had a point. I won't go into it further. I simply wanted to point this out to Professor Röling as an extremely important fact. I want to ask him . . .

CHAIR: One more minute . . .

MR. TANAKA: Sorry, one more minute will do. There are mistakes in the majority judgment that are truly elementary, or perhaps careless, or perhaps irresponsible. What I want to say is this: How could this happen?

General Matsui Iwane was killed only for his alleged involvement in the Nanjing [Nanking] Incident. He was found innocent of participation in the alleged conspiracy and, indeed, on every other count against him, except Nanjing. In the introduction to the majority judgment, which cost him his life, under the heading "The Nanking Massacre," the judgment states that more than two hundred thousand people were killed, and that twenty thousand women were raped. There are things I want to say; but I have only one minute, so I won't. However, in the individual judgment against Matsui, the figures have become more than ten thousand people killed and several thousand women raped. Which statement is right? He was killed for this. But even an amateur can see from examples like this that there were elementary defects in the judgment.

Again, Araki Sadao was never prime minister, but the judgment designated him as the director of the Materials General Mobilization Plan, an *ex officio* post of the prime minister. Even more ridiculous was the designation of Hirota Kōki, a civilian, as Military Affairs Counselor. It was due to this designation that Hirota was killed. The majority judgment contains major errors like these. Was Professor Röling aware of these mistakes? Or, as I asked earlier, was it not true that you and the other dissenting justices were excluded from the deliberations by the "gang of six" that drafted the majority judgment—that in the end all you could do was submit your own opinions separately? This is what I want to ask Professor Röling.

CHAIR: Professor Röling has already pointed out that there were a number of mistakes in the text of the judgment. As to how these mistakes arose, there is the problem that emerged earlier of professional ethics, which makes it difficult for him to discuss these issues publicly even at this late date. I ask your understanding.

Concerning the minority opinion written by Judge Pal, the minutes will record your comments as a personal opinion. Professor Ōnuma has a question for Professor Ienaga.

The Danger of Legalism

PROFESSOR ŌNUMA: In his presentation, Professor Ienaga stated that he felt great shame for the failure of the Japanese to prosecute war criminals, especially in light of the fact that West Germany is prosecuting German war criminals even now. I agree that it is cause for serious reflection, as Mr. Kinoshita argued in his paper, that the Japanese were not able to pursue the issue of war guilt themselves. I also agree that this problem, as such, is an extremely important one. However, and this is related to the arguments presented yesterday by Professor Paik, as well as to the issues raised yesterday and today by Professor Ipsen, I think there may be differences, in terms of their respective historical backgrounds, between the cases of Germany and Japan that explain why Germany has had to continue prosecuting war criminals. As I said yesterday, while it is true that acts corresponding to crimes against humanity were committed in the areas under Japanese control, the scale and degree of these acts were a little different from those of the crimes against humanity committed by the Nazis. To lump Japanese war crimes together with Nazi crimes would be ludicrous.

This in no way contradicts Mr. Tsurumi's proposal concerning the importance of having a method by which we can think about the Tokyo trial and war responsibility from an Asian perspective. On the contrary, I intend to continue to assert precisely the same point.

Other Means of Questioning War Responsibility

However, I feel that we should not place excessive demands on the role that can be played by law. Of course, as a scholar of international law, I find it unfortunate that law cannot fulfill in fact what it can fulfill in theory. For example, I received something of a shock from Mr. Tsurumi's presentation. Dr. Röling had pointed out earlier that the question of the individual's duty of disobedience toward the state was raised in both the Tokyo and Nuremberg trials. Mr. Tsurumi said that he was surprised to hear this, and that it was too bad that the peace movement had not been aware of that fact. We international legal scholars have taken it for granted that the principle of the individual's duty not to obey illegal orders of the state had been established by the Tokyo and Nuremberg trials. But this obvious legal principle has not been communicated. In this sense, the law, and perhaps we legal scholars, have not performed the function that is intrinsic to the law and to legal scholarship. I find this failure extremely unfortunate. But I wonder if it is not a mistake to expect too much of the role that should be played by law. Yesterday, I stated that the concept of leaders' responsibility emerged at Nuremberg and Tokyo, and that this was an extremely significant legal concept. At the same time, I added that this concept should not necessarily be limited to criminal responsibility.

Professor Ipsen has stated that today, when no international criminal court exists, the pursuit of individual responsibility must be considered highly dubious. But I don't think we should rely exclusively on the individual's *criminal* responsibility. As I suggested yesterday, aren't there other ways to question the responsibility of state leaders? Moreover, the pursuit of individual responsibility for those who are not national leaders can be taken over by other forums than criminal courts. Indeed, such alternatives are sometimes preferable.

For example, it is not that easy to determine which is preferable: to pursue responsibility for the acts committed by Japan against colonial peoples under the old imperial system through criminal proceedings, or for this and succeeding generations to take over and pursue the problem in other ways. Personally, I find it difficult to accept the opinion that Japanese should be ashamed because we did not pursue responsibility in criminal tribunals. I would like to hear Professor Ienaga's response to these points.

CHAIR: Thank you, Professor Ōnuma. Professor Ienaga, would you care to respond?

Law for the People

PROFESSOR IENAGA: The comments Professor Ōnuma refers to were added on the spur of the moment, and I fear they have caused some confusion. What I said was that I felt ashamed that there were almost no Japanese who died fighting against their own government—that there were no Dietrich Bonhoeffers, no Italian Resistance. I did not say that I was ashamed at the failure of the Japanese to pursue criminal responsibility. This is a trivial problem of words. In fact, as I stated in my conclusion, I believe that responsibility should be pursued in ways independent of state power. On that point my position is not necessarily opposed to Professor Ōnuma's.

However, if this leads, then, to the question of whether we need not pursue legal responsibility, I refuse to join either those who believe in the omnipotence of law or those who subscribe to legal nihilism. I believe that the law should be used, positively, relatively, and vigorously, to protect the rights of the people and prevent abuses of state power. And I am in fact using the law in that way today.

In general, I think the problem has its roots in the fact that the people of Japan were not able to end the war through their own efforts, and that they were not able to bring to justice with their own hands those who promoted and provoked the war. In my presentation, I gave the examples of Bonhoeffer and the Italian Resistance without mentioning the people of Germany.

It is true that the German people were not able in the end to overthrow their Nazi masters. However, as one can see in such books as *Lautlose Aufstand* [Silent Insurrection], a vast number of Germans died struggling against the Nazis. Their struggle ultimately was in vain, but that is one kind of struggle. In Italy, an insurrection of the people had liberated the north before the arrival of the Allied armies. In contrast, the Japanese had not been able to end the war in this way, so that pursuit of responsibility for the war by the Japanese people themselves was already impossible right at the outset. Herein lies the problem.

As I have argued in an article in *Hōgaku semina*, I believe that, legally speaking, it is possible even today to pursue the legal responsibility of those who started the war, even under domestic Japanese law. But what I think is most important today, as I stated in my conclusion, is the kind of pursuit of responsibility that was suggested by Sartre in his statement opening the Russell tribunal. On this point, again, I am not in fundamental disagreement with Professor Ōnuma.

CHAIR: Thank you very much. Professor Ipsen has a question or comment on this discussion.

Nazis Prosecuted for Crimes under Existing German Law

PROFESSOR IPSEN: Thank you, Mr. Chairman. I would like to comment briefly on what Professor Ōnuma just said. There is indeed a basic distinction between the crimes of Japan and Germany. Until 1933, Germany had a well-established legal system. This legal order was violated more and more blatantly during the ensuing twelve years by the Nazi regime. It is for this very reason that we were able to prosecute war crimes, and that we are able to continue to do so today. It is not, as Professor Ōnuma suggests, only a distinction in the magnitude of the crimes. The fact is that we are prosecuting and punishing war criminals according to the laws they violated during the war. This was our national law. We are applying an existing penal code, and this, I think, is the principal difference between the Japanese situation and the German situation.

I would also like to comment briefly on the question of individual responsibility in international law. If I were asked whether there should be individual responsibility for criminal matters in international law, I would of course say, yes, there should be. If I am asked, as an international lawyer, if individual criminal responsibility already exists under international law, my answer must be no. As an international lawyer, I have to look to a rule of treaty law or of customary law, and in this respect I can only state that there is neither a rule of treaty law nor a rule of customary law that actually affirms individual responsibility in criminal affairs. Thank you, Mr. Chairman.

The Extension of Responsibility to Leaders

DR. RÖLING: The statement that at this moment international responsibility for committing international crimes is not recognized in the world is amazing to me.

In the Red Cross conventions, for example, international criminal responsibility is treated extensively. In this respect, it is perhaps worthwhile, even at this late moment, to stress the differences between Nuremberg and Tokyo. Nuremberg only prosecuted and condemned those who had committed the crimes themselves or had ordered the crimes. In the case of the Tokyo trial, it was far more difficult to find general orders to commit crimes. And the leaders that were accused did not commit the crimes with their own hands. Thus, in Tokyo, the main question was the responsibility for omission—the failure to prevent the continuation of crimes of which the leaders were aware and which they had the power and the duty to prevent. In this respect, legally, the Tokyo trial contributed to the development of an international responsibility, which was later confirmed in the treaty that was added to the Geneva Convention of 1949, in which it was codified that responsibility exists not only for those who have committed the crimes or ordered them but also for those who failed to put an end to crimes. This latter responsibility exists legally under three conditions: that they knew of the crimes, that they had the power to prevent them, and that they were responsible in that specific field. That is important, because in the heat of battle people easily commit crimes. If the responsibility also extends to those who sit quietly behind tables, it is much easier for them to approach the question of what is expected of them under international law.

A second point, and it is just a question to Professor Ipsen, is this. I had the impression that at this moment in Germany trials take place only for crimes against humanity, and that conventional war crimes are no longer tried. Could Professor Ipsen give me some information on this point?

War Trials Based on German Criminal Law

PROFESSOR IPSEN: To answer Professor Röling's question, it is quite true that the crimes that are tried before German courts at this time are crimes that could be termed crimes against humanity. However, they are tried and punished as murder on the basis of our national criminal law.

If I may make a second brief remark, I was one of the negotiators on the additional protocols to the Geneva Convention, which Professor Röling has just quoted. I have this protocol before me. It states, in article 68, paragraph 1, ''The High Contracting Parties and the Parties to the conflict shall repress grave breaches, and take measures necessary to suppress all other breaches of the Conventions or of this Protocol which result from a failure to act when under a duty to do so.'' All negotiating states were in accord that this means the trial and punishment of violators by the respective national laws of the parties to the convention. Thank you.

CHAIR: Thank you. I think we often do not understand that the prosecution of Nazi war crimes is conducted only against crimes against humanity, and that they are prosecuted on the basis of domestic German law.

There have been some complaints, especially from Professor Ōnuma, that we have not heard enough from younger members of the audience. I would now like to recognize a question from a junior at Aoyama Gakuin University. It is a question for Professor Ienaga.

Pointing Out the Defects of the Tokyo Trial in Textbooks

QUESTION: In his paper, Professor Ienaga touched on the textbook problem, and I would like to ask him just one question about that.

The problem of whether the Tokyo trial was conducted with proper legal procedure, and that of the rightness or wrongness of Japanese actions in modern history, are not problems that completely overlap, but separate issues. It is quite clear that a recognition of the legal defects in the Tokyo trial is not an affirmation of Japan's acts of war.

Unlike Professor Yokota Kisaburō's work at Hattori House at the time, current scholarship is exposing the underside of the trial and also clarifying the minority opinions. The fraudulent character of the Tokyo trial under international law is an objective truth, attested to by the fact that there is no legal scholar who doesn't recognize this. Based on this, I believe that textbooks should record the fact that the trial was legally flawed under international law. I would like to ask Professor Ienaga for his thoughts on this point. And, if he disagrees, I would like to hear his grounds for disagreeing.

CHAIR: Thank you. Professor Ienaga, would you care to comment?

PROFESSOR IENAGA: The problem I raised is that of the Ministry of Education's intentions in demanding revisions of textbooks. The demand that I excise the truth that it was a reckless war and the demand that I write that the Tokyo trial was a one-sided affair carried out by the victors are a matched set. That is where I perceive the problem to be. Basically, I cannot agree to write merely that the Tokyo trial was a trial with flaws.

CHAIR: Thank you. Here is a related question.

Concerning the Unfairness of the Tribunal's Findings

QUESTION: I too am in the generation that grew up in the postwar period. My education, from the top of my head to the tips of my toes, was that of the postwar period. I don't know if it was Professor Ienaga's book, but I had to study a textbook of Japanese history. I would like to ask Professor Ienaga this question: Looking back now on these Japanese history textbooks, aren't almost all of them highly colored by the Tokyo tribunal's view of historical fact?

Professor Ienaga stated that the tribunal had defects, that aspects of it were unfair. For example, there was the fact that the victorious countries judged the defeated country, or that the misdeeds of the victors were ignored, and that the indictments were political, that is, motivated by expediency. Professor Ienaga raised all these points. But I would like to ask about the unfairness of the trial from a slightly different viewpoint.

I have not seen the complete transcript of the trial, but a great deal of the evidence submitted by the defense was dismissed as irrelevant. I will not attempt to give all of the examples, but consider the case of hearsay evidence. The defense must have had more hearsay evidence than the prosecution, but the prosecution's hearsay evidence was accepted by the tribunal while that of the defense was rejected. Again, evidence in the form of newspaper articles submitted by the prosecution was accepted, but newspaper evidence submitted by the defense was ruled irrelevant. There are countless examples of this kind of unfairness in the selection of admissible evidence.

What I would like to say here is that a true trial bases its findings on a comprehensive selection of evidence, whether the testimony of witnesses or documentary evidence. If that selection was so unfair . . . At the end of his minority opinion, Judge Pal listed several examples of evidence that was not accepted by the majority judgment. Many of the areas covered by this evidence are related to the issues raised by Mr. Kojima: evidence related to the state of public order in China before Japan's entry, evidence related to how the situation changed after Japan began operations in China, and evidence that the signatories to the Pact of Paris reserved the right of self-defense. From my viewpoint, the tribunal's findings of fact were assembled on the basis of an extremely unfair selection of evidence.

As someone stated yesterday, the Tokyo tribunal, unlike its Nuremberg counterpart, issued a condemnation of history. I would like to ask Professor Ienaga whether his statement that there were defects in the trial, and that it was an unfair trial, includes this unfairness in the selection of evidence.

CHAIR: Thank you. Professor Ienaga?

PROFESSOR IENAGA: Since I have not compared the huge volume of evidence and the specific findings of the judgment, I would like to reserve comment on the question of the court's findings on historical fact. As I said earlier, however, I recognize that the trial was not necessarily fair. At the same time, if you listened to all of my presentation, you will have understood that my conclusion is that the unfair aspects of the trial do not mean that we should totally reject it. That is why I could not suddenly write that the trial was unfair in my textbook. There are many mistaken judgments closer to hand, in the trials that take place in modern Japanese courts, but you cannot write about every single one of these cases in a textbook. In my textbook, I limited myself to recording the facts concerning the Tokyo trial, without offering any particular evaluation, because to do so would have required an enormous amount of space. Overall balance required that I do so.

CHAIR: Thank you. I believe Professor Yu would like to speak to this issue.

Thieves Judging a Thief

PROFESSOR YU: Concerning the problem of the evaluation of the Tokyo trial, I would like to state my thoughts about the fact that aspects of the Tokyo trial were extremely unfair.

I stole, but you stole too. This has been a topic of our discussions already. From that angle, both parties are the same. And seen from this perspective, I think it is a reasonable proposition. From the Chinese standpoint, the first people who stole from China were the English. At the Tokyo trial, however, England was on the side doing the judging. Then came the Dutch, and then the French, and finally the Americans. In the Chinese view, they were all thieves. So those who had stolen judge one who had stolen—thieves judging a thief. [Laughter.] There is an aspect of unfairness in this. However, I would like to say this: the Tokyo trial was a trial of a limited historical period, but, one day, mankind will sit in judgment on colonialism from a longer historical perspective. It may be one hundred years of history; it may be two hundred years. But mankind will eventually sit in judgment.

Still, in terms of the historical period on which the trial sat in judgment, the Tokyo trial was a trial of those who had stolen in the limited period from 1928 to 1945. Therefore, I think the concept of historical limits is essential in this discussion. The question boils down to who was the worst thief at this stage in history.

The Villains: First England, Then Japan

In the Chinese view, when we take a longer historical look, England was the first thief. England opened China's doors to aggression by the great powers. In this perspective the Chinese people see England as the villain. But in the twenties, the thirties, and first half of the forties, the enemy most feared by the Chinese people was Japan. Thus, if one asks who provoked the most savage war against the people of the world in the period from the twenties to the first half of the forties, there is no hiding the fact that it was the fascist states of Germany, Italy, and Japan. Therefore, evaluations of the Tokyo and Nuremberg trials are no good unless they take into account the fact that they were the principal trials of the principal culprits.

Of course, there was an aspect of unfairness—people who had stolen were part of the tribunal, and they were not prosecuted for their criminal responsibility. And it was because these people did not learn the lessons of the Tokyo trial that such conflicts as the Vietnam War would occur.

The United States entered the world stage as a superpower after the collapse of the Axis powers and, as a new aggressive state, launched its war in Vietnam. Professor Minear has suggested that this can be viewed as an extension of the ideology of the Tokyo trial, and I think this is true. However, while I believe there is a connection in terms of thought, I wonder if, from a temporal view, it would not be better to see the two periods as separate. There are aspects of the trial, in terms of law and ideology, that connect to the preceding period, and aspects that connect to the subsequent postwar period. However, I think it is essential to precisely define the period under discussion when evaluating the trial. [Applause.]

CHAIR: Thank you very much. Two people have their hands raised in the back. Are your questions relevant here? . . . Very well, you have the floor.

The Problem of How Mankind Should Live

QUESTION: Thank you. I am a graduate student specializing in modern Japanese history. But I would like to speak as a member of the younger generation born after the war, rather than as a person specializing in history, and ask the opinion of my seniors gathered here.

I was born after the war, in 1952. As was suggested in one of the papers yesterday, Japan has not been directly involved in a war since World War II; it has maintained peace, somewhat paradoxically, by means of article 9 of the constitution [which renounces war]. However, if we look realistically at recent conditions (and I think this was also Professor Ienaga's point), we see that a structure that can be termed a "tendency to the right" is developing very rapidly. The reality is that, despite article 9, Japanese military capabilities are expanding. Of course, there may be various ways to interpret this, but when I was little, the Self-Defense Force was not the large military force it is today. Up to this moment, I myself have not been able to do anything to stop this expansion. But I cannot conceive of this continuing military expansion, despite the "peace constitution," as the action of a country that desires world peace.

I am greatly impressed that international legal scholars should discuss world peace and efforts to eliminate crimes against humanity. But I wonder if we wouldn't get more positive results by studying the issues in terms that are more concrete. How can we Japanese make the most of the Japanese constitution's orientation toward peace? How can we relate it to the world peace that is sought in international law? And what actual achievements should we leave behind in the quest to create peace?

In this sense, I think there were some points in Mr. Tsurumi's paper that were misunderstood. As a Japanese, I too feel strongly that the legal consciousness of the Tokyo trial has not taken root among the Japanese people. However, I do not believe that this fact makes the trial meaningless. Rather, I think the biggest problem facing us today is how to go beyond the complex structure of peace that exists in contemporary Japan. We young people are the ones who will go on living and having children. And having listened to the discussions of the last two days, I find it hard to take that the greatest theme, that of how mankind can live in the future—and this includes the threat of nuclear war—has been reduced to a matter of whether the Tokyo trial was fair or not. I would like to ask the opinions of the speakers. [Applause.]

CHAIR: Thank you very much for this opinion. Another young person had his hand up. Yes, you have the floor.

One Side Condemning Another

QUESTION: I'm a twenty-three year old American. This question is directed to Professor Minear, or to anybody who would like to answer. Leaving all the legal jargon aside, and all the noble intentions, its seems that the Nuremberg and Tokyo trials did very little to stop violence in the postwar period. There are obviously as many wars going on now as ever. Not only did it do very little, but I wonder if it did harm, in that it gave the victorious powers, let's say the USSR and the United States for example, a sense of moral supremacy that allowed them in later years to throw their weight around the world, thinking simply that they were right.

I realize there has to be some kind of forum not to forget the realities of war, but it seems to me that a forum in which one side condemns another can only do harm. It gives the condemning side the feeling that what they have done is right and that they can continue their actions, which is what seems to have happened since then.

Now I wonder, first of all, if you think it might have been better had there not been a trial at all—whether, if this situation comes up again, it would be better to avoid having such a trial, and whether there isn't some other kind of forum in which to remember these things, and keep a high consciousness about these things, without anybody condemning anyone else, or without anybody using any kind of shield of moral supremacy.

One example is: if you have a definition of a war of aggression and of a war of liberation—well, to Israel, the PLO is waging a war of aggression. But to the PLO it is waging a war of liberation. Now, if you have those definitions, you can wage a war of aggression and hide behind the definition of a war of liberation. So the definition is not only meaningless, it might do harm, in giving the person who is waging a war of aggression a shield behind which to hide. If you have any comments about that, I'd appreciate it.

CHAIR: Thank you very much. [Applause.] Professor Minear, might I ask you to respond?

Limited Revenge

PROFESSOR MINEAR: In response to your first point, about the creation of moral supremacy, I agree entirely. I am almost tempted to suggest that you read a piece of my book [laughter], because that was part of my argument for the dangers of the Tokyo trial in terms of American thinking.

In that sense, if I could refer again to Vietnam, I think the role of Vietnam has been to destroy that dangerous American sense of supremacy, moral superiority, or to begin to undermine it.

As to your point about alternatives to a trial, that is a difficult question. As you know, Stalin and Churchill spoke, apparently in a joking manner, about executing some fifty thousand Germans, and presumably a similar number of Japanese, without trial. One function of the Tokyo trial, it seems to me, for all its weaknesses, was to limit the amount of revenge exacted. If there had not been a trial, there would have been more people put to death. If there had not been a trial, there would not have been minority opinions. There would not have been defense counsel like Mr. Furness taking an active role. So I think there can be positive things said about a trial. But I go back ultimately to Professor Röling's earlier comment, that the next time around there may be nobody to be defendant or prosecutor.

CHAIR: Thank you very much. Dr. Pritchard has a few words to say.

The Benefits of the Evidence of the Trial

DR. PRITCHARD: In response to several of the questions from the floor, I think that—both in regard to rejection of defense evidence and, indeed, on the question of any alternatives to a trial—had there been anything other than a trial, we wouldn't have the benefit of the terrific amount of evidence that has been produced and can be debated by historians, and, perhaps through textbooks, can eventually be transmitted to the rest of the population. Obviously, the final word has not been spoken in terms of any of these textbooks. The records of the trials have not been fully utilized.

There is, in fact, a rough parity in the evidence that has been produced on both sides. A great deal of defense evidence was rejected wrongly. Nevertheless, there are some 26,800 pages, by a rough calculation I've done just now, of the transcripts on just the defense case, compared to some 21,200 pages on the prosecution's case. I wouldn't actually quibble about the bits between them, but there's a rough parity there. So I think from the historian's point of view it would be very deplorable if that amount of evidence, or that kind of evidence, were not available for discussion and debate.

Obviously, if there are legal advantages to having a trial in the progression of international law, then that's an additional benefit. But, strictly from the historian's point of view, it would have been a shame had there been no trial. I come to that conclusion reluctantly, because I myself have very great reservations about the fairness of any international trial. Nevertheless, there's the evidence. And we no longer have to be bound by the judgment. We can look at the evidence. That's where you should look, not at the judgment. Be guided by the judgment and the separate opinions, by all means, but look at the records.

CHAIR: Thank you very much. Professor Awaya?

Subjective Feelings of Responsibility Among the Japanese Themselves

PROFESSOR AWAYA: I would like to say something in relation to the earlier discussion concerning the Japanese constitution. Actually, I had not yet entered elementary school when the Tokyo trial began, and I too have no real feeling of that period. Recently, I looked at the press coverage of the trial at the time; the censorship carried out by GHQ at the time may have been a factor, but the newspapers carried reports almost totally supportive of the trial.

Even in their editorials about the trial, the various newspapers argued that for the sake of preventing future wars, the Japanese people must themselves reflect not only on the responsibility of individual wartime leaders but also on the war responsibility of Japan itself as an aggressor state, and that the nation must push boldly ahead on the course of a peaceful state as prescribed by the new constitution.

Of course, the editorial tone of the press may have changed thereafter; but this tone was characteristic not only of newspapers at the time, but also of the thought of Japan's intellectuals. Mr. Tsurumi seems not to have a very high regard for intellectuals, but consider, for example, the subsequent development of the Japanese peace movement. It emerged from discussions among intellectuals in such groups as the Heiwa Mondai Danwa-kai (Peace Studies Group), which recognized Japan's war responsibility as of primary concern and dealt specifically with its relation to article 9 of the peace constitution. This movement was by no means unrelated to the thought of the masses.

Concerning the editorial stance of the newspapers at this time, I am particularly interested in the editorials by Ishibashi Tanzan in the *Tōyō keizai shinpō* [Oriental Economist]. I was attracted to them partly because Ishibashi pointed to the issue of the responsibility of the Allies, but essentially Ishibashi perceived the trial from the viewpoint of the self-conscious sense of guilt shared collectively by the Japanese. His viewpoint, which linked this collective sense of guilt to article 9 of the constitution, failed subsequently to be convincing, not just to intellectuals but also to the great majority of Japanese. However, it seems to me that such a current existed even in the contemporary context, and that it continues today. This may be a strained interpretation, and I would very much like to hear Mr. Tsurumi's reaction to it.

CHAIR: Mr. Okamoto has a question for Professor Ienaga. I believe the gist of his argument is that what the trial tried was "emperor-system fascism." Mr. Okamoto, please elaborate.

Emperor-System Fascism and the Problem of the Newspapers

MR. OKAMOTO: Professor Awaya just spoke about the editorial stance of the newspapers toward the trial, and I would like to comment briefly on this point.

In Professor Ipsen's West Germany, the principal newspapers were forced to close during the war or went out of circulation voluntarily. In the case of Japan, unfortunately, not a single newspaper ceased publication. This is an important point in considering the newspapers of the time and, say, their editorial positions.

My second point is that while it is probably true that the trial had defects, it did pass judgment on prewar Japan. It did pass judgment on the fascist politics carried out by the Tokkō [Special Secret Service Section], the Kenpei [Military Police], and other groups. The trial even raised the issue of women, who had not been allowed to participate in politics under the fascist regime. I think the trial deserves high praise on all these points, and I believe that this was the candid perception of the Japanese people at the time. I would like to ask Professor Ienaga's opinion on this point.

CHAIR: Thank you. Professor Ienaga?

PROFESSOR IENAGA: It is extremely difficult for me to answer if the question is limited to whether or not the tribunal passed judgment on "emperor-system fascism." There are various objections to the phrase, and I do not use it myself. However, if I understand your main point correctly, I think that the trial did have that aspect, too.

Moreover, as Professor Awaya has suggested, the reception given the trial by the newspapers at the time was relatively favorable. I still have a clear memory of the harsh criticism directed at the motion for dismissal in defense counsel Kiyose's opening statement. My own interpretation is that this was by no means an opportunistic attempt by the newspapers to ingratiate themselves with GHQ. Rather, I believe that these editorials reflected the feelings of the Japanese people of the time very much as they were.

CHAIR: Thank you. A younger member of the audience has his hand up in the back of the room.

The Extension of Leaders' Responsibility to Pollution

QUESTION: Thank you. I'm not all that young, but . . . [Laughter.]

Perhaps what I have to say will not directly address the subject at hand. I have been deeply impressed by the discussions since yesterday, and especially the remarks by the panelists. They have been highly suggestive, and suffused with a special kind of passion, especially concerning the question of how we can make the best use of the Tokyo trial from now on—where we can discover its positive significance. In this regard, I would like the participants to discuss—or, since that may be impossible in this symposium, to think about—one concrete direction for the future that has not been taken up so far.

It is related to the concept of leaders' responsibility, which has been one of the topics of debate since yesterday. Professor Ōnuma argued that leaders' responsibility was not merely responsibility under criminal law but could be pursued in other ways. I do not understand what he means in concrete terms, but in my own opinion I wonder if we cannot make use of this idea in a way that will go beyond the new legal concepts, such as crimes against peace and crimes against humanity, that were lodged against the defendants in the Tokyo and Nuremberg trials at the end of World War II—in a way that would go beyond even the concept of restrictions on war or on military activity. Indeed, I have often wondered if we cannot establish a system of legislation and legal concepts that could be used more broadly and more actively against mistakes or defects in policy making and execution.

Environmental pollution, for example, is a very modern problem that has become extremely serious today in the advanced industrial nations. Especially in Japan, a large part of the pollution problem can be traced to mistaken policies, or policies that did not go far enough. I am not suggesting the death penalty for anyone, but a system of legislation based on leaders' responsibility would enable the various citizens' groups that are protesting against pollution problems to pursue the responsibility of the government officials concerned—to establish clearly that illegal acts were committed by policy makers and public administrators.

The concept of national reparations is firmly established in capitalist countries today. Of course, there is the contradiction that while the responsibility for reparations is borne by the state, it is the taxpayer who ultimately has to pay. But since this is a conference where there are many legal scholars and other people connected with the law, I wonder if we cannot use the remaining time more effectively by discussing how we can move in this direction in the future? The example I have given is only one idea, but I hope it will encourage further discussion along these lines. [Applause.]

CHAIR: Thank you. An even younger person has his hand up.

Japan's Responsibility toward Asia

QUESTION: I am a twenty-eight year old laborer, and I am attending a citizens' lecture series dealing with Japan's aggression in Asia. I would like to say two or three things about my reactions to the discussions yesterday and today.

All of the panelists have emphasized that the Tokyo trial was unfair in various senses and that it was a political trial. And, at the same time, they have discussed how we can understand its positive significance today. Professor Ōnuma argued yesterday that the Fifteen-Year War was the inevitable result of Japan's modern history and that the Japanese people as a whole bear responsibility for that history. I agree completely with Professor Ōnuma's opinion. A little while ago, the term *Fifteen-Year War* became an issue, with discussion of whether or not it had continuity. However, as Professor Yu from the People's Republic stated, when we think of Japan's war responsibility toward Asia, we should consider the war to have begun with the deployment of troops to Taiwan in 1874.

Japan's responsibility toward Asia for the war has been mentioned over and over again, but, in fact, it has not been discussed very much. Professor Than of Burma pointed out that not enough evidence was gathered from Asian countries and argued that crimes committed in Burma should have been tried in Burma by the Burmese people. I think that is true.

I have studied some history, and I think the research that has been done since the seventies has gone a long way toward uncovering exactly what Japan did in Asia. Yesterday, Professor Awaya said that there is a need to make the facts even clearer by using the documents submitted to the Tokyo tribunal, and I think that is true. But people like me, who received our educations after the war, didn't learn very much about what Japan did to the rest of Asia, and I think it is more important for people in my generation to make crystal clear for themselves what Japan's war in Asia was all about.

In 1980, Professor Ōnuma wrote an article in the *Asahi shinbun* of 18 and 19 December. One problem, he suggests, is that even though Japan's existence as a colonial power was negated by its defeat, Japan itself did not realize this. I too wonder if that is not the biggest problem.

In particular, I think we need to consider the fact that, during the Pacific War, Koreans and Taiwanese were conscripted and mobilized, and, moreover, that Indonesians were mobilized as laborers or forced to act as paramilitary reinforcements to the Japanese army. Don't we need to think more about that issue? After listening to the discussion yesterday and today, I have the feeling that the perspective on Japan's war responsibility toward other Asian countries is not clear enough, so I have taken this opportunity to state my views.

CHAIR: Thank you for your opinion. Professor Ōnuma, would you please comment.

The International Significance of the Peace Constitution

PROFESSOR ŌNUMA: I would like to say just a word. A little earlier, among the questions from members of the younger generation, there was one which stated an opinion something like this: Japan has a peace constitution, but in reality isn't Japan gradually pursuing a line of military expansion? I would like to point out that when I said in my own paper that Japan has held the rate of military expenditures to a low level, I very carefully emphasized that I was speaking *comparatively and relatively* and *in international terms*.

Isn't it true that up to now we have used the peace constitution only passively? I am referring to the excuse we have used in response to American demands that Japan rearm itself—the argument that "we have article 9, so we can't respond to your demands." Speaking from an international perspective, there is a different aspect to this argument. That is, we cannot plead the exigencies of our internal situation and refuse to take actions based on international agreements, or principles of international cooperation, and expect that refusal to be seen as anything but national egoism. For instance, it is the same with the problem of Japan's refusal to accept refugees. It would be strange indeed if the argument from domestic conditions—that because, as some people say, Japan's population density is so high it cannot accept refugees—were to be accepted at the international level.

It is precisely in this sense that I have misgivings about the fact that Japanese constitutional law has always been used passively, as an excuse based on internal conditions. Rather, I believe we should take a stance that asserts much more actively the positive significance of the Japanese constitution, and that we should do so on the basis of a problem consciousness which asks how we can make the fullest use of vital aspects of Nuremberg and Tokyo—how we as Japanese citizens can exploit the concepts of leaders' responsibility and the duty of the individual to disobey illegal orders by the state.

Thus, I am not arguing for an across-the-board legitimization of Japan's conduct since World War II. What I am saying is that Japan's conduct, at least since the war, has been *better* than that of the superpowers—the United States and the Soviet Union. I am saying that despite pressure from the United States, Japan has maintained its peace constitution and, on the basis of that constitution, has limited military expenditures as a percentage of GNP to a much lower level than the United States, the Soviet Union, and other powerful countries. And, finally, I am saying that despite the advanced level of its technology, Japan has not embarked on a program of arms sales. Japan has not played the merchant of death to any great extent. Of course, these statements are made strictly in comparison with the United States and the Soviet Union, or with Britain and France.

In this sense, I think we can assert more strongly the significance of the Japanese constitution and say that Japanese actions can become a model for emulation, at least in the sphere of the use of military force in the postwar world; I think we can have that much confidence. This is by no means to give blanket approval to all of Japan's actions since World War II. It is only to say that Japan's behavior has been superior to that of the United States, the Soviet Union, and others. I cannot emphasize this too strongly, for I do not want to be misunderstood on this point.

Japan's Responsibility toward Asia, and the Importance of Civil Disobedience

A previous speaker stated the opinion that Japan's responsibility vis-à-vis Asia is an important issue. I agree completely. This young person said he got the impression that discussions on this point at the symposium had been vague. But I would like him to think that part of the significance of this symposium lies in the fact that such viewpoints at least came to the surface. Up to now, discussions of the Tokyo trial have completely ignored this point. Only Judge Pal of India, in his minority opinion, put his finger on this question. Moreover, even Judge Pal's minority opinion, like Professor Minear's *Victors' Justice*, has been made use of in Japan, most unfortunately, as an argument for

"Japan's innocence," as an argument affirming wholesale Japan's actions in the past.

Under these conditions, while it is only a very small step forward, the fact that a viewpoint encompassing Japan's responsibility toward Asia has emerged in this symposium, a subject previously ignored, has provided a perspective for future study of the Tokyo trial.

Finally, I would like to call attention to another important viewpoint, emphasized by Dr. Röling. It is the question of how we can link the concept of civil disobedience to international law. I think this view deserves recognition as a vital first step, one of the most important raised by the symposium. Thank you very much.

CHAIR: Thank you, Professor Ōnuma. Professor Hata has a comment that returns us to an earlier argument. Professor Hata?

PROFESSOR HATA: Rather than returning to an earlier argument, this has to do with a point raised in the question just before Professor Ōnuma's remarks. That is, what can we do from now on? How can we make the Tokyo trial into an effective instrument in the present and the future? I am certainly not qualified to answer this question, but it occurred to me that up to now we have been discussing the Tokyo trial and its implications largely from the point of view of international law. I wonder if we have forgotten its implications for domestic law.

I say this because many of the problems dealt with by the Tokyo trial arose from contemporary Japanese state institutions, and particularly from the corruption of the military. At the time, Japan was a modern nation-state with an established system of law. There was a system of criminal law; the military too had a system of criminal law. Under the latter, men such as Kōmoto Daisaku, whose name came up in our discussions yesterday, Ishihara Kanji, Itagaki Seishirō, and Matsui Iwane would have been given the death penalty as a matter of course. That is, all of them had committed acts that were subject to the death penalty under Japan's own code of military criminal law. The fact that they could not be punished, but on the contrary were made into heroes, is one aspect of the stark reality of Japan at the time.

Matsui Iwane, for example, knew something of what had happened in the Nanjing (Nanking) Incident but chose to overlook it. But even if he knew nothing at all, the fact remains that he was not able to control his subordinates. Even under Japan's old martial code of *bushidō* [the way of the warrior], this is completely inexcusable. That is why Matsui broke down in tears when he apologized to the emperor for the incident. Matsui should have been punished under Japanese domestic law.

But the case of Hirota is extremely difficult. In his actions as foreign minister, there was certainly dereliction of duty. That is, despite the fact that he could have resisted the military, he did not. I think that is dereliction of duty. But it is problematic whether he would have been subject to punishment under Japanese law.

My point, however, is that if Japanese domestic law had been functioning properly, Japan's actions before the war would have been much different. Therefore, one of things that we should do now and in the future is to establish and maintain an effective system of domestic law. Moreover, we must use this system effectively to check the actions of our government. The same holds for other countries, too. I think there is a good deal of room for us to consider the issues raised by the Tokyo trial not only from the perspective of international law but also from that of domestic law. Thank you.

CHAIR: Thank you very much. Whether we call it dereliction of duty or a failure of leadership, I think that Hirota's piloting of the Japanese ship of state was badly mistaken in what were, after all, areas of vital importance. In terms of the decision-making process, for example, I think he must bear a good deal of the responsibility for the policies that were adopted in this period.

There is a question from the floor. Please go ahead.

QUESTION: I have a question for Dr. Röling. It may be out of place in this atmosphere, but . . .

CHAIR: We have just reached a high point in the discussion. I hope you won't destroy the mood . . .

QUESTION: I consider Dr. Röling to be an outstanding representative of Dutch good sense, and I would very much like to ask him this question. I believe that the Dutch, given their long history of involvement with Japan since first establishing their trading concession on Dejima [in Nagasaki harbor], understand Japan better than any other foreigners. When negotiations were going on between Japan and Holland, and Japan asked Holland to sell it oil, why did the Dutch refuse? [Laughter.] And why did the Dutch blindly go along with the United States and Britain in their oil embargo? If the Dutch had been so kind as to sell oil to Japan, then the Greater East Asia War would never have happened, and Holland would not have lost the Dutch East Indies. That is the gist of my question. It is an extremely difficult question, but I would like very much to hear your views on this point. [Laughter.]

The Oil Embargo and the China Question

DR. RÖLING: Well, I was not in a position to know all the circumstances that led the Dutch government to join its allies in countermeasures with respect to Japan.

It has already been said in this discussion that the link between the Sino-Japanese War and the Pacific War was exactly that the Allied powers reacted against what happened in China, and that reaction implied the embargo on oil. I think it was a justified measure. I don't know the exact motives of the Dutch government, but from the documents we saw during the trial, it was quite clear that if war began, Holland and Indonesia would not have been excluded from Japan's endeavor to drive out all of the colonial powers from Asia. So I don't think Holland was to blame for taking part in the embargo of oil. It was a consequence of what happened in China. I realize that, at that time, there was a kind of warning from the Chinese that if these severe measures were not taken, they would not be able to withstand the Japanese. And I got the impression that the Cordell Hull note was delivered under pressure from Chiang Kai-shek [Jiang Jieshi]. Thus, it is quite clear that the ABCD reaction concerning oil was closely related to the Chinese issue.

CHAIR: Thank you very much, Dr. Röling. Mr. Tsurumi?

The Irrelevance of University Education to Whether Or Not One Commits Atrocities

MR. TSURUMI: Thank you. I have been thinking about the questions raised by Professor Awaya and, before that, by one of the speakers from the floor.

Professor Awaya pointed out that intellectuals have been involved in the Japanese peace movement throughout the postwar period, through such activities as the Heiwa Mondai Danwa-kai. He suggested that I fail to recognize the importance of these activities because of my dislike for intellectuals. But I myself have participated in these activities. I have participated in them, and I believe that it is better not to make too much of them.

That is something I learned during the war. In short, I realized that whether one commits atrocities or not is not a matter of whether one has received a university education. This became the basis for my feeling that one must not make too much of intellectuals.

When intellectuals are forced into a corner, most of them will act just like ordinary people, the masses. I am not saying that, therefore, the masses are superior beings. I am saying that when they act in an extreme situation, Japanese intellectuals are no different from the masses. Their language is the same, too. Then, if they're no different from the masses, when the masses do something wrong, are intellectuals wrong in the same way? Yes, they are. Therein lies the problem.

It is one's thought as a member of the masses that supports one's daily life, so even intellectuals can be depended on to some degree if they think as one of the masses. Even if something pretty bad happens, they can stick it out to the end. That is, they can keep both feet firmly on the ground. And then think from there. In short, if intellectuals would think always in the context of their own lives, then, for the first time, they could produce ideas that are relevant to their own lives.

Memorizing what Kant said about something has little relation to thinking. That is one point.

The Necessity of a Broad Movement

This is related to the question about the turning point. Last night, in a conversation with Professor Hosoya, I confirmed a belief that I have always held. There is always a turning point—to the very end. During the war, I decided that if worst came to worst, there was still the final act of suicide. That is, I myself have the means to commit suicide. Suicide is a tiny option, but human beings always have it. And that choice remains to the bitter end.

That's why the further back you go, the wider the range of choices. To state my own conclusions, the range of choices was extremely wide in the period after 1918. It was during that period that people like Yoshino Sakuzō emerged. But the young people who received their training from Yoshino immediately "went beyond him." Yoshino's democracy is old hat, they said. Someone even did a cartoon of him entitled [in approximate translation] "Yoshino the Democracy Hick." There is something wrong with this way of doing things—something wrong with the fad among intellectuals for refining concepts and constantly going beyond them.

The ideas Yoshino was talking about in that period were those of ordinary democracy—democratism. They would have abolished the misuse of the supreme military command. I understood this yesterday, listening to Professor Ienaga's presentation. Had there been a broad movement in the period of Taishō democracy to stop the army chief of staff and the navy chief of staff from arrogating to themselves access to the emperor and arbitrarily making decisions on a broad range of actions, I have a feeling things would have been much different later.

There are of course many reasons why this did not happen, but I think intellectuals bear a great deal of the responsibility. They're doing the same thing today: in the antiwar movement they try to separate people who are antiwar from those who are tired of war. They dismiss them as being "merely" tired of war or "merely" disliking war. But I think those people are extremely important. Just sticking to a position of being tired of the war in 1939 and 1940 wasn't easy. It wasn't easy at all.

Responsibility for Starting the War and Responsibility for Losing the War

There is a second issue that relates to responsibility for starting the war and responsibility for losing the war. Some intellectuals say it makes little sense to pursue only the responsibility for losing the war, that responsibility for starting the war should also be pursued. But responsibility for losing the war is something that concerns every Japanese. That so many had bitter experiences or were killed is all related to the question of responsibility for Japan's defeat. So if there is a wide consensus on pursuing that responsibility, then it should be done.

What is important is to create a place where responsibility for starting the war and responsibility for defeat overlap. What is important is to create a place where people who are antiwar and people who are merely tired of war—people who will not declare categorically that they are against war—can come together, a place where those two groups overlap.

But when intellectuals insist on refining concepts, they wind up distrusting anyone who doesn't have the same motives and the same temperament that they have. It's these people, I feel, who can't be relied on, and that is where my dislike of intellectuals comes from. I can't stand that type. [Laughter.]

When an intellectual starts talking about Kant or something like that, I think: "Kant? Ho, ho, ho . . ." [Laughter.] All through the war, they were singing "The Imperial Support Association, flawless gold," and now that the war is over, they're talking about Kant? I'm not attacking Kant, you know. I respect Kant. But when some Japanese professor of philosophy says "Kant," I feel like saying, "Kant? Ho, ho, ho, ho . . ." That feeling developed into my antipathy toward intellectuals.

When you have been through a war, you become extremely nihilistic like that, but this is relevant to the question of how to build a movement from here on. To this extent, I think very highly of Yoshida Mitsuru. Even after becoming an executive of the Bank of Japan, he never stopped pursuing responsibility for losing the war; he continued to call for such an accounting. And he did so from a position of considerable prestige. I think he was a great man. I don't want to think Yoshida was not on our side just because he held a "prestigious" position in the Bank of Japan.

CHAIR: Thank you very much.

Professor Ienaga commented today that he believes Japan violated the Soviet-Japan neutrality pact first. Professor Ienaga, I wonder if you would elaborate on that point.

PROFESSOR IENAGA: I have argued this point in great detail in my debates with Hayashi Kentarō, former president of Tokyo University, and those who are especially interested in my opinions should refer to the published accounts of this debate. Briefly stated, the argument centers on the "special operation of the Guandong [Kwan-tung] Army" [Kantōgun Tokushu Enshū], usually shortened to Kantokuen. This was no mere operation to improve military preparedness. It was clearly based on decisions made at a meeting in the emperor's presence held on 2 July 1941, and received the emperor's sanction. Following this meeting, army headquarters issued a wartime mobilization order, amassing eight hundred thousand troops on the Soviet border. The preparations for war went so far as to include plans for the military occupation and administration of Siberia and decisions on how to deal with Manchuria once war had begun. That the army did not push these plans to the point of actual hostilities was due only to the fact that objective conditions did not allow it. It was by no means the case that they stopped because they spontaneously decided to remain faithful to the neutrality pact with the Soviet Union.

Now to bring up a legal concept—and I may be scolded again by Professor Ōnuma—Japanese criminal law in effect at the time contained a provision whereby in cases of grave crime, the preliminary plot was also a crime. A person involved in a preliminary plot to carry out hostile acts against a foreign country was to be sentenced to not less than three months and not more than five years of imprisonment. This was a general principle of law that had been established not only in Japan but in every civilized nation.

Paragraph 1 of article 38 of the statute of the International Court of Justice recognizes the application of this general principle of law to international problems. In this light, the special operation of the Guandong Army was clearly a preliminary plot to commit aggression against the Soviet Union and hence was an illegal act.

I was afraid that this was my own arbitrary opinion, but I found an article in the September 1981 issue of *Rekishi to jinbutsu* [History and People] written by Mr. Nomura Minoru, a career soldier now retired, who heads the Military History Research Library of the Defense Agency. Mr. Nomura states clearly that Japan, and not only the Soviet Union, is in the position of having attempted to violate the Soviet-Japan neutrality pact. Labeling Japan's action an "attempted crime" is even harsher than my own evaluation. If a person like him makes such a statement, I think it is clear that my views are by no means far-fetched.

The Enduring Problem of Japanese Attitudes

CHAIR: Thank you very much.

We have spent the last two days discussing the Tokyo trial. I think it is clear that in terms of the law a number of problems still remain. It is equally clear that there are various interpretations of the historical facts considered by the tribunal, and, indeed, a number of differing opinions have been expressed here. But this symposium was not intended to be a forum where we might arrive at a consensus on the Tokyo trial or make final decisions on anything. If it has provided an opportunity for us to discuss our views and to give more thought to the issues, then it has succeeded.

However, there is something that hasn't been touched on very often in our discussions. I think that the tribunal committed many errors in its interpretation of the facts, and that some of the wartime leaders convicted in the postwar trials may have been condemned unjustly. Yet at the same time the tribunal passed judgment, I think, on prewar Japan's political and social institutions, and on the attitudes of the Japanese people. I believe that the problem of Japanese attitudes is still with us today.

Somebody used the word *contempt* to describe the Japanese attitude toward other Asian peoples, suggesting that people looked upon Asia as if it were on a lower plane. That view gave rise to all sorts of behavior. Conversely, there existed a kind of inferiority complex toward the United States.

This is something of a digression, but the other side of the coin may be seen in the arrogance toward the United States and Europe that is now making its appearance among some Japanese. This attitude forms part of the psychological background of the present trade friction between Japan and the United States and between Japan and Europe.

I would like to have discussed this problem of our attitudes more fully, but there was insufficient time really to go into it. I myself have also written a book on the Soviet-Japanese neutrality pact, and I would very much have liked to participate in the discussion on the point of no return. As Chair, however, I have attempted to behave myself. [Applause.] Thank you very much.

I understand that Dr. Röling has a final statement. Dr. Röling.

Closing Remarks

DR. RÖLING: Mr. Chairman, ladies and gentlemen, I have been invited to say a few words as a representative of the foreign participants, first of all to express our gratitude at having been invited here to enjoy Japanese hospitality. I can tell you that when we want to describe a kind of hospitality as very extensive and very amiable, we call it Japanese hospitality. We enjoyed it very much, and we are very grateful for it.

The second thing I would like to do is to give expression to our feeling of appreciation for the fact that the initiative was taken to discuss the Tokyo trial—to discuss it from every angle, to evaluate it, to weigh the different aspects, the legal, the historical, the peace research aspects.

As I listened to the discussions here, it was clear that one could approach the Tokyo trial in two different ways. One can, of course, look back to it with a kind of anger, because we all agree, I think, that it is almost humanly impossible to have a postwar trial that is absolutely fair. It is impossible because of the war propaganda, because of the emotions that still prevail. One can emphasize that aspect of the unfairness, but I think this is a bit sterile. There is the other aspect, not to look so much at those features, but to emphasize the role the trial can play in historical development.

The Need to Abolish War

The world is at a turning point. Up to the present, we have never experienced so keenly the need to abolish war, but that need is now apparent, for the first time since humanity has faced the question of war. If we look at the Tokyo trial in that respect, and ask what it can do, then I think we can appreciate the positive significance of the trial, and especially the contribution which the condemnation of war made to the general feeling that war should be outlawed. This is an opinion that the world needs.

The outlawing of war, and the emotional disapproval of war, is a condition of human survival. In this respect, Japan, having suffered more than many nations from this war, has the relevant experience. Its historic mission, which was sometimes mentioned during our debates, might be, on the basis of that experience, to play a great role in pushing the world toward a general conviction that wars are no longer tolerable.

It was said earlier in the discussions that governments are still pursuing their national interests. But we have become aware of the significance of the environment. The environment of the state is the world. Every human being needs a favorable environment. And when the world is the environment of every national state, it is in the national interest to have a peaceful environment. Here, I think, is the very reason for the observation in one of the papers that patriotism and the universal principle of mankind are no longer in opposition.

The Tokyo trial, and Nuremberg, may inspire people to compel their governments to act more reasonably than they do at the present time. Therefore, the impact of our conference may be furthered if the discussions and the papers here can be published, and if possible not only published in Japanese but made available to the whole world. We foreign participants hope that we will be able to see the publication of this symposium in a language we can read.

The Tokyo Trial in Light of the Japanese Peace Constitution

The Tokyo trial has been described several times here as a kind of revolution. That revolution is not over. It now turns to the governments still in power. And I believe that this revolution does not end with the restriction on the state's right to use armed force. It implies a further step—the restriction on the state's right to possess armed power.

Here perhaps is the relation of the Tokyo trial to article 9 of Japan's constitution. Japan's historic mission, on the basis of this constitution, might be to act together with other nations to have a generally-agreed-upon arms control. In striving for peace, aggressive, destabilizing, and excessive armed power should be banished and prohibited. And I know that Japan takes initiatives. I have seen them—initiatives in arms control. I wish that Japan would act still more actively in this field.

Mr. Chairman, I would like to conclude with the wish that this symposium will stimulate further research, not only on the Tokyo trial, but on the problems of war and peace—will stimulate not only peace research, but also peace action. And I hope that peace action can be based on research by scholars and intellectuals—notwithstanding the fact that some of us have some misgivings about intellectuals. [Laughter and applause.]

CHAIR: Thank you very much for this final message. Your presence at this symposium has given it life, and we hope that all of you will come back to Japan soon.

NOTES

Introduction: B. V. A. Röling (pp. 15–27)

1. We should mention especially Bradley F. Smith's *The Road to Nuremberg* (London: Andre Deutch, 1977), in which one can read of the difficulties in drafting the indictment, the problems concerning trial procedure, and the decision-making in the case of each defendant. All these problems are also covered in a book by Ann Tusa and John Tusa, *The Nuremberg Trial* (New York: Atheneum, 1984).

2. R. John Pritchard and Sonia M. Zaide (eds.), *The Tokyo War Crimes Trial: The Complete Transcripts of the Proceedings of the International Military Tribunal for the Far East*, 22 vols. and 5 supplementary vols. (New York: Garland Publishing [in association with the London School of Economics and Political Science], 1981).

3. Report to the President by Mr. Justice Jackson, 6 June 1945, document VIII in "Report of Robert H. Jackson US Representative to the International Conference on Military Trials, London 1945," Dept. of State Publication 3080 (Washington 1949), 46.

4. The top personnel managed to escape to Japan after destroying the laboratory and buildings and killing the remaining prisoners of war. But some of the officers were captured by the Soviet Union. They were put on trial in Khabarovsk from 25 through 30 December 1949, after the sentence of the IMTFE had been pronounced. A book has been published about the Khabarovsk trial: *Materials on the Trial of Former Servicemen of the Japanese Army Charged with Manufacturing and Employing Bacteriological Weapons* (Moscow: Foreign Languages Publishing House, 1950). In his final statement (p. 443) the prosecutor stated explicitly that the results of the interrogations were reported to Chief Prosecutor Joseph B. Keenan in Tokyo, but no date is mentioned. The book about the Khabarovsk trial leaves an impression of unreliablility because some of the Japanese defendants state that their crimes were committed by explicit command of the Japanese emperor. Later publications of official American documents affirm that immunity from prosecution was promised to those who were willing to supply information about the criminal experiments. See John W. Powell, "A Hidden Chapter in History," *Bulletin of the Atomic Scientists* (October 1981), 43–52.

5. It is noteworthy that accountability was not yet recognized in the four Red Cross treaties of 1949. They mention "persons alleged to have committed, or to have ordered to be committed" "the grave breaches" of the conventions (I art. 40, II art. 50, III art. 129, IV art. 146). Responsibility for "the failure to act" was recognized explicitly in 1977 by the four Red Cross conventions in Protocol I, articles 86 and 87.

6. The American court-martial of Lt. William Calley for the murders at My Lai was brought about by the American press and ended in a mild sentence, which was soon followed by a pardon. General Samuel Koster, who was involved in the effort to cover up the affair, lost one star and his post as superintendent of West Point. However, he was given a general parade when he left, and his farewell address, in which he protested against the role of the press and the public in the affair ("Don't let the bastards grind you down"), led to a standing ovation by the cadets. See Joseph Ellis and Robert Moore, *School for Soldiers: West Point and the Profession of Arms* (New York: Oxford University Press, 1974), 164 ff.

7. The conviction that a lessening of the threat of war as posed in the weapons themselves

can best be sought in a strategy of "defensive deterrence" needs to be expressed in a mutually agreed upon reduction in offensive strategic weapons. It is a mistake to see the Strategic Defense Initiative (the so-called Star Wars plan) as the embodiment of a defensive posture. Instead, this is an attempt to obtain one-sided protection against certain offensive weapons of the adversary while retaining offensive weapons of one's own. In short, it is a military measure to secure superiority.

8. Department of Defense Authorization for Appropriations for Fiscal Year 1982 (Washington 1981), 93.

9. Hearings on Military Posture and HR 5968 (Washington 1982), 46.

10. Annual Report Fiscal Year 1981 (Washington 1980), 75.

11. Report to the Congress on the Fiscal Year 1984 (Washington 1983), 32.

12. Not only the governments of powerful states, but also many prominent jurists, among them Julius Stone, are of the opinion that international law does not prohibit military action when vital interests are threatened or violated by nonmilitary means. An elaborate rebuttal of this opinion can be found in an article of mine: "On the Prohibition of the Use of Force," A. R. Blackshield (ed.), *Legal Change: Essays in Honour of Julius Stone* (London: Butterworth, 1983), 274–98.

13. The "case concerning military and paramilitary activities in and against Nicaragua" (ICJ Reports 1984, pp. 69–207) was brought by Nicaragua on 9 April 1984. On 10 May 1984 the court ordered provisional measures. The court held unanimously that "the United States of America should immediately cease and refrain to or from any action restricting, blocking or endangering access to or from Nicaraguan ports, and, in particular, the laying of mines." By fourteen votes to one the court declared: "The right to sovereignty and to political independence possessed by the Republic of Nicaragua, like any other State of the region or of the world, should be fully respected and should not in any way be jeopardized by any military and paramilitary activities which are prohibited by the principles of international law, in particular the principle that States should refrain in their international relations from the threat or use of force against the territorial integrity or the political independence of any State, and the principle concerning the duty not to intervene in matters within the domestic jurisdiction of the State, principles embodied in the UN Charter and the Charter of the Organization of American States" (p. 187). The American judge, Schwebel, cast the dissenting vote. His detailed motivation (pp. 190–207) concerns in particular the circumstance that Nicaragua itself was also militarily active and rests not in the least on any suggestion that the absolute ban on violence is invalid.

14. As an example we may mention James T. Johnson's *Just War Tradition and the Restraint of War: A Moral and Historical Inquiry* (Princeton University Press, 1981). Johnson objects stringently to the now accepted distinction between aggression and defense (p. 328). He speaks of "the rediscovery of just war tradition by theological ethics as a source of relevant moral wisdom of the contemporary age" (p. 357).

15. Partial Test Ban Treaty 1963, art. 4; Treaty of Tlatelolco 1967, art. 30; Nonproliferation Treaty 1968, art. 13; Seabed Treaty 1971, art. 8; Biological Weapons Treaty 1972, art. 8; Antiballistic Missile Treaty 1972, art. 15; SALT I 1972, art. 8; Threshold Treaty 1974, art. 16. In addition, the usual *clausula rebus sic stantibus*, as mentioned in the 1969 Vienna Convention on the Law of Treaties (art. 62), remains valid.

16. Barry Buzan, *People, States and Fear: The National Security Problem in International Relations* (Wheatsheaf Books, 1983), 96.

The Tokyo Trial: Ōnuma Yasuaki (pp. 45–52)

1. To be sure, the tribunal in Nuremberg was established by the Four-Power Agreement on the Charter of the International Military Tribunal, which stated that a "tribunal shall be established for the just and prompt trial and punishment of the major war criminals of the European Axis," and that "the Tribunal established by the Agreement . . . shall have the power to try and punish persons who, acting in the interests of the European Axis countries, whether as individuals or as members of organizations, committed crimes against peace, war crimes, or crimes against humanity." The International Military Tribunal for the Far East was established on the basis of the Potsdam Declaration and the Instrument of Surrender signed by the Allied powers and Japan. Therefore, the fact that neither of the trials

was able to judge the acts of the Allied powers during the war was not the responsibility of the tribunals themselves. However, in evaluating the Tokyo trial—and no less in the case of Nuremberg—it is essential that we not limit discussion to the proceedings of the tribunals, but also consider the trials holistically, including their charters, which as substantive law limited their actions. In this broader sense, it is undeniable that the trials were one-sided and unfair.

2. This fact was fully recognized by R. H. Jackson himself, who played the most important role in creating the major postwar war crimes tribunals. See Ōnuma Yasuaki, *Sensō Sekinin-ron Josetsu* [Prolegomenon to a Theory of War Guilt] (University of Tokyo Press, 1975), 293.

3. However, as I shall point out below, the principles of Nuremberg were cited by the antiwar movement in criticizing US intervention in Vietnam and its prosecution of the Vietnam War in violation of the laws of war. In this sense, the postwar trials have played an important role in the antiwar movement.

4. Ōnuma, op. cit.: 14, 277, 303.

5. Ibid.: 320–24.

6. Ibid.: 58–59, 334–35.

7. The atrocities committed systematically and on a large scale by Germany, based on the Nazi myth of racial supremacy, were widely known even in the early stages of the war, and were consistently condemned by the Allied powers throughout the war. In this sense, even though "crimes against humanity" had not actually been incorporated into international law by the time of the outbreak of World War II, it can be said that there was a strong consciousness of their criminal nature from the earliest stages of the war. Indeed, it was precisely this widespread condemnation of the horrible atrocities committed by the Nazis against Jews, Slavs, and other "non-Aryan" peoples—a condemnation which was truly an expression of the basic sense of justice held by ordinary people—that provided the substantive basis for the postwar tribunals.

8. On this point, however, it should be noted that even in regard to conventional war crimes, which are recognized even by the critics of the Tokyo and Nuremberg trials, only the illegality of the acts themselves had been established by international law. Individual criminal responsibility had not been established in the letter of international law as it existed at the time. Therefore, the problem of distinguishing between "crimes against peace" and "crimes against humanity" on the one hand, and conventional war crimes on the other, is not as simple as critics of the trials suggest.

9. In the period when the three-mile limit on territorial waters was considered to be general international law, it was clearly an illegal act—in the absence of a bilateral treaty—for a nation to exercise jurisdiction over a vessel that was polluting the ocean twenty nautical miles off its coast. However, pollution of the oceans is an act that involves the universal interests of mankind, and there is no room for doubt that the exercise of jurisdiction over such a vessel is a legitimate act under current international law. In fact, it is a general phenomenon that acts that become the starting point for new laws in succeeding periods are often illegal under the existing legal order.

10. J. N. Shklar, *Legalism* (Harvard University Press: 1964).

11. Under traditional international law, responsibility for illegal acts by a state was termed "state responsibility." However, if we focus on where the burden of responsibility actually rested in applying the law, it is clear that responsibility in fact was interpreted as "national responsibility" (i.e., "responsibility of the people of the state").

12. There are many examples of this. The categorical distinction between citizens and aliens based on nationality, which existed under traditional international law, is gradually being made relative by the development of international guarantees of human rights. Similarly, sovereign immunities based on the traditional concept of the state are shifting from the absolute to the relative. And the concept of sovereignty itself, which traditionally has had the special quality of exclusive territorial rights based on national territoriality, is gradually being replaced by the concept of functional jurisdiction in the fields of maritime and economic law.

13. This does not mean that I approve of the way in which the peace constitution is being eviscerated by increases in the budget for the Japanese Self-Defense Forces or the strengthen-

ing of the US-Japan Security Treaty. However, speaking comparatively and relatively, Japan's conduct in the international community has been far superior to that of the former Allied powers, especially the United States and the Soviet Union.

The Tokyo War Trial: John Pritchard (pp. 89–97)

1. *The Tokyo War Crimes Trial: The Complete Transcripts of the Proceedings of the International Military Tribunal for the Far East*, vols. 1–22, *Transcripts of the Proceedings in Open Session*, annotated, compiled and edited by R. John Pritchard and Sonia Magbanua Zaide, Garland Publishing (in association with the London School of Economics and Political Science), New York, 1981: Vol. 1 [Transcript pages (T.) A-2097], T. 21.

2. For a cross-section of Japanese views: "Summary of Censorship Intercepts Commenting on the War Crimes Trials, September 1945 to March 1947," prepared for Justice Röling by Civil Censorship Detachment, Civil Intelligence Section, Military Intelligence Section, General Staff, GHQ, SCAP, under cover of Letter from Col. C. S. Myers, Executive Officer, to Justice Röling, 10 April 1947, Röling Papers (I am deeply indebted to Professor Röling for entrusting this collection of some of his papers to my care).

3. Professor Röling, Interview with the author, 14 December 1982.

4. Observed by Keenan and confirmed by Sir George Sansom at a meeting of Committee 5 (War Criminals) of the Far Eastern Commission, Washington, D.C., 25 June 1946, FO 371/57432, Public Record Office, Kew.

5. *Proceedings*, Vol. 1, Historical Introduction by Donald Cameron Watt, p. xvii; Letter, Robert Donihi to the author, 30 May 1977; Pre-Trial Briefs produced by the Executive Committee of the International Prosecution Section, SCAP General Headquarters, 1945–1946. The only collection of the latter which I have been able to discover in Europe is to be found in FO 648 at the Imperial War Museum in London.

6. *Proceedings*, Vol. 11 [T. 25258–27838] Vol. 12 [T. 27839–30420], T. 27796–27963; DX 3109–3123. The only references by the prosecution were at *Proceedings*, Vol. 2 [T. 2098–4679], T. 3209–3285, and in Brendan Francis Brown's draft, *The Juridical Implications of the Proceedings of the International Military Tribunal for the Far East*, Tokyo, tss, 1947, chapter VII, p. 14: Röling interlineated on Brown, "Not proved." Pal, *Separate Opinion*, in *Proceedings*, Vol. 21, makes the same point, pp. 1058–9.

Significance of the Tokyo Trial: Ienaga Saburō (pp. 165–70)

1. Uchimura Kanzō, *Uchimura Kanzō chōsakushū* [Works of Uchimura Kanzō] III, Iwanami Shoten, 1954.

2. Kimura Tōru, *Yokohama jiken no shinsō* [The True Facts of the Yokohama Incident], Chikuma Shoten, 1983.

3. Uchimura, op. cit.

4. Ienaga Saburō, *Kyōkasho kentei* [Textbook Approval], Nihon Hyōronsha, 1965.

5. *Sekai* [World], no. 42 (June 1949).

6. Ōgata Kōhei, *Nitchū sensō to Indo iryō shisetsudan* [The China-Japan War and Indian Medical Teams], Sanseidō, 1982.

GLOSSARY

Anti-Comintern Pact: International agreement concluded between Japan and Germany on 25 November 1936, providing for their cooperation and the exchange of information concerning Comintern activities; later adhered to by Italy.

Araki Sadao (1877–1966): Defendant at the Tokyo trial; career army (placed on the reserve list after abortive revolt of 26 February 1936), general, army minister (1931–34), education minister (1938–39); sentenced to life imprisonment.

Axis alliance (Tripartite Pact; 27 September 1940): The military alliance of Germany, Italy, and Japan; regarded by some historians as the "point of no return" for Japan in the course of events leading up to the Pacific War. During the war, cooperation among the Axis countries was much less effective than that among the Allies.

Bacteriological experiments: Shortly before the symposium took place, research disclosed the existence of a Japanese station in Manchuria (Unit 731) at which POW's were used as live guinea pigs in experiments to develop bacteriological weapons of war, and often killed in the process. The United States apparently traded immunity from prosecution for the results of the experiments; no evidence was submitted at the Tokyo trial.

Bernard, Henri (1899–?): French judge at the Tokyo trial, author of minority opinion that argued all defendants were innocent because of procedural defects of the trial.

Changgufeng (Ch'ang-ku-feng) Incident. *See* Khassan Incident.

Chang Tso-lin. *See* Zhang Zuolin.

China Incident: The official designation by the Japanese government for the Sino-Japanese War; the usage of "incident" rather than "war" was based on highly political considerations.

China-Japan War. *See* Sino-Japanese War (2).

Class B and Class C war criminals: The Tokyo trial defendants (and a few others who were detained but never indicted) were considered Class A (or major) war criminals— the most important ones politically. Some 5,700 individuals in the Japanese military, including a number of Taiwanese and Koreans, were charged in various countries as Class B and Class C (or minor) war criminals; of these an estimated 920 (figures vary) were executed.

Convention on Non-Applicability of Statutory Limitations to War Crimes and Crimes Against Humanity: International treaty adopted by the General Assembly of the United Nations on 26 November 1968, providing for non-application of statutory limitations to certain war crimes and crimes against humanity. Entered into force on 11 November 1970.

Eastern Conference (summer 1927): Conference of Japanese policy-makers convened by Prime Minister Tanaka Gi'ichi concerning the crisis occasioned by deployment of Japanese troops in Shandong (Shan-tung); endorsed vigorous pursuit of Japan's interests in Manchuria and China.

Eighth Route Army: The military arm of the Communist movement in China; involved in fighting against both Japanese forces and the forces of Jiang Jieshi (Chiang Kai-shek).

Far Eastern Commission: The Allied organ that determined basic policies for the occupation of Japan, its decisions were transmitted through the US government to SCAP (Supreme Commander of the Allied Powers for the Occupation of Japan). Located in Washington, D. C., it was composed of the nine signatory nations of the instrument of Japanese surrender, as well as India and the Philippines, with Burma and Pakistan as subsequent members.

Fifteen-Year War: A sequence of wars and battles between Japan and China, commencing with the Manchurian Incident (1931) and concluding with the end of the Pacific War (1945).

GHQ: Acronym for General Headquarters of SCAP, the Supreme Commander for the Allied Powers (Gen. Douglas MacArthur for most of the Occupation), 1945–1952.

Greater East Asia War: official Japanese designation for the Pacific War. Its purported purpose was the establishment of the Greater East Asia Coprosperity Sphere, whose members were to include (with variations) Indochina, Southeast Asia, the Philippines, China, Manchuria, Korea, and Japan.

Guandong Army (Kwan-tung Army): The branch of the Japanese military stationed permanently in the Guandong leasehold (1905–45); initiated the Manchurian Incident and thereafter exercised great influence over the Japanese puppet state of Manchukuo (established 1932).

Guomindang (Kuomintang): Chinese Nationalist Party, established by Sun Yixian (Sun Yat-sen) in 1912. After Sun's death, Jiang Jieshi (Chiang Kai-shek) assumed leadership; the party formed the backbone of the Chinese government. After a long struggle with the Chinese Communist Party, it was defeated and took refuge in Taiwan in 1949.

Hata Shunroku (1879–1962): Defendant at the Tokyo trial; career military, general, and commander in chief of the expeditionary force in central China (1940–44); sentenced to life imprisonment.

Hirota Kōki (1878–1948): Defendant at the Tokyo trial; career diplomat, foreign minister (1933–36), and prime minister (1936–37); sentenced to death and hanged. The fairness of his sentence has been the object of considerable debate.

Hull Note: US proposal made during the last stages of Japan-US negotiations immediately before the Pacific War. Drafted by secretary of State Cordel Hull, it included among its demands the complete withdrawal of the Japanese army from China and recognition of the Jiang Jieshi (Chiang Kai-shek) government. Regarding the note as an ultimatum, Japan decided for war.

Instrument of Surrender (2 September 1945): The formal surrender document between Japan and the Allied powers, stipulating acceptance of the Potsdam Declaration and subjection of the emperor and the Japanese government to the authority of the Supreme Commander of the Allied Powers (SCAP).

Itagaki Seishirō (1885–1948): Career military, colonel involved in Manchurian Incident, general, chief of staff of Guandong (Kwan-tung) Army (1936–37), and army minister (1938–39); sentenced to death and hanged.

Jackson, Robert H. (1892–1954): American statesman, attorney general (1940–41), justice of the US Supreme Court (1941–54); American delegate to the London Conference and American prosecutor at the Nuremberg trial.

Japan-China War. *See* Sino-Japanese War (2).

Japanese constitution. *See* Meiji constitution; peace constitution.

Kellogg-Briand Pact (Pact of Paris; 27 August 1928): Pact signed in Paris condemning recourse to war for the solution of international controversies, and renouncing war as an instrument of national policy. The proponents of the pact—Kellogg, the American secretary of state, and Briand, the French foreign minister—were supported by public sentiment in favor of outlawing war.

Khassan Incident (also known as Changgufeng [Ch'ang-ku-feng] Incident): Fighting in 1938 on the border of Korea, Manchuria, and Siberia between the Soviet Union and Japan; subject of negotiated settlement in the same year.

Kido Kōichi (1889–1977): Defendant at Tokyo trial; statesman, minister of education (1937), minister of welfare (1938), home minister (1939), and lord keeper of the privy seal (1940–45); sentenced to life imprisonment.

Koiso Kuniaki (1880–1950): Defendant at the Tokyo trial; career military, general, chief of staff of Guandong (Kwan-tung) Army (1932–34), minister of colonial affairs (1939–40), and prime minister (1944–45); sentenced to life imprisonment.

lex ferenda: Latin phrase meaning "law as it should be"; that is, law proposed for the future.

lex lata: Latin phrase meaning "law as it is"; that is, existing law.

London Conference (July-August 1945): Negotiations among the Big Four that produced the charter for the Nuremberg trial. The most crucial issue at the conference was the criminality of "crimes against peace," which was finally recognized.

Manchurian Incident (September 1931–February 1933): The conquest and pacification of Manchuria, beginning with a bomb planted by the Guandong (Kwan-tung) Army and ending with the seizure of Manchuria, the establishment of the client state of Manchukuo, and the Japanese withdrawal from the League of Nations.

Marco Polo Bridge Incident: Clash between the Japanese and the Chinese armies that occurred on 7 July 1937 around Marco Polo Bridge in the suburbs of Beijing (Peking); marks the beginning of the Sino-Japanese War.

Matsui Iwane (1878–1948): Defendant at the Tokyo trial; career military, general, commander in chief of Japanese forces in central China (1937–39; hence during the Rape of Nanjing [Nanking]); sentenced to death and hanged.

Matsuoka Yosuke (1889–1946): Defendant at the Tokyo trial; career diplomat, foreign minister (1940–41); died during the trial, and no verdict was handed down.

Meiji constitution: Japanese constitution promulgated in 1889 under the reign of Emperor Meiji. It provides that "the emperor is the head of the empire, combining in himself the rights of sovereignty." It was replaced by the current Japanese constitution in 1946, which is based on the principle of people's sovereignty.

Minami Jirō (1874–1955): Defendant at the Tokyo trial; career military, general, commander in chief of Guandong (Kwan-tung) Army (1934–36), placed on reserve list after the abortive revolt of 26 February 1936; governor general of Korea (1936–42); sentenced to life imprisonment.

Moscow Declaration (1943): Proclamation issued following the Moscow Conference of foreign ministers of the United Kingdom (Eden), USSR (Molotov), and USA (Hull), stating that punishment of German officers and members of the Nazi Party responsible for atrocities would be carried out in the countries in which the crimes took place, and that "major criminals" whose offenses had no particular geographical location would be punished by a joint decision of the Allied governments.

Nagano Osami (1880–1947): Defendant at the Tokyo trial; career military, admiral, navy minister (1936–37), chief of naval general staff (1941–44); died during the trial, and no verdict was handed down.

Nanjing (Nanking), Rape of: Widespread violence on the part of the Japanese army following the Japanese capture of Nanjing on 13 December 1937; the single most notorious Japanese atrocity of World War II.

Nomonhan Incident: Fighting on the border of Outer Mongolia and Manchuria between Soviet and Guandong (Kwan-tung) Army troops in the summer of 1939; subject of negotiated settlement in same year.

Northern Expedition: the military operation (beginning in South China and moving north) of the forces of Jiang Jieshi (Chiang Kai-shek) in 1927; resulted in the (temporary) unification of China and brought to the forefront the issue of the Japanese position in Manchuria.

nullum crimen sine lege: Latin phrase meaning "unless there is a law, there can be no crime." One of the basic principles of law prohibiting retroactive legislation, particularly in criminal matters; incorporated into many modern constitutions guaranteeing fundamental freedoms and human rights.

Ōkawa Shūmei (1886–1957): Defendant at the Tokyo trial; civilian, ideologist; declared unfit for trial, so no verdict handed down.

Pacific War (1941–45): That part of World War II fought in the Pacific theater between Japan and the Allied powers, starting with the attack on Pearl Harbor and ending with the Japanese surrender.

Pact of Paris. *See* Kellogg-Briand Pact.

Pal, Radhabinod (1886–1967): Indian judge at the Tokyo trial; author of massive dissenting opinion that attacked the trial's legal foundations, procedure, and philosophy, finding all defendants innocent of all charges.

peace constitution: Japan's postwar constitution (3 May 1946); so-called because article 9 reads: "Aspiring sincerely to an international peace based on justice and order, the Japanese people forever renounce war as a sovereign right of the nation and the threat or use of force as a means of settling international disputes. (2) In order to accomplish the aim of the preceding paragraph, land, sea, and air forces, as well as other war potential, will never be maintained. The right of belligerency of the state will not be recognized."

Potsdam Declaration (26 July 1945): Declaration issued at Potsdam Conference (attended by Churchill, Attlee, Stalin, and Truman), stating: "We do not intend that the Japanese shall be enslaved as a race or destroyed as a nation but stern justice shall be meted out to all war criminals, including those who have visited cruelties upon our prisoners."

Puyi (P'u-i; 1906–67): The last emperor of the Qing dynasty; later enthroned as the emperor of Manchukuo by Japan. After the end of World War II, he was arrested by the Soviet Union and took the witness stand at the Tokyo trial.

Qing government: Last of the Chinese dynasties; of Manchurian origin; ruled the country from 1616 to 1912; overthrown in the Xinhai Revolution.

Rape of Nanjing. *See* Nanjing (Nanking), Rape of.

Russell Tribunal (also known as Stockholm Tribunal; May 1967): Unofficial tribunal convened by Bertrand Russell, a vehement critic of US intervention in Vietnam, to consider American actions there; wholly without official authority or power, it relied on moral suasion. The "Nuremberg principles" were among the major norms it sought to apply.

Self-Defense Forces: The official designation of Japan's military, designed to obscure any possible conflict with article 9 of Japan's postwar constitution.

Shanghai Incident (January–May 1932): Military confrontation in Shanghai between China and Japan. One of the series of "incidents"—Manchuria, Marco Polo Bridge, and China—that formed an integral part of Japan's Fifteen-Year War.

Shigemitsu Mamoru (1887–1957): Defendant at the Tokyo trial; career diplomat, foreign minister (1943–45 and, after the war, 1954–56); sentenced to seven years' imprisonment.

Sino-Japanese War: (1) The war between China and Japan over special interests claimed by both countries in Korea; declared on 1 August 1894 and concluded on 17 April 1895. Japan's overwhelming victory made it the dominant power in East Asia. (2) That part of the Fifteen-Year War that started with the Japanese invasion of China proper in 1937 (Marco Polo Bridge Incident) and ended in 1945 with Japan's surrender.

South Manchurian Railway: The chief artery of Japanese expansion and control in Manchuria. With its beginnings in the Russian railroad ceded to Japan in the Portsmouth treaty of 1905, it came to cover the whole of Manchuria as Japan extended its influence in the area, reaching over 10,000 kilometers in length at the end of World War II.

Soviet-Japanese Neutrality Pact (13 April 1941): Neutrality pact, denounced by the Soviet Union in April 1945 prior to the Soviet attack on Japan in August 1945, but by its own terms still in effect until April 1946. The Soviet Union has claimed that Japan had in fact violated the pact long before, when the Special Maneuvers of the Guandong (Kwantung) Army were held in Manchuria (1941).

Sun Yixian (Sun Yat-sen; 1866–1925): Chinese statesman, revolutionary, and founder of the Chinese Nationalist Party. At the time of the Xinhai Revolution, which overthrew the Qing dynasty, he was elected provisional president of the revolutionary government and the Republic of China was proclaimed. However, when Yuan Shikai (Yüan Shih-k'ai) became president of the republic and exhibited dictatorial tendencies, Sun fought against him, the result being civil war.

Tanaka Gi'ichi (1864–1929): General, prime minister (1927–29).

Tōgō Shigenori (1882–1950): Defendant at the Tokyo trial; career diplomat, ambassador to Germany (1937), ambassador to the Soviet Union (1938), foreign minister (1941–42, 1945); sentenced to twenty years' imprisonment.

Tripartite Pact. *See* Axis alliance.

Twenty-One Demands (1915): Japanese call for Chinese concessions during World War I, including Japanese rights in Shandong (Shan-tung), Southern Manchuria, and eastern Inner Mongolia, a Japanese role in Chinese mining, and the installation of Japanese advisors in the Chinese government; aroused strong Chinese resentment.

war crimes: *Conventional war crimes* are acts prohibited by traditional international laws of war, such as murder of prisoners of war and the murder or ill treatment of civilians. To these established categories, the Nuremberg charter added *crimes against peace* (planning, preparation, initiation, or waging of a war of aggression) and *crimes against humanity* (systematic persecution and inhumane acts committed against any civilian population, such as the German atrocities committed against the Jews). Differences of opinion exist as to the criminality of the new categories.

Webb, Sir William (1887–1972): Australian judge and president at the Tokyo trial;

author of separate opinion arguing against any death penalties on the ground that the emperor had not been indicted.

Yamashita Tomoyuki (1885–1946): Career military, general, victor at Singapore; tried by an American military commission in the Philippines, condemned to death, and executed. His trial was the most famous of the Class B and Class C proceedings, in part because of Yamashita's fame, in part because it was appealed to the US Supreme Court.

Yoshida Mitsuru (1923–79): Veteran of World war II, banker, and writer. His *Senkan Yamato no saigo* (English trans, 1985: Requiem for Battleship Yamato) is one of the best of Japanese postwar writings on war.

Zhang Zuolin (Chang Tso-lin; 1875–1928): the most influential warlord in the northeast region of China during the 1920s; killed in 1928 in a train explosion set off by the Japanese army as he was fleeing from the army of Jiang Jieshi (Chiang Kai-shek).

INDEX

(numbers in boldface indicate prepared papers and comments delivered at the symposium)

Afghanistan, 22, 46, 162
aggression, 26, 32, 105, 195; against China, 63, 98–99, 135, 149, 169, 183, 193; in Tokyo charter, 40; and individual, 50, 162; international criminality of, 107-8; international law and, 127–28; Japanese translation of, 107; motives of Japanese war of, 132; and Vietnam war compared to Japan's war in China, 140
aggression (definition of): attempt at, 40; as authoritative interpretation of UN charter, 178–79; in Tokyo charter, 34; in UN General Assembly Resolution 3314 (XXIX), 23, 66, 67, 107, 125
aggressive war. *See* aggression
American Catholic bishops, 163
Angola, 22
Anti-Comintern Pact, 36
apartheid, 49–50, 64
Araki Sadao, 186
Argentina, 91
arms control, 24–25
Asia for Asians, 132
atomic bombings, 23, 45, 51, 80–81, 86, 128, 138, 140, 168
atomic weapons, 24, 132
Auschwitz, 49, 50, 150
Australia, 69, 92
Awaya Kentarō, **79–87**, 115–16, 196–97
Axis, 32, 33, 50, 81, 193

bacteriological warfare (experiments) in China, 18, 19, 62, 85–86, 96, 116, 131, 138
Beard, Charles A., 160
Beijing (Pei-ching, Peking), 71, 72, 75
Beiqing (Pei-ch'ing) Incident, 71, 98
Belgium, 91
bellum justum, 23
ben'itai (*bianyidui*), 58, 59
Bernard, Henri, 19, 96, 153, 154

Biddle, Francis J., 126
biological warfare. *See* bacteriological warfare
biological weapons, treaty concerning, 24
Bismarck, Otto von, 178
Blakeney, Ben Bruce, 104, 120
Bonhoeffer, Dietrich, 166, 188
Borah, 127
Boxer Rebellion. *See* Beiqing Incident
Brecht, Bertolt, 151
British colonial empire, 91
British Commonwealth, 93
Brooks, Alfred W., 65–66, 121
Brown, Brendan, 97
Brown, Harold, 22
Burma, 91, 101–2, 143, 199
bushidō, 201

Cai Zhikan, 73
Canada, 35, 69
Canton (Kuandong), 72
Carpenter, Alva C., 83
Chang Hsüeh-liang. *See* Zhang Xueliang
Chang Tso-lin. *See* Zhang Zuolin
Changchun (Ch'ang-ch'un), 60, 71
Changgufeng (Ch'ang-ku-feng) Incident. *See* Lake Khassan Incident
charter (Tokyo trial), 33–34; amendment of, 57, 90–91; conspiracy in, 40, 42; and crimes against peace, 125, 128; and criminal nature of groups, 84; definition of crimes against humanity in, 42; definition of crimes against peace in, 40; definition of war crimes in, 41; drafting of, 36, 46, 56; in excess of then existing international law, 41; international customary law and, 40; and jurisdiction of tribunal, 38, 39–40; and number of judges, 90–91
Chiang Kai-shek. *See* Jiang Jieshi
China, 69, 136, 143, 183, 192; aggression against, 63, 98–99, 135, 149, 169, 183, 193; Communism in, 132; crimes against humanity in, 53; germ and chemical warfare in, 85; Hamaguchi cabinet and policy of rapproche-

ment with, 75; Japanese aggression invited by weakness of, 76–77; Nationalist government in, 75; and oil embargo, 202; Potsdam Declaration and, 33, 34; protection of Japanese residents in, 72–73, 106; and relationship to Japan before Manchurian Incident, 70–77; summary execution by Japanese army in, 80; and Twenty-One Demands, 71–72; war crimes trial in, 142; war of national liberation in, 60

China, People's Republic of, 59

China Incident, 63, 87, 99, 135, 185

China-Japan War. *See* Sino-Japanese War (1937–45)

Chinese Communist Party, 72, 77, 100

Ching-chou (Jinzhou), 184

Ch'ing (Qing) dynasty, 71

Ch'inhuang-tao (Qinhuangdao), 71

Churchill, Winston S., 16, 195

civil disobedience, 201. *See also* state orders

Clausewitz, Karl von, 26

Club of Rome, 132

cold war, 18, 83

collective security system, 178

colonialism, 46, 48, 52, 132

combatants, 60

Communism, 21–22, 132

Comyns-Carr, Sir Arthur S., 16, 92, 95

conspiracy, 47, 95, 97, 136; in Tokyo charter, 40, 42; Japanese leaders incapable of, 76; among Japanese leadership, 99; in Manchurian Incident, 109–10; meaning of, 108–9

Constitution of the Empire of Japan, 45, 76

Constitution of Japan, 117. *See also* peace constitution

Convention on the Non-Applicability of Statutory Limitations to War Crimes and Crimes against Humanity, 35, 66–67, 152, 177

Convention for the Pacific Settlement of International Disputes, 127

conventional war crimes. *See* war crimes (conventional)

Costello, William, 169

courts-martial, 20, 39, 41, 42, 43, 80; and American deserter during Vietnam War, 174; of Japanese and Allied soldiers compared, 175; of Japanese army, 81

Craigie, Sir Robert, 90

Cramer, Myron H., 91–92, 126

crimes against humanity, 21, 32, 53–54, 198; committed against peoples under Japanese rule, 85, 113, 114, 115; committed by Unit 731 and Unit 1644, 85; defined in Tokyo charter, 34, 42; of Nazi Germany and Japan compared, 187; and *ex post facto* law, 47; and indiscriminate bombing of Japan, 80; and international law, 49, 54; jurisdiction of Tokyo tribunal for, 42–43; relation to war

crimes, 55, 115; relevancy to crimes against peace, 55; and Tokyo trial, 53, 85, 113; and trials by German courts, 20–21, 190

crimes against peace, 21, 32, 83, 126, 198; concept of, 47; defined in Tokyo charter, 34, 40; evolution of concept of, 125–28; and *ex post facto* law, 47; and international armed conflicts since Nuremberg and Tokyo trials, 177; and international law, 132, 178; in Nuremberg and Tokyo charters, 125, 128; and Shigemitsu Mamoru, 17; *in statu nascendi*, 130; in Tokyo charter, 39, 40

Cuba, 22

Czechoslovakia, 22

Dandō Shigemitsu, 168

Declaration of Atrocities. *See* Moscow Declaration

disarmament, 24–25

Doihara Kenji, 93

Dominican Republic, 22

Donihi, Robert, 95

Doolittle Squadron air raids, 80

Draft Code of Offences against the Peace and Security of Mankind, 44, 67

Dürrenmatt, Friedrich, 181

Dutch colonial empire, 91

Eastern Conference (*tōhō kaigi*), 73–74

economic security, 23, 132, 178

Eden, Sir Anthony, 16

Eichmann, Adolf, 162

Eighth Route Army, 60, 100, 169

Eisenhower, Dwight, 24

Emergency Imperial Decree (Draft), 81–82, 87–88

emperor, 20, 82, 87, 102, 121; included in list of major war criminals, 90; movement for abdication by, 86; war responsibility of, 45–46, 81, 86–87

emperor-system fascism, 197

environmental pollution, 198

ex post facto law, 41, 43, 44, 47, 53, 80, 168

Falk, Richard A., 161, 162

Far Eastern Commission, 57, 83, 84, 95

fascism 36, 77, 100, 166, 185

Fifteen-Year War, 116, 119, 166; chances to end, 184–85; continuity of, 182–84; in Ienaga's textbook, 168; Japanese responsibility for, 51–52, 170, 198–99; Japan-US negotiations during, 185; origin of, 149; overall picture of, 137–38 Tokyo trial on illegality of, 170. *See also* China Incident; Greater East Asia War; Manchurian Incident; Pacific War; Sino-Japanese War (1937–45)

France, 32, 69, 94, 119, 127, 192, 200

freedom fighters, 60

French colonial empire 91

Fritzsche, Hans, 17
Fujimura Michio, 136
Fujishima Unaki, 148–49
Furness, George A., 57–58, 104, 119, 120, 154–55, 174

Gandhi, Mahatma, 169
Gangloff, Eric, 96
Geneva Convention Relating to the Treatment of Prisoners of War of 1929, 41, 42, 43
Geneva Protocol of 2 Oct. 1924 (Protocol for the Pacific Settlement of International Disputes), 40
Geneva Red Cross Conventions, 189–90
germ and chemical warfare. See bacteriological warfare
German emperor. See kaiser
German High Command, 84
German-Soviet Nonaggression Pact (Stalin-Ribbentrop Agreement), 126
Germany, Federal Republic of, 18, 35, 61, 84, 187
Germany (postwar), 15, 21, 54, 66, 84, 146
Germany (prewar, including Nazi Germany), 50, 63, 77, 78, 132, 183, 193; and aggression, 64, 70; appeasement toward, 119; conspiracy in case of, 76; crimes against humanity by, 114; and Nuremberg tribunal, 32; and relations with Soviet Union, 36; people of, and struggle against Nazis, 188–89; systematic murder of Jews by, 51; in war against Soviet Union, 33 58, 62
Gestapo, 84
GHQ, 81, 82–85, 137, 196, 197. See also Supreme Commander for the Allied Powers
Goering, Hermann, 15, 16
Great Britain, 32, 33, 34, 35, 69, 71, 118, 140, 200; and aggression against China, 192–93; and appeasement of Germany and Italy, 119; Japan's war with, 169; and oil embargo against Japan, 202; and policy of ending Tokyo trial, 82–83; recruiting defense counsel from, 93; and reservations to Pact of Paris, 108
Greater East Asia War, 87, 91, 135, 137, 167–68, 169, 182–83, 202–3
Grenada, 22
Grossraum, 131
Grotius, Hugo, 23
Guandong (Kwan-tung), 71
Guandong (Kwan-tung) Army, 74–75, 85, 99, 184, 205
Guatemala, 22
guerrillas, 58, 59, 80
Guomindang (Kuomintang, Nationalist Party), 60, 77, 100

Hagiwara Nobutoshi, **104**, 185
Hague Peace Conference (1907), 23
Hague Regulations respecting the laws and

customs of war on land (1907), 35, 38, 42, 43, 55
Hakone conference, 153
Halhin Gol (Nomonhan) Incident, 17, 36, 61
Hamaguchi Osachi, 75
Hart, Liddell, 138, 140
Hashimoto Shinobu, 141
Hata Ikuhiko, **103-4**, 111-12, 182–83, 185, 201–2
Hata Shunroku, 19, 131
Hayashi Kentarō, 205
Hegel, Friedrich, 167, 170
Heiwa Mondai Danwa-kai, 203
Higashikuni cabinet, 81, 82
Hirota Kōki, 92, 95, 139, 201; and "Asia for the Asians," 132; death sentence to, 17, 153, 155, 156; designation of, at Tokyo trial, 186; and failure to prevent war crimes, 17, 19; Röling on, 19, 131
Hitler, Adolf, 17, 102, 104, 109
Hosokawa Karoku, 166, 167
Hsin-hai (Xinhai) Revolution, 72
Hull Note, 183, 185, 202
Humphreys, Christmas, 91, 95
Hungary, 22, 46, 179

ideological security, 22, 132
Ienaga Saburō, **165–70**, 183, 188–89, 191, 192, 197, 205–6
Imperial Support Association (Taisei Yokusan Kai), 204
India, 69–70, 91, 102, 169
indiscriminate bombing, 80–81
individual responsibility (including individual criminal responsibility), 26, 63, 64, 66–67, 181, 189–90; for aggression, 125; for crimes against peace, 40–41, 43, 53; differences between Nuremberg and Tokyo concerning, 190; established by Tokyo charter, 42; and Pact of Paris, 127; UN discussion of, 44. See also international responsibility; leaders' responsibility; responsibility; state responsibility
Indo-China, 94
Indonesia, 199, 202
Instrument of Surrender, 34, 38
International Court of Justice, 23, 205
international crime, 40, 131, 132, 189
international criminal law, 38, 41, 43–44, 67, 178
International Law Commission of UN, 43, 44, 67
international military order, 24–25
International Military Tribunal for the Far East. See tribunal (Tokyo)
International Peoples' Tribunal on Israel's invasion of Lebanon, 51
International Prosecution Section, 85, 94, 95
international responsibility, 40–41. See also individual responsibility; leaders' responsibili-

relationship between China and Japan concerning, 70–76
Manchurian Empire, 58, 76
Manchurian Incident, 63, 87, 110, 111, 119, 135; and Chinese people's war of resistance, 183; essential nature of, 112; and last chance to prevent war, 184–85; prehistory of, 70–76; and question of conspiracy, 71, 76, 99; and relation to Pacific War, 182–83; responsibility for, 103
Manchurian Railway, 74, 111
Manchurian Rehabilitation Pact, 71
Mansfield, A. J., 92
Marco Polo Bridge Incident, 63
Matsudaira Kōtō, 61, 62, 116–17
Matsui Iwane, 58, 186, 201
Matsuoka Yōsuke, 93, 108
Meiji constitution, 45, 76
military-industrial complex, 26
Minear, Richard H., 15, 96, **159–64**, 181–82, 195, 200
Mongolia, 73
Morimura Sei'ichi, 85
Moscow Declaration, 32, 35, 125, 126
Murase Okio, 84
Muste, A. J., 163–64
Mutō Akira, 95
Mutual Progress Society of War Criminals of Korean Nationality, 112
My Lai incident, 44

Nagano Osami, 93, 95, 108
Nanjing (Nanking), 49, 50, 72
Nanjing (Nanking) Incident (Rape of Nanjing, Nanjing Massacre), 17, 58–59, 110–11, 160, 186, 201
Napoleonic War, 129
national liberation movements, 59–60, 100
Nationalist government in China, 75
Nationalist Party. See Guomindang
NATO, 22
Nazi Party, 32, 84, 109, 147
Nazi regime, 19, 189
Nazis, 21, 33, 126, 150; atrocities committed by, 114; crimes against humanity committed by, 49; German struggle against, 189; persecution and extermination of Jews by, 15, 85; summary execution plan against, 16
Nazism, 77
ne bis in idem (principle of double jeopardy), 82
Netherlands, 69, 140, 169, 192, 202
neutrality pact between Japan and Soviet Union, 36, 54, 117–18; differences of opinion concerning, 57–58; Soviet violation of, 45, 61–62; violation by Japan, 33, 168, 205–6
New Zealand, 69
Nicaragua, 22, 23
Nine Power Treaty, 91

Nomonhan (Halhin Gol) Incident, 17, 36, 61
Nomura Minoru, 205
Norman, E. H., 116
Northcroft, Erima H., 91, 92, 93
Northern Expedition, 72–75, 98
Nuclear Nonproliferation Treaty, 24
nuclear war, 125, 163, 194
nuclear weapons, 24, 26, 46, 163
nullum crimen sine lege, nulla poena sine lege. See ex post facto law
Nuremberg charter, 32, 34, 35, 84, 125, 127, 128
Nuremberg judgment: conviction for conspiracy in, 108, 109; on crimes against humanity, 85; historic significance of, 34–35; on Nuremberg charter, 38–39; quoted in Tokyo judgment, 40; trial of Nazi war crimes based on, 84; UN and, 35; on war crimes, 19
Nuremberg principles, 35, 44, 132, 176–77
Nuremberg and Tokyo trials, 31–32, 46, 54, 70, 101, 200; effectiveness of law of, 177–78; and evolution of customary international law, 55; and examination of legality of charters, 129; historical significance of, 34–35, 48; legal basis for, 48–49; motive for holding, 55–56; and progressive development of international law, 37–38, 130. See also Tokyo trial; tribunal (Tokyo)

occupation of Japan, 83–84, 117, 136–37
oil embargo, 202-3
Okamoto Aihiko, 112–13, 141, 197
Ōkawa Shūmei, 32, 93, 108, 109
Okinawa, 149
Okuhara Toshio, **54–56**, 60, 108–10, 114–15, 176–77
Ōnuma Yasuaki, **45–52**, 59–60, 64, 106, 113–14, 171, 187–88, 199–201
Ōoka Shōhei, 80
Ōshima Hiroshi, 185
Oświęcim (Auschwitz), 49, 50, 150
Ōta Kinjirō, 93

Pacific War, 91, 94, 95, 98, 103, 135, 164; compared with World War I, 104–5, 118; conspiracy in, 99; essential nature of, 119; as extension of war in Europe, 118; and Japan's responsibility toward Asia, 199; and oil embargo against Japan, 202-3; and relation to Sino-Japanese War (1937–45), 182–83, 202. See also Fifteen-Year War; Greater East Asia War
Pact of Paris (Kellogg-Briand Pact), 21, 40–41, 107, 126, 127
Paik Choong-Hyun, **52–54**
Pal, Radhabinod, 137, 154, 155; on Allied war crimes, 168; anti-Communist ideology of, 169; on atomic bombings, 186; Costello on, 169; on crimes against peace and war

crimes, 152-53; on criminal nature of aggression, 107; on evidence, 192; on Japanese aggression in Asia, 106; on Japan's responsibility toward Asia, 200; and justification of Japan's aggression against China, 169; and movement to revive Japanese militarism, 167; on Tokyo trial, 186

Patrick, Lord, 92

peace constitution, 51, 86, 193-94, 196, 197, 199-200, 207-8. *See also* Constitution of Japan

peace movement, 26, 133, 196

Peace Studies Group (Heiwa Mondai Danwakai), 196

Pearl Harbor, 53, 128

Peking (Pei-ching). *See* Beijing

Pei-ch'ing Incident. *See* Beiqing Incident

People's Liberation Army (Eighth Route Army), 60, 100, 169

People's Provisional Government in Beijing, 59

people's war, 60, 183

Permanent Court of International Justice, 42

Perry, Admiral, 182

Philippines, 53-54, 70, 84, 91, 102, 143

PLO, 195

Poland, 22

Port Arthur (Lüshun), 71, 103

Porter Convention, 127

Portugal, 91

Potsdam Declaration, 33, 34, 117, 129, 179; and concept of major war criminals, 90; and elimination of former political leaders of Japan, 130; Japan's acceptance of, 167; and legal basis of Tokyo trial, 38; and postwar trial, 81

prisoners of war, 35, 60; bacteriological experiment on, 18, 62; massacre of Chinese, 111; mistreatment of, 20; punishment of, for war crimes committed prior to capture, 41; summary execution of, 80

Pritchard, R. John, 15, 56-57, **89-97**, 111, 119, 171-72, 175, 195-96

Protocol Additional to the Geneva Conventions of 12 August 1949, and Relating to the Protection of Victims of International Armed Conflicts (1977), 60, 190

Pusan, 112

Puyi (P'u-i), 76

Qigihaer (Tsitsihar), 99

Qing (Ch'ing) dynasty, 72

Qinhuangdao (Ch'inhuang-tao), 71

Rape of Nanjing (Nanking). *See* Nanjing Incident

Reagan, Ronald, 22

reasons of state, 163, 165, 180

Red Cross Conventions, 189-90

responsibility: under international law, 55; of

leaders, 66; for losing war, 103, 135-36, 137, 139, 204, 205; for omission, 190; for starting war, 103, 118, 135-36, 137, 138, 140, 189, 204; for war, 79, 82, 83, 146-47, 173, 188, 196-97, 198-99, 200-201. *See also* individual responsibility; international responsibility; leaders' responsibility; state responsibility

Röling, B. V. A., **15-27**, 66, 120, **125-33**, 152-53, 154, 156, 178-80, 189-90, 202-3, 206-8; on amended Tokyo charter, 91; on crimes against peace, 130; on Hirota, Shigematsu, Tōgō, Kido, and Hata, 19, 131; minority opinion of, 104, 168

Roosevelt, Franklin D., 116, 118, 127, 138

Rozhdestvenskii, Admiral, 103

Russell, Bertrand, 125, 162, 163

Russell tribunal, 51, 162-63, 170, 189

Russo-Japanese War, 71, 98, 103, 118

Rüter, C. F., 15

Saionji Kinmochi, 185

SALT I Treaty, 22

SALT II agreement, 179

Sanminzhuyi, 72

San Francisco Peace Treaty, 86, 117, 138

Sartre, Jean-Paul, 162, 170, 189

SCAP. *See* Supreme Commander for the Allied Powers

Schutzstaffel (SS), 84

Seiki no isho (Testaments of the Century), 141

self-defense, 21, 106, 107, 108; and Pact of Paris, 127; right of, 23

Self-Defense Force (Japan), 194

Shandong (Shan-tung), 184

Shanghai Incident, 135, 185

Shanhaiguan (Shan-hai-kuan), 71

Shan-tung (Shandong), 184

Shidehara, Baron, 91

Shidehara cabinet, 82

Shigemitsu Mamoru, 17, 95, 120, 155, 161; and failure to prevent war crimes, 19; Röling on, 18, 19, 131; sentence on, 17, 131

Shiroyama Saburō, 139

Singapore, 143

Sino-Japanese War (1894-95), 74, 93

Sino-Japanese War (1937-45), 98, 103, 119; link with Pacific War, 202; and oil embargo against Japan, 202-3; and question of conspiracy, 99; and relation to Pacific War, 182-83

Smith, Bradley, 126

Son My (My Lai) incident, 44

South Africa, Republic of, 34l. *See also* apartheid

South America, 35

South Manchurian Railway, 71

Soviet Union, 32, 33, 34, 54, 63, 69; atrocities in Manchuria and northeastern China by, 168; and bacteriological warfare Unit 731,

62, 85; entrance into war with Japan by, 33, 58; Japanese detainees in, 84; Japan's aggression motivated by threat of, 76, 99; and legal ground for participation in Tokyo trial, 36; and massacre in Katyn Forest, 17, 50–51; position of, on war crimes trial in Japan, 84; and postwar confrontation with US, 18, 21–22, 80, 83, 100; postwar military intervention by, 22, 46; and postwar policy on war criminals, 35–36, 57; questions on postwar international conduct of, 24, 46, 51, 161–62, 200; and selection of accused in Tokyo trial, 17, 95; war between Germany and, 33, 185; war crimes trial in, 84, 142; and war in Afghanistan, 162. *See also* neutrality pact between Japan and Soviet Union

Stalin, Josef, 17, 125–26, 195

Stalin-Ribbentrop Agreement (German-Soviet Nonaggression Pact), 126

state orders, duty to disobey, 49–50, 114, 187, 200, 201

state responsibility, 40

Stessel, Anatoli M., 103

Stevenson, C. L., 143

Stimson, Henry L., 127, 131

Suez Canal incident, 46, 179

Sugamo prison, 112, 120

summary execution, 50, 52, 79, 80–81, 83

Sun Yixian (Sun I-hsien, Sun Yat-sen), 72

Supreme Commander for the Allied Powers (SCAP), 33–34, 38, 65, 90, 138. *See also* GHQ; MacArthur, Douglas A.

Sweden, 91

Switzerland, 81, 91

Taisei Yokusan Kai. *See* Imperial Support Association

Taishō democracy, 204

Taiwan, 52, 113, 143; crimes against humanity in, 114, 115; Japanese invasion of, 98, 199

Taiwanese, 199

Takano Yūichi, 63–64

Takayanagi Kenzō, 93, 168

Takigawa Seijirō, 58–59

Tanaka Gi'ichi, 73–74, 75, 116

Tanaka Masaaki, 153–54, 186–87

"Tanaka Memorandum," 73

Taylor, Telford, 44

Terazaki Yoshinari, 87

textbook censorship, 160, 168, 191

Than Tun, **101–2**

Thompson, E. P., 162, 163

Three People's Principles (Sanminzhuyi), 72

Three Power Declaration. *See* Moscow Declaration

Tianjin (T'ien-chin, Tientsin), 71, 119

Tōgō Shigenori, 18, 19, 131

Tōjō Hideki, 81

Tokkō, 197

Tokyo trial: benefit of evidence of, 195–96; as compared to summary execution, 50, 52; and criminal nature of groups, 85; defects of, 36–37, 102, 143, 191; defendants in, 32; doubts on universal nature of, 46–47; editorial stance of newspapers toward, 86, 196, 197; evaluation from Chinese standpoint of, 192–93; and function of limiting revenge, 195; historical significance of, 51, 97; and implication for domestic law, 201–2; and individual resistance to acts of state, 164; influence of US Far Eastern policy on, 100–101; and Japanese scheme for autonomous trial, 81–82; and neglect of crimes against humanity, 53–54, 85; compared with Nuremberg trial, 16–19, 84–85, 108–9, 117, 131–32; political character of, 45–46; and possibility of retrial, 117; problem concerning conclusion of, 82–84; selection of defendants in, 95; and trial concerning Pearl Harbor, 128; US initiative in, 80; US occupation policy and, 83–84, 100–101; and US policy in Indochina, 160; and view of history, 77–78, 103–4, 182. *See also* majority judgment (Tokyo trial); Nuremberg and Tokyo trials; tribunal (Tokyo)

Tōkyō keizai shinpō, 196

Toyoda Kumao, 120

Treaty of Versailles, 129

tribunal (Tokyo): appointment of president and chief prosecutor of, 36, 56, 57; as compared with common court-martial, 57; defense counsel at, 19–20, 37, 92, 93–94, 104, 119, 120–21; educational function of, 50, 65–66; and indictment on criminal nature of groups, 84; legal basis of jurisdiction of, 39–43; participation of judges in, 155; prerequisite for membership on, 91; unbalanced representation of judges of, 46; unfairness of procedure and findings of, 19, 131, 191–92. *See also* Nuremberg and Tokyo trials; Tokyo trial

Tripartite Pact, 36, 183, 185

Truman, Harry S., 100

T'sai Chi-kan, 73

Tsar, 103

Tsitsihar (Qigihaer), 99

Tsukuba Hisaharu, 174

Tsurumi Shunsuke, **134–45**, 172–74, 175–76, 183–84, 203–5

Tusa, A. and J., 16, 17

Twenty-One Demands, 63, 71–72

Uchimura Gōsuke 142

Uchimura Kanzō, 165–66, 167

Umezu Yoshijirō, 95

Unit 731, 62, 85. *See also* bacteriological warfare in China

Unit 1644, 85. *See also* bacteriological warfare in China

United Nations, 178; charter of, 161; and extradition and punishment of war criminals, 35; and problem of international criminal jurisdiction, 43–44; charter of, and prohibition of war, 23, 24; reaffirmation and formulation of Nuremberg principles by, 35, 44, 132, 176–77

United Nations War Crimes Commission, 90, 91

United States, 32, 33, 34, 69, 71, 92, 118, 192; and appointment of Indian and Philippine judges, 91; and nonprosecution of Unit 731 at trial, 18, 85–86, 131; indiscriminate air raids on Japanese cities by, 168; influence on Tokyo trial of Far Eastern policy of, 100–101; Japan's war with, 169; and Nicaragua, 162; and oil embargo against Japan, 202; policy and action in Indochina of, 160; policy of, and crime of aggressive war, 126–27; and policy of terminating trials in Japan, 82–84; position on trial of kaiser, 126, 129; postwar confrontation between Soviet Union and, 18, 21–22, 80, 83, 100; postwar military intervention by, 22, 46; question on postwar international conduct of, 24, 46, 51, 161–62, 200; and Star Wars, 22; Tokyo trial and occupation policy of, 83–84, 100–101; and war in Indochina, 160, 163; and war in Vietnam, 46, 140, 163, 193; and war crimes in Indochina, 162; war criminals hiding in, 35, 57

US Neutrality Act (1935), 126

US vs. Calley, 44

Utsumi Aiko, 113, 142, 174

Uzawa Sōmei, 93

van der Post, Laurens, 164

Vietnam, 22, 46

Vietnam War, 46, 139, 163, 193, 195; American deserter from, 157–58, 174; criminality of, 170; similarity of, to Japan's aggression in China, 140

von Glahn, Gerhard, 107

Wakatsuki Reijirō, 99

Walser, Martin, 150

Wang Zhaoming (Wang Chaoming), 180

war: concept of illegality of, 47, 48; of national liberation, 59–60, 100, 195; prohibition of, 23–25, 125, 132

war crimes (Class B and C), 82, 110; British trials of, 171–72; of Koreans and Taiwanese, 85; and language barriers, 174; possibility of international research on, 175–76

war crimes (conventional), 21, 32, 81, 114, 190; by Allied powers, 168; bacteriological experiment in Manchuria as, 131; defined in Tokyo charter, 34, 41; failure to prevent, 17, 18, 19; failure to prosecute, by Japanese people, 166–67; jurisdiction of Tokyo tribunal for, 41–42, 43; massacre of Chinese prisoners of war as, 111; and punishment of American warplane crews by Japan, 80–81; and relation to crimes against humanity, 115; in Tokyo charter, 40; British trials of, 171–72, 175; trials of, in China, 142; trials of, in Soviet Union, 84, 142; trials of, in West and East Germany, 84

war criminals (Class A), 97; of European Axis, 32; of Japan, 32, 80, 82, 83, 84, 90, 103, 148

war criminals (Class B and C), 81, 84, 95, 103, 173; Korean, 112–13, 141, 142; and possibility of retrial, 117; Taiwanese, 112–13, 141

war criminals: extradition of, 57; pardon of suspected, of Japan, 102; and Potsdam Declaration, 33, 38; punished by German court after World War II, 61, 166; UN and extradition of, 35–36

war criminality, 18, 20

war responsibility. *See* responsibility

Webb, Sir William, 17, 89, 91, 92, 96, 154; against death sentences. 156; on emperor, 121, 156; minority opinion of, 168

Weinberger, Caspar, 22

Xinhai (Hsin-hai) Revolution, 72

Yalta Conference, 33

Yamashita case, 41, 44

Yanagida Kunio, 135

Yanai Hisao, 120

Yokohama Incident, 166

Yokota Kisaburō, 168, 191

Yonai Mitsumasa, 145

Yoshida Mitsuru, 144–45, 205

Yoshino Sakuzō, 203–4

Yu Xinchun, **98–101**, 192–93

Yuan Shikai (Yüan Shih-k'ai), 72

Zhang Xueliang (Chang Hsüeh-liang), 75, 183

Zhang Zuolin (Chang Tso-lin), 74, 75, 111, 116, 184